What They Say

"*Go Ahead and Shoot Me!* is a significant contribution as it tells another side of the story in the criminal justice system—not one many people are familiar with."

— *Dr. J. Thomas Dalby, Forensic Psychologist*

"Doug Heckbert encourages us to rethink what many have come to believe about criminal offences and the people who commit them. While never excusing criminal behaviour, he clearly explains that most crime results from poor decision making in difficult circumstances. Doug's lifelong contribution to criminal justice education continues in this entertaining and thought-provoking account of his experience working in Canada's criminal justice system."

— *Michelle R. Andrews BSW, MCA, Criminal Justice Educator*

"I have witnessed many ordinary families torn apart by their child's drug abuse and crime. With the right help and continued love and support of their child, many eventually return to normalcy, both for the child and the family. This is a common experience as shown in many of the stories in *Go Ahead and Shoot Me*. This is a compelling read based on informed reality that offers hope and strength to many community members."

— *Don Pare, former Sr. Mgr., Correctional Services of Canada and Chairman, RvC Inc. Venture Capital & Mentoring (retired)*

What They Say

"In my six years with drug court I have experienced multiple highs and lows; seeing participants struggle to find recovery from drugs, struggle even more when they must face the trauma that led them into addiction, struggle to rebuild a life that had been shattered into pieces. I have seen some falter and unable to cope with the reality of their trauma and walk away, while others refuse to face their reality and instead stay with their criminal ways and be terminated from the drug court program. There are those that have overdosed and those that die, each one leaving a mark in my soul. It wears at me to see the constant battles. But the rewards far outnumber the heartache and disappointment of a participant that does not succeed; those rewards are in the graduations. There is no greater joy or cause for celebration than seeing a broken life become whole and flourish."

— Grace Froese, Director of Provincial Drug Court Development and Sr. Mgr, Edmonton Drug Treatment Court Service, John Howard Society, Edmonton, Alberta

"Doug Heckbert has provided us an important insight into the human condition as he tells the stories of real people who have committed crimes. Although the label "criminal" is used to describe people in this book, the stories help us understand who these people are and how they ended up where they did. If we truly believe in crime prevention we must understand more than statistics and labels, we must understand the people and the reason terrible choices were made in their lives."

— Robin Murray, President and CEO, John Howard Society, Edmonton, Alberta

GO AHEAD AND SHOOT ME!

And Other True Cases About

Ordinary Criminals

〤

The Durvile True Cases Series

Tough Crimes: True Cases by
Top Canadian Criminal Lawyers (2014)
Edited by C.D. Evans and Lorene Shyba

Shrunk, Crime and Disorders of the Mind:
True Cases by Forensic Psychiatrists and Psychologists (2016)
Edited by Lorene Shyba and J. Thomas Dalby

More Tough Crimes: True Cases by
Canadian Lawyers and Judges (2017)
Edited by William Trudell and Lorene Shyba

Women in Criminal Justice: True Cases By and About
Canadian Women and the Law (2018)
Edited by William Trudell and Lorene Shyba

Florence Kinrade: Lizzie Borden of the North (2019)
Written by Frank Jones

Ross Mackay, The Saga of a Brilliant Criminal Lawyer:
And His Big Losses and
Bigger Wins in Court and in Life (2020)
Written by Jack Batten

Go Ahead and Shoot Me!
And Other True Cases About Ordinary Criminals (2020)
Written by Doug Heckbert

After the Force: True Cases by
Law Enforcement Officers (upcoming 2021)
Edited by Det. Debbie J. Doyle (ret.) and Lorene Shyba

〤

DOUG HECKBERT

GO AHEAD AND SHOOT ME!

And Other True Cases About Ordinary Criminals

Foreword by Howard Sapers

Afterword by Debbie J. Doyle

DURVILE IMPRINT OF DURVILE & UPROUTE BOOKS
CALGARY, ALBERTA, CANADA
DURVILE.COM

Durvile Publications Ltd.

DURVILE IMPRINT OF DURVILE AND UPROUTE BOOKS

Calgary, Alberta, Canada
www.durvile.com

The publisher and author wish to acknowledge the ancestral and traditional territory of Treaty 6 and Treaty 7 Nations of the Cree, Dene, Saulteaux, Nakota Sioux, Blackfoot, Stoney Nakoda, Tsuut'ina, as well as the Métis. They help us steward this land, as well as honour and celebrate this place.

LIBRARY AND ARCHIVES CATALOGUING IN PUBLICATIONS DATA

Go Ahead and Shoot Me!
And other true cases about ordinary criminals
Heckbert, Doug, author | Shyba, Lorene, editor
Book Seven in the True Cases Series

1. True Crimes | 2. Probation Officers
3. Canadian Law | 4. Canadian History

ISBN: 978-1-988824-34-5 (print pbk) | ISBN: 978-1-988824-64-2 (e-book)
ISBN: 978-1-988824-50-5 (audiobook)

Cover illustration, Rich Théroux.
Editing and design, Lorene Shyba.

Canada Alberta
Government

Durvile Publications would like to acknowledge the financial support of the Government of Canada through Canadian Heritage Canada Book Fund and the Government of Alberta, Alberta Media Fund.

Printed in Canada
First edition, first printing. 2020

This book is dedicated to the men and women who have successfully turned their lives around from criminal activity, either instantly or over time, and who are no longer a concern to the community. Many are quietly living ordinary lives and many are seen as role models.

CONTENTS

XX

CONTENTS

𝕏

FOREWORD

HOWARD SAPERS

A FEW YEARS AGO, I heard from my friend and colleague Doug Heckbert with news that he had started a writing project about clients he had worked with over his years as a probation officer. As always, I was happy to hear from him and felt that he was onto a good idea.

Doug and I had originally met in the mid 1980s when he was Director of Training for the Native Counselling Services of Alberta and I was Provincial Executive Director for the Alberta John Howard Society. A little later in our careers, we worked together as faculty members in the Correctional Services program at what is now MacEwan University in Edmonton. I knew him as a fair-minded professional who, like me, believed that true justice requires compassion and an ability to separate the acts that have been committed from the person who committed them.

As we spoke more about the project over time, I was surprised when he told me that his book was to be published with the provocative title of "Go Ahead and Shoot Me!" I was afraid that Doug was about to move away from his principles and turn some real-life tragedies into pulp fiction, but I should have known better. In the book, Doug actually offers a sensitive and insightful treatment of his clients, pulling the phrase from a story about a woman he called Sally for the purpose of his writing. The phrase "Go ahead and shoot me" was what Sally's husband screamed as he taunted her to shoot him with a rifle he had to teach her how to use. So at his insistence she shot him and was charged with attempted murder. By the time Doug took her on as a client, she had come to see her offence as being pretty stupid.

The criminal justice system is far from perfect. To the extent that it works at all, it does so only when actors in the system remember that behind the case numbers and criminal records are mothers and fathers, sons and daughters, husbands and wives. Doug reminds us that when people commit a crime, they are criminal only in that moment. They have lives and ambitions beyond their crimes and the system is supposed to help them find their place in society once their debt is paid.

Throughout the stories in the book, Doug digs deep into his motivations and examines his own morality as he provides honest portraits of men and women in conflict with the law. Readers catch a glimpse of real people—often at their worst but sometimes at their best—with real problems and real obstacles to their success. In telling their stories, Doug tells his own. We can feel the turmoil not only in the lives of his clients, but also in Doug as he learns and then masters the work of a probation officer. Some of the stories about his most memorable clients are tales of success, others are riddled with ambiguity. He writes about Juanito, a long-time addict who finds compassion in a drug court and with some support and guidance finally sees a way to face his addiction. And Joseph, who could easily turn his chronic criminality into a career, instead finds a way to make better choices as he learns how to avoid violence. He recalls the story of Mary, weary beyond her years and trapped in a life the justice system can't make better. The cast of characters is rich and as we meet them, the rough terrain of criminal justice is revealed along with Doug's insights about how to navigate it.

Our criminal justice system relies upon public confidence for its legitimacy. For the public to be confident, it must be informed. Sadly, too much of the public discourse is distorted by fear mongering, half-truths, outright lies, and the manufacture of entertainment. *Go Ahead and Shoot Me!* presents an antidote to the misinformation about crime and justice. While it focuses on only one component of the system, community corrections, its content can easily be broadly applied. Readers become more knowledgeable about how the system works, some of its frailties and how discretion and judgment are just as important as rules and procedures. Understanding this leads to an appreciation of not only the challenges associated with the administration of justice, but also of the principles such as restraint and proportionality upon which it is based.

Nitty-gritty everyday life is the fuel stock of the system. The lives of those in conflict with the law intertwine with the lives of the people who administer it. Good days, bad days, disappointments and distractions all factor into the how and why of crime. The same is true of the successes and failures of the men and women who work in our courts and jails, police and community corrections offices. *Go Ahead and Shoot Me!* takes us from the front of the house to backstage. In so doing, we are treated to some good story telling as well as some memorable and important lessons.

— Howard Sapers,
Correctional Investigator
of Canada (2004 – 2016)

PREFACE

THIS BOOK, *Go Ahead and Shoot Me!* is about people I supervised when I worked as a probation officer and also contains a few cases I came to know about during the process of researching and writing the book. The title was chosen to model the reality that I have had to deal with over the years, the phrase "Go Ahead and Shoot Me!" being the utterance that motivated the crime in the first story in the book, and the subtitle reflecting the fact that there are very few serious offences in the book, but many very ordinary offenders. This will become evident as you work your way through the stories and meet the people. They represent, in my view, the majority of actual offenders in our system— ordinary people who made questionable decisions, were investigated and charged by police, appeared in court and, if found guilty, ended up in corrections.

In the early part of my career, spanning a period of nearly ten years, I worked as a probation officer, a parole officer and a caseworker in a minimum security prison. In the latter part of my career, spanning a period of over thirty years, I was involved in staff training, career development at the college/university level, and research in criminal justice. Throughout my years of practice, I must admit that I dealt with some horrific crimes committed by people who were a real hazard to the community, but fortunately these dangerous offenders formed a small minority of my clientele. The people I mainly dealt with had committed crimes that rarely come to the attention of the public.

People who appear in these pages could easily be the guy or gal next door or who is even part of the family. In my view, it is ordinary people who commit most of the crimes on any given day in any community and in any region of the country.

As a story teller, I have changed the clients' names to ensure confidentiality. In my view, there is nothing helpful for the reader to know exactly who I am talking about. Also, I have disguised other personal details, such as exactly where they lived, where they worked or where they went to school. Again, knowing these precise details would not, in my view, be helpful. You will also note that I refer to 'the city' without naming any particular city. This practice on my part contributes to privacy and confidentiality, ensuring that the people in these stories will not be individually recognized even by location of where they lived. I would prefer that you focus your attention on the character, behaviour and attitudes of these people, not just on where they lived, worked, went to school, their actual names or the details of their crimes.

In order to tell their stories, I have revived my memory, and have tried to be as accurate as possible. As I would write about one case, details of other cases came flooding over me, and this has become a wonderful nostalgic journey. I have intentionally kept information about legal processes to a minimum in the book, but include some aspects of criminal law when a legal context might illuminate the

world in which criminals operate. I have also tried to minimize the use of slang we used back in the day that might
now be perceived as incorrect, but old-fashioned slang
sometimes sneaks into authentic dialogue as I remember it.
It is not meant to offend and I try to justify its use.

In my work, I tried hard not to get mad at the people I
worked with. It was easy to be frustrated by the behaviour
or attitude of some clients, but I found it counter-productive
to get angry. I tried to see the good in people and to work
with those strengths, as opposed to harping on the offence
or other problems and circumstances over which I (or they)
had no control. I soon came to realize that personal change
takes time and rarely occurs with the snap of a finger. I quite
often saw the look of amazement, almost wonderment, on
people's faces when 'the lights came on', that is when they
realized something in their life experience that was a major
influence in changing their behaviour in a positive way.

The people I have written about have all made a lasting impact on me personally. One of my greatest lessons
was the importance of prevention. Our system depends
very heavily on laying charges, getting convictions and sentencing people to terms of probation or imprisonment. If
only we could summon the will and resources to focus on
preventative measures rather than devote so much of our
time and resources on reacting to someone's problematic
behaviour, we'd be much further ahead.

I challenge you, the reader, to seriously think about the
popular phrases, "Let's get tough on crime," and "You do
the crime, you do the time." After reading about the people in these stories, how would "getting tough" or "do the
time" with them (or anyone else) make our communities a
safer place? Might better thoughts be, "Let's get smart about
crime," or "Let's get real about crime"?

I also hope you reach a point where you understand
what many of us working in criminal justice have come to

understand; that there is a fine line between those who commit crimes and those who don't. Or, stated another way, that many people are just one event or one decision away from becoming an offender. As Lorene Shyba, my publisher commented, the ordinary offender and the ordinary person can be simply a hairsbreadth away from each other on the moral compass.

So, get comfortable, relax and read about some of the folks that I dealt with. The crimes and people I write about are real. These are not actors. These folks are not larger than life, they live real lives. They are part of the thousands of offenders whose names and crimes rarely or never receive any attention from the media. Some of the crimes they committed were serious, some were stupid, some were funny, and some were sad. That is what most true crime is actually about and what most real people who commit crime are like— rather ordinary people who could be your neighbour or even a member of your family. My hope is that by reading this book you will come away with a better understanding of crime, people who commit crime, and the criminal justice system.

— *Doug Heckbert BA, MA*
Criminal Justice Educator

PART I

UNDER MY SUPERVISION

INTRODUCTION TO PART I

Back in 1966, I showed up for my first day on the job as a probation officer. Reporting to the receptionist, I gave her my name and asked to see Mr. Campbell, the senior probation officer. Emily, the receptionist, looked through various filing drawers, then returned to the reception wicket and said to me, "I'm sorry but I can't find your file. When were you placed on probation?" I paused, and replied, "I'm the new probation officer!" She was most apologetic, then scurried off to find my personnel file somewhere before ushering me in to meet the director, Mr. Campbell. Later, Emily and I had a good laugh about this incident, and we worked well together for five years until I left the city for another probation office.

I found it interesting that even Emily, with all her experience in dealing with people who commit crime coming into a large probation office, initially figured I was a client, not a staff member. Could she not tell the difference? Or, maybe there is not much obvious difference? Could people who commit crime be as "normal" or "ordinary" as people who don't commit crime? I was not embarrassed by this mix-up, but it did get me thinking right from day one about the types of people that I would end up dealing with. How normal/ordinary would they be?

I was twenty years old when hired as a probation officer; the legal drinking age at the time was twenty-one, so my colleagues sometimes bootlegged for me over the next couple of months when I wanted a case of beer. I was one of the first young probation officers who was hired with a university degree. I joined at a time when probation administrators were looking to hire university graduates for their staff, which up to then had often been ex-military, church pastors or retired policemen. All were men— women would not begin to work their way into the ranks of probation officers until a few years later.

I was assigned to a unit headed by one of the former police officers. These men took me under their wing and helped me learn about law, people who commit crime, and what criminality was all about. I think I brought a youthful exuberance and scholarly discipline to the office. I fit in well with most of the staff and quickly settled into the job of a probation officer which entailed preparing pre-sentence reports for the courts and supervising a caseload of adults who were on probation for a variety of offences. I handled some probationers in the city but also supervised cases and attended courts in nearby, smaller communities. Towards my latter time in the city office, I was assigned to the courthouse and ended up spending most of my day at the courthouse, representing the probation branch in its dealings with judges, crown prosecutors, defence counsel, the clerk's office, the media, representatives of various agencies, offenders, their families and a few victims. As well, I became involved in developing programs for young adults on probation to help them increase their employment and interpersonal skills.

My close friends have always been interested in the work I do and I have always been willing to talk about issues regarding crime and justice. I find it helpful for others to understand my roles in the justice system by telling them stories about the people I have worked with, both staff and clients. My friends would make interesting comments like, "You a probation officer? Knowing some of the things you have done, you should be on probation!" Or, "You have lived a really sheltered life. What do you know about real life, the law, people who commit crime and what life is like on the wrong side of the tracks?" Regardless of these views, both of which I believe are accurate, I loved my first full time job as a probation officer. I considered my caseload of probationers to be interesting people who got themselves into interesting situations. I was friendly towards these folks, but I was not their friend, although I did end up curling, (curling the sport not curling as in hair styling) with a former client one winter after he successfully completed his period of probation under my supervision.

Early in my career, I realized that the general public, including my friends, did not know very much about criminal justice. Some of what they thought they knew was actually totally wrong. People can have strong opinions about justice; but, sadly in my view, their opinions are often based on faulty information. This is not a good situation for people in a democracy, where making criminal law or having input into very serious matters such as crime and justice, but basing some of that input on wrong information, really calls into question the value of the resulting laws and related policies.

What I have noticed is that many people with strong, negative opinions about crime and justice often soften their views when presented with quality, accurate, and realistic information about the individuals I dealt with and their circumstances. One point I always try to drive home is that the person (criminal) is not the behaviour (crime). There is much more to the person than just their criminal behaviour.

THIS BOOK *Go Ahead and Shoot Me* is in two parts. The first part deals with clients, also known as probationers or offenders, who were under my supervision as a probation officer. The second part deals with some folks with criminal records who I came to know as a result of researching and writing this book. All the people I write about as well as their offences are ordinary in one way or another and all the chapters in the book explore this idea in more detail.

The criminal justice system is best understood in terms of its four components:

1. Community (including the general public, offenders, victims and legislative bodies which make criminal law).
2. Police (including national police services, provincial or state police services; and municipal police services).
3. Courts (including judges, prosecutors and defence lawyers).
4. Corrections (including community based services, like probation and parole, and institutional services such as remand centers, correctional institutions and penitentiaries).

Corrections is unique in that it has two goals or functions:

1. To protect the public.
2. To assist offenders to become law-abiding citizens.

How do we achieve these goals? Well, we protect the public by controlling offenders. The amount of control offenders need is determined by the perceived risk they pose to the public.

This risk is determined by examining information such as the current offence(s), their previous criminal record, and their social circumstances, such as age, family dynamics, education, employment, mental health, physical health, influence of peers, use of alcohol and drugs and their financial situation. Armed with this information, justice professionals can protect the public quite well by controlling offenders only as much as necessary. Some offenders need a lot of control; thus the existence of maximum security penitentiaries to house high risk offenders. Most offenders, however, need much less control; thus the existence of sentences like probation, with conditions such as directing them to keep the peace, be of good behaviour and to report to a probation officer as required.

A common form of sentence for criminal charges is a fine in the form of a financial penalty. Once the fine is paid, no further action is required by the offender. A fine is often, but not always, enough to protect the public in that the offender usually does not commit another crime—no further control is needed.

The other goal of corrections is to assist offenders to become law-abiding citizens. This involves assessing the offender's social circumstances mentioned above and developing a case plan to work with the offender to change those circumstances that were thought to be somehow lacking for that person. We believe these circumstances contributed, at least in part, to them becoming in conflict with the law; and we are obligated to be part of a process to change those conditions, thereby, deterring or preventing future criminal acts. Correctional workers assist offenders to become law-abiding citizens by helping offenders as much as possible to make changes in their lives so they don't become repeat offenders. Some offenders actually need very little help from justice professionals. They simply decide to live within the confines of the law from now on; and that is what they do—totally on their own with little or no help from criminal justice or other professionals.

However, in my experience, many offenders need a hand at sorting things out in their minds. They are often unclear as to what they want to do with their lives or where to go to seek help—some aren't even aware just yet that they have a problem. Correctional professionals can be very helpful to folks like this, assisting them to gain focus and control over their lives and, thus, staying out of future conflict with the law. There are some offenders, however, that, no matter how much help they are offered, simply do not want to (or don't yet know how to) change their behaviour. These folks soon re-offend. In these cases, correctional professionals accept the fact that they did what they could in the time prescribed through the Court's sentence and with the resources available through the correctional service and in the community.

So, to sum up the dual goals of corrections, we control offenders as much as necessary and we help offenders as much as possible. This was my job as a probation officer. I guess I was pretty good at it because I was asked by my employer to take on duties of increasing responsibility within the first office in which I worked and later within the correctional service in a supervisory capacity.

You will see in some of these stories, such as Sally (Go Ahead and Shoot Me!) that the initial charge (attempted murder) was very serious; yet, by the time all the court appearances were over and a new charge emerged to better represent the actual circumstances, the new charge was much less seriousness (dangerous use of a firearm). No doubt the media paid a fair bit of attention to the initial incident, but I doubt if anything later appeared in the media as to the actual sentence. The public may have learned something about the initial incident, which seemed extremely serious at first; but, upon conclusion of the court process, the public probably learned absolutely nothing about what actually happened.

All the chapters in Part I, with the exception of Barry, are about ordinary people living fairly normal lives who somehow found themselves in trouble with the law. That is where I became involved. In Barry's case, he came from an unstable background and got himself into a fair bit of trouble. It turns out that cases like Barry's are quite common, rather typical—there are quite a number of folks we encounter in criminal justice who fit this profile. Most of the other cases are about ordinary people living fairly normal lives before getting into trouble. Initially in my career, I was surprised by the number of "ordinary", "normal" and "average" cases I dealt with. I was not surprised, however, by the fairly large number of people experiencing personal instability who committed crime—these were "common" and "run-of-the-mill" encounters for those of us working in the justice system. Thus, the concept of ordinary applies to both the people and to the crimes they commit.

CHAPTER 1

SALLY: GO AHEAD AND SHOOT ME!

SALLY WAS ASSIGNED to my probation caseload following a series of court appearances she had made over the period of about a year. Her length of probation was twelve months—the charge, "Dangerous Use of a Firearm." The usual conditions applied such as keeping the peace and being of good behaviour but in addition, she was directed to "take counselling as required." This condition is a fairly common one, ordered by the Court when there are concerns about a client's personal stability, emotional well-being, and/or possible mental illness. I had not been trained as a psychologist, but had taken counselling workshops and would routinely sit and listen to clients who were upset by something in their lives, or when there appeared to be some deviance in their background.

I was on my way to the police station to read the police report on another client so I decided to ask for Sally's police report at the same time. When I gave the clients' names to the officer, he told me that my first client's file was normal size, but, he added, "You better have a while to look at Sally's report. She was originally charged with attempted murder!"

As I waited for the officer to return with the reports, the words "take counselling, attempted murder, and dangerous use of a firearm," danced in my head. "What was this Sally going to be like," I wondered? "More intriguing than most, I expect."

The officer arrived, using both arms to carry two heavy banker-style boxes. He plunked the boxes down in front of me on the counter and on top of the boxes was a thin file folder. I reached for the thin folder first that summarized my first client's case and it took about five minutes to read it all and write my summary notes. Then I turned my attention to Sally's files. The officer asked me, "You sure you got the time to go through all this?"

Normally, police report files were quite brief, as was the one I had just read, with succinct statements of what happened to form the basis of the charge and what the disposition was in court. But Sally's police reports comprised dozens of folders jammed into the two boxes. Some folders were very thick, while a few only had a few pieces of paper in them. I had to be quick as I had other appointments to go to so I took the most recently dated file and opened it. There was a summary: "Accused pleaded guilty in Court to one count of dangerous use of a firearm; sentenced to one year probation with conditions. Plea to lesser charge OK'd by Prosecutor."

I am no stranger to firearms, having hunted migratory birds such as ducks and geese as well as upland game birds including grouse and partridge since I was a teenager. Firearms to me were an important tool, to be used with respect and care, and not something to be afraid of. I had only experienced one incident involving the misuse of firearms and that had been a few years before. My dad and I were hiding in a hand-dug pit, waiting for geese to come to our decoys when an idiot drove his red pickup truck into the field about two hundred yards from us and started shooting at our decoys, in line with the pit, with a rifle. We hunkered down as far as we could in the pit while bullets whizzed by and hit the ground nearby. Dad grabbed his white handkerchief, stuffed a corner of it into the end of his gun barrel, thrust the barrel out of the pit and waved it back and forth vigorously. The shooting stopped right away. We heard the truck start and then it roared away from the field. Aside from this personal experience, I also knew from media reports that some people had been tragically injured or killed by others who used firearms inappropriately.

Now I had at least a brief picture of what had happened in Sally's case. I started thumbing through the other files, but there was very little information giving further details. What I did learn is that at some of Sally's court appearances, bail was the issue and at other court appearances, the case was remanded upon the request of Sally's lawyer.

I returned the boxes and folders to the officer, saying that I had to get going but might be back to gather more information. On the way back to the office, the picture that developed in my mind was that Sally was initially charged with attempted murder but the prosecutor and the defence lawyer eventually agreed to a reduced, less serious charge of dangerous use of a firearm. The judge accepted the reduced charge and had suspended Sally's sentence for twelve months, releasing her on a probation order with the usual conditions plus the added condition to take counseling. A fascinating mental image was forming in my mind, one that was of extreme seriousness—attempted murder—and one that was very routine—twelve months probation.

"Aaaah," I sighed. "This will be quite something to deal with." A day or so later, I called Sally to book an appointment to see her at her home. The plan was that I would gather information about her such as age, finances, education, work record, health, marital situation, and the offence, then develop a case plan with her for the period of probation. The appointment was for two days time, at her home.

I arrived at Sally's address in the north-central part of the city. As I pulled up in front of the house, I noted it was an older bungalow, about 1100 square feet with a well-kept yard featuring grass lawns, shrubs, flowers, and trees. The outside of the home was a combination of grey stucco and brown wood panels, in good condition. Nicely kept houses and yards were on either side of Sally's.

I head to the front door which faced the street. The woman who came to the door introduced herself as Sally. I estimated her to be about forty years old, of average height, weight, and build. Once inside the home, she introduced me to Roger, her husband. He was about the same age as Sally, about five feet ten inches and 170 pounds, with slightly greying wavy hair. Sally led us through the front room into the kitchen where she offered coffee. I accepted and we all sat down at the kitchen table; Sally, Roger, and me.

I started out the interview by explaining that the purpose of this meeting is to review the probation order, to be sure she understood what had happened in court, to gather information about her, and then to develop a case plan that covered what she needed to do to complete her probation.

As I worked through the probation order, phrase by phrase and condition by condition, Sally said she fully understood what probation was, and what she had to do. Sally relayed her information to me in a pleasant, easy-going manner with no hint of anger, no hesitation. Roger sat quietly at the kitchen table, listening intently to our discussions but not saying very much.

In response to my questions about their home, Sally told me that they had lived at this address for nearly twenty years. She worked part-time as a clerk in a downtown department store and Roger had worked for many years in a warehouse in the north end of the city. They had two children, both girls, who were doing well in high school. Both Sally and Roger had attended high school in the city and both reported to be in good health. I noticed the furnishings in the house are relatively new, so on the surface it appeared that Sally and Roger were doing well financially.

I wanted to hear about the offence; but it was a matter to be explored with solemnity, tact and respect. Attempted murder is a very serious charge. When I judged that the interview was going well and we were comfortable with each other, I decided it was time to explore what the offence was all about. "Thanks for all the information about your house, family, and work," I said. "Now, can you tell me what the charge is all about?"

There is a long pause. Sally and Roger looked back and forth at each other, neither speaking nor displaying overt facial expressions. Eventually, Sally cleared her throat and began to speak. Roger just sat there at the table, quiet. Over the course of the next while, I listened and digested the scenario that had taken place right over in the next room.

"Well," she said. "For years, Roger would go out for beers with some of the guys from work, nearly every Friday after work. He wouldn't get home until eight or nine in the evening, and sometimes he was pretty drunk. For a while, I accepted this behaviour and didn't say a thing. He then started to come home later and later, saying he was hungry and horny. This really bugged me, but again I didn't say anything. But it continued and I started telling him that I was not the least bit pleased that he came home drunk and demanding. He normally didn't say much when I got after him, but he did not change. It just kept happening."

"So this one time," she continued, "about a year ago, he came home drunk and wanting sex. I had enough of being treated this way so I really lit into him." When I asked her where this all happened she got up from her chair and pointed down the hall to the room we'd just walked through. "We were in the living room, just over there," she said. She spun around and then started re-enacted the scene as if was happening all over again.

'You son of a bitch!' I yell at him. 'You come home drunk and being a jerk, expect me to do everything for you. Well, that's all gonna change right now and I won't be putting up with this shit any more. So, you get out of here and sober up!'

"I was furious and I don't usually swear," she tells me, "but I'd had it up to here with him!" she said, waving her hand across her throat. She continues:

> He's staggering around and slurs, 'I ain't going nowhere and you can't make me. This is my house, too. What are you gonna do? Pick me up and throw me out?' Then he kinda laughs so I scream at him, 'No. I know I can't throw you out. But I'm so mad I could kill you.' He has this weird twisted smile on his face, you know, and says, 'Oh, how you gonna do that? How you gonna kill me?' 'Well, I'll shoot you!' I yell back at him, mad as hell. 'Oh, I see,' he sneers at me. 'And where's your gun?' I say, 'Well, you have your rifle downstairs. I'll use that!' Then he just snorts at me and says, 'Do you want me to go get the gun? You probably don't even know where it is!' 'Alright, asshole,' I tell him. 'You go get the gun!' So he does.

By her own account, Sally was enraged by this time. She'd had enough. The way she tells it, Roger staggered across the living room to the hallway, lurched his way down the stairs to the basement, found the storage room, grabbed the rifle (a 308 Winchester he used for hunting deer) and stumbled his way back up the stairs to where she was waiting and fuming. Pacing back and forth across the kitchen, she carries on telling the story.

> 'Here, bitch,' he yells at me, then hands me the rifle, and staggers back across the living room, leaving about eight paces between us. I sling the rifle over my shoulders for a second, all defiant, then I point it straight at him. 'Where's the bullets?' I yell. 'They're downstairs,' he says. 'Want me to get them?' So I scream, 'Yeah, asshole, you go get the bullets!' So he does!

The way she tells it, Roger again staggered across the living room to the hallway, lurched his way down the stairs to the basement, found the storage room, grabbed the shell package and stumbled his way back up the stairs to where Sally was still waiting, and still fuming. Sally explains:

> When he comes back upstairs he says, 'Here you go,' and hands me a box of shells. He even opens the box and pulls one out, 'You'll need this,' he says. So I hold the rifle in one hand and the shell in the other. I don't know what to do next so Roger holds out his hands palms upwards like this, and says, real sarcastic, 'You want me to load it?' So I say, 'Sure,' and he grabs the rifle, slides the cartridge into the chamber, slams the chamber shut with the bolt and hands it back to me. 'There you go!' he shouts. And then he staggers back to about eight paces away, like before. It takes me a couple of seconds to consider my move; should I or shouldn't I, but I raise the gun up to my shoulder and point it straight at him. Then I pull the trigger. But nothing happens. Then he yells, 'You stupid bitch! The safety is on!' So he rushes over to me, grabs the rifle, flicks off the safety and back he goes, eight paces away and yells, real loud, 'Go ahead and shoot me!'

So this time she did! The rifle boomed and the recoil sent Sally staggering backwards a few steps, where she tripped over a chair and fell to the floor. The gun had jumped from her hands and skidded to a halt under a table. The bullet hit Roger in the left shoulder, passed through his body causing a flesh wound and slammed right on through the wall of the living room.

Both Sally and Roger were stunned. Roger moaned due to the searing pain of his wound, and he grasped his shoulder. Blood slowly oozed between his fingers and he unsteadily sank to his knees, then toppled over onto his side. Sally started to sob uncontrollably.

After what seemed an eternity, Sally got up from the floor, went to the kitchen and sat down at the table. Roger crawled from the floor onto a sofa and remained in the living room. And this is how the police found them about twenty minutes later. The offence part of this story ended here. The consequences continued.

I never had the time to review all the police reports in the two banker boxes, but they were exhaustive, with documentation that a bullet hit the house next door, blasting through the exterior wall of that house and ricocheting around their kitchen, eventually coming to rest on the floor. The lady of the house screamed, yelling to her family to get on the floor. That's who called the police.

Police cars would have swarmed the area, closing off roads and stopping traffic. A dozen officers fanned out on foot, going from door to door, directing residents to stay indoors and away from windows. The area would have been effectively sealed off as a public safety precaution.

I can only imagine the reaction of the police officer who eventually came to Sally and Roger's front door to warn them to stay indoors as there was a shooting incident in the neighbourhood. The officer would be expecting to meet residents in a quiet residential area who then became shocked and alarmed when they learned that there could be a shooter in the area.

Instead, the officer found Roger bleeding from his shoulder, in a lot of pain, and in shock, unable to talk. The officer found Sally unharmed, and she had composed herself well enough to make an initial statement regarding what had just happened.

The community shut down was soon thereafter lifted.

OVER THE NEXT FEW WEEKS, I interviewed Sally and Roger several times. I was very concerned that the level of domestic tension in the household could again reach crisis levels, but each time we met, they assured me they were now okay in that regard. This conclusion was reinforced when I spoke to them individually as well. This message was repeated throughout the twelve months of probation. No further incidents were noted from the court record which I reviewed daily from the courts or from police records.

The condition of the probation order "take counselling as required" was fulfilled when Sally and Roger sought the counselling services of their pastor. They attended sessions on a regular basis for a year and when I spoke with the pastor, he assured me that notwithstanding privacy issues, he was confident the violent behaviour would not be repeated.

While Sally was on probation, we met once a month for a year, either at the family home or in my office. I learned that Roger had quit drinking and no longer went out with his work buddies on Fridays after work. I also learned that Sally wanted nothing further to do with firearms, and this resulted in Roger giving away his rifle to a friend.

When I closed Sally's file at the end of the twelve-month period, I concluded that the probation order had been completed successfully and that there was little likelihood of further weapons or violent incidents.

On the day I'd first met Roger and after I'd heard the details of the shooting, I looked at him and said, "You should be charged with stupidity. Maybe you're the one who should be on probation, not your wife."

Roger grunted, "Yeah, you're right," and hung his head.

So far as I know, the criminal law does not include a charge of stupidity but I have heard a lot of offenders conclude, "Yeah, what I did was pretty stupid, wasn't it!"

I suspect the criminal justice system will continue dealing with stupidity for generations to come.

CHAPTER 2

RON: DO I CALL POLICE OR NOT?

O NE OF THE DUTIES of a probation officer is to supervise offenders placed on probation by the court. Some people are placed on probation after the judge considers a pre-sentence report, which is prepared by a probation officer at the judge's request to assist in deciding on a sentence for someone who has pleaded guilty or has been found guilty at a trial. This report contains a host of factual information such as age, gender, education, work experience, financial situation, health, family, criminal record, friends, involvement in the offence, and personal interests, all things a judge takes into account when deciding on a sentence. Most accused end up pleading guilty as charged—this shows that police and prosecutors have done their jobs effectively. Some people are placed directly on probation by the judge, without the benefit of a pre-sentence report.

Ron was placed directly on probation for a period of fifteen months on four charges of "Theft Over $50." A similar charge these days would be "Theft over $5,000." No matter the difference in dollar amounts, it is a fairly serious charge but a common one, both in the past and nowadays as well.

He was assigned to my caseload by the senior probation officer; and he appeared at the office right after he had been in court, which was only three blocks away. My office at the time was in an old brick building with a terrific view of a notorious all-night café which was a gathering place for hookers, drug dealers, alcoholics, and street people. Other government services were also available from our building, which bordered the upscale city centre and the notorious inner city, also commonly known as "the drag." The café was about the only place in the downtown area of the city where anyone could go for coffee or a snack late at night. I had been there a few times while going to university a few years earlier when a few friends and I drifted in there for coffee after the bars in the city had closed for the night. I recalled feeling excited by being "close to the action"—a far cry from the stable lifestyle I grew up with in a small town. I also recalled feeling a youthful exuberance at the time as we, eighteen- or nineteen-year-old half-drunk, university students (males), swaggered into the café for a pee before we caught our last bus to the south side and to our residences at the university. I know I also felt an element of fear—there were some pretty scary looking people there, not the types I met in my hometown or at the university.

RON WAS WITH HIS MOTHER. We met in my very plain office which was four painted walls, a wooden desk with a large desktop ink blotter, a telephone, a small grey metal filing cabinet, a small wooden bookcase, a chair for me and two chairs for visitors. I had a few pictures on the walls, a bulletin board with a calendar and a few cartoons pinned to the board.

Ron looked like many young people of the day, wearing faded jeans and a well-worn t-shirt, faintly displaying a rock band. He was of average height, weight and build—nothing outstanding in terms of his physique. His brown, straight hair was near shoulder length, again in keeping with the trends of the youth of the day. He was polite with me and did not seem to be uncomfortable dealing with a probation officer for some fairly serious charges. He did not come across as defiant or rebellious, unlike many of the other young people who I had on probation.

However, his mom fidgeted and seemed very nervous. Her eyes darted back and forth between her son and me, and around the room as well. No doubt she was trying to get a read on me. What would I be like, supervising her son. She seemed motherly, maybe somewhat overprotective, reminding Ron to sit down and answer the questions I would surely pose to him.

The first item of business was to go over the probation order with Ron to ensure he understood what it meant and what impact it would have on him for the next fifteen months. There were some conditions on the order that he had to follow:

1. Report to a probation officer once a month or as required,
2. Keep the peace and be of good behaviour,
3. Report any changes of address or employment to the court or probation officer,
4. Remain within the jurisdiction of the court, and
5. Appear before the court when required to do so.

I reviewed the order with him, and I was of the view that he knew full well what the order meant and what was in store for him while he was on probation. I judged right away that he was a pretty smart kid.

I say kid in the sense that he was seventeen years old. (The juvenile or youth age at the time for males was up to fifteen years; for females, up to seventeen.)

Ron's mom said her husband did not know of Ron's charges nor that he had appeared in court. She stated she did not want her husband to know that he was on probation. She did not say this in a threatening or pleading manner, just matter-of-factly. She explained that the family was well known in the city, particularly in the business community where the family name appeared in the business name. I recognized the name right away.

IT WAS A LITTLE UNUSUAL that Ron appeared in the office on the same day he was placed on probation, right after being in court. Sometimes, probationers avoid seeing their probation officers, who then have to spend a lot of time trying to track them down. Another unusual fact was his mom's presence. Often, young people didn't want a parent with them or the parent did not even know their son or daughter was in trouble; or, as was sometimes the case, the parent just did not care. Yet, here were Ron and his mother, and they appeared to get along reasonably well.

Once we went over the probation order, I indicated that I would like to individually interview them both to complete a Social History, which is a report of the offender, the circumstances of the offence and the nature of his relations in the family, at school and at work.

The picture quickly emerged of a young man with lots of potential who had become mixed up with the wrong crowd. There was no financial hardship in the family. Ron's father was busy at work and active in the wider business community; his mom did a lot of volunteer work in the community and raised the kids; and he got along pretty well with his younger brother and sister. Ron, himself, was not doing so well in grade eleven at high school—his attendance (or rather the lack of attendance) had become a concern to the family and to the school, as well; and his marks had dropped noticeably over the past year. From time to time, he worked in the family business. His health was fine. He reported that he rarely used alcohol or drugs.

I then turned our attention to the crimes that led Ron to being on probation. He outlined that over the past year, he wanted to be more independent from his family and their lifestyle; and he became attracted to other young adults who he felt led what he perceived to be a more adventurous life that involved stealing on an organized scale. Ron admitted that he periodically stole small items from the home, such as loose change left on a counter top or candy bars from the neighbourhood corner store, but what his new friends did was significantly more exciting—and more rewarding. He and some accomplices decided what they wanted to acquire and then planned how to steal those items from a department store in the nearby shopping centre.

Here's how they operated. Ron and an accomplice would enter the store and engage a clerk in the sporting goods section in a discussion about an item, such as a set of downhill skis. Once the clerk was actively engaged in the sales pitch, including holding up and examining the skis, two other accomplices would enter the store and loudly demand the clerk to show them something as well. The minute the clerk's back was turned to deal with the two accomplices, Ron and his friend would pick up the first item, such as the pair of skis, and walk from the store. The four offences for which Ron was on probation were committed this way. He indicated the process was not hard to carry out as staff never seemed to catch on to what was happening. This was at a time before merchants attached security chips to every item for sale.

Ron's mom sat quietly through this part of the interview. She seemed almost more embarrassed than he was. Ron said he was sorry he had let his parents down this way. No doubt she felt she was an ineffective parent, who had somehow let her son down. Ron pledged he would not be involved in this sort of behaviour again.

For each person under supervision on a probation order, a case plan is completed. The plan outlines what will happen in terms of supervision (such as reporting to the probation officer once a month or as required) and activities to be performed by the client, intended to assist in turning their lives around (such as staying in school, maintaining employment, or taking counselling). The case plan we worked out for Ron was that he would follow the conditions of his probation order, channel his energies into school, continue to work part-time in the family business, and pull himself away from the associates that he had been hanging around with for the purpose of stealing.

I visited the home the following week, gathering a few more details to complete the Social History. The home was in the city's west end, in a well-to-do neighbourhood, not lavish; but clearly the family had money to maintain a nice home.

Ron reported to my office in person a few weeks later and indicated things were improving at school. He said he was getting along fine with his family and no longer associated with those that he used to get into trouble with. A few days later, I called his mom, and she confirmed what he had reported. I felt that Ron was off to a good start on probation.

SEVERAL MONTHS went by with Ron reporting how well he was doing and this was confirmed by phone calls to mom.

About five months into Ron's probation, I called his school counsellor who indicated he was now attending full time and doing very well in all subjects. I quickly came to the conclusion that Ron had decided to behave better at home and at school, and that he was doing very well in terms of living a pro-social lifestyle. In my dealings with

Ron, he was pleasant and focused, stressing the positive things he was doing. He spoke with me in an adult, business-like way and I concluded that he would not likely be in any more trouble with the law.

However, a few days later, Ron called me, saying he had something important to discuss with me in private and that he did not want his mom to know. He asked me to come to his home, at a time when his mom would be gone. I was a bit surprised at the request but agreed to meet him two days later.

When I arrived, just he and I were there. He seemed nervous and ill at ease; but I was not concerned for my safety by meeting alone with him. Ron showed me downstairs to his bedroom. His brother and sister also had bedrooms in the basement as well; his was at the far end of the basement hallway. When he opened the door to his room, I could readily see it was full of sporting equipment and electronics….skis, ski boots, fishing rods, tackle boxes, lures, hunting rifles, hunting vests, colour television sets, stereos, and dozens of large boxes that surely contained other items. The room was full of these goods, piled from the floor to the ceiling, stacked against the walls, and some pushed under the bed. Before I could think of how to respond, Ron explained that all this stuff was stolen by him and his accomplices over a period of almost a year and was being stored in his room because his parents never went into his room. By a quick estimate, I concluded the stolen goods were worth thousands of dollars.

Ron then looked directly at me and posed a question, "What should I do about all the stolen property?"

Now, what do I say? And, what do I do?

My mind kicked into overdrive! I was a probation officer, a public servant, whose job it is to protect the public in addition to helping offenders. I have a professional relationship with Ron, not a personal relationship. I am friendly with him, but I am not his friend. I liked Ron and could see a lot of potential in him, but he is now admitting to much more crime than originally charged. What was I to do? How should I respond to his request? He had posed a troubling question—now, how can I deliver a suitable answer?

I was in an ethical dilemma; I knew I had an important decision to make.

Was there anything in my personal life I could draw upon in times like this? I decided my days of stealing a few (well, actually quite a few) golf balls or "exploring" abandoned buildings (actually break and entering) as a kid were not much help in this regard.

My immediate concern was that Ron could face a lot of additional charges regarding the stuff in his room; and, if convicted, he may very well receive a prison sentence. How would jail affect him, given all the positive changes he had made in the past six months?

A thought whirled through my mind, "Were there any other cases that I was dealing with that might shed some light on what I could do in Ron's case?" "Ahhh," I thought, "Fred."

I WAS IN THE PROCESS of completing a pre-sentence report on Fred, a single man who lived with his mother. He was thirty-nine years old, steadily employed as a warehouse labourer, and had been charged with twenty-eight counts of Break, Enter, and Theft from apartments. He was currently in custody, pending the outcome of the sentencing hearing. Fred would break into apartments by using a vice-grip tool to grasp and break the handle on the door, then enter the suite and steal whatever was lying nearby on a table or countertop near the doorway.

When we come home, most of us hang up a coat or

jacket and put items like car keys, wallets, and purses on the nearest stand or small table. It took Fred no more than sixty seconds to break open a door, step inside, grab valuables that could be used immediately or fenced (sold on the black market for about ten percent of the real value), and then leave. If no one was visible in the hallway, he would repeat the process next door. If he saw someone in the hallway, he would casually walk away from the person and head for the stairway, going to another floor to start the process again. If he discovered someone in the apartment, as he broke open the door, he would say, "Oops, sorry, wrong apartment!" close the door and walk briskly to the stairway and leave the building. He told me most people who were home at the time he broke in were so surprised and startled that they often froze in their tracks and did nothing for a few seconds. This gave him enough time to get away from the scene before the victims could clearly recall his features.

Fred was an interesting fellow. It turned out he was quite meticulous about some things and liked to keep lists of things to do, people to see, etc. I learned this, along with lots of other information, from his mother when I first interviewed her for the pre-sentence report.

A few days later, Fred's mother called me as I was finalizing the report. She said she had found a notebook while cleaning his room. It had some lists in it. She thought I would be interested in the notebook and asked what she should do? I made an appointment to visit her at the home later in the day.

When I arrived, she showed me to the kitchen, invited me to sit down at the table, poured me a cup of tea, and then gave me the notebook. It was a plain, common notebook, with a metal coil binding and 6 cm x 12 cm pages, about 1 cm thick. I casually thumbed through the notebook and noted a pattern of dates, addresses and list of items such as cash, watches, credit cards, and even a passport. My first reaction, which I tried to conceal from mom, was that this is a list of the places he broke into—hundreds of them! There was page after page with dates, places and items. I told mom I thought I should keep the notebook. She said, "Okay." I finished my tea and immediately returned to the office.

I then called the city police detective who had done the investigation to bring the initial twenty-eight charges to court. We agreed to meet at the police station the next day where I gave the notebook to the detective. He called me a few days later to say thanks again, and indicated that more charges would be laid against Fred.

I submitted my pre-sentence without reference to the potential new charges. Nothing had been proven yet in court or admitted by Fred. I learned that day from the probation officer who attended court for most of the day to act as the court liaison that the case had been further adjourned for one week.

When Fred's day in court for sentencing arrived, I went to the courthouse and looked for the docket posted in the hallway outside the courtroom. A docket is a printout of the names and charges of everyone appearing in that courtroom on that day. There was Fred's name, appearing on not one, not two, but on six pages! I was right—there were hundreds of new charges against Fred. I stayed for awhile to hear the charges being read out to Fred, methodically one charge at a time. It took all morning for the clerk of the court to read out the charges. When one clerk became hoarse, another clerk came in to the courtroom to continue the reading of the charges. Three clerks were needed that morning to read all the charges to Fred. He pled guilty to each one, a total of about three hundred charges—all the same types of charge and all the same method of committing this crime. Fred was remanded in custody for another week so the judge could think about an appropriate sentence. When he was eventually sentenced, he received eight years in a federal penitentiary.

I felt okay with my decisions in Fred's case. Without his mom calling me, without me calling the detective, without the detective reviewing the information with the Crown prosecutor and without the prosecutor laying a raft of new charges, Fred would have gotten away with a lot of crime.

Although Fred's and Ron's cases were quite different, they had one feature in common—the discovery of additional information which could dramatically affect their sentence.

THE WHOLE CASE involving Fred flashed through my mind as I stood in Ron's room, and it raised a dilemma for me. What should I say to him? Should I call the police, as I did in Fred's case? I knew Ron had been involved in criminal behaviour—lots of it—now what the hell do I do?

Another chain of events whirled around in my mind. One thing new probation officers did at the time as part of their ongoing training was to ride along with city police officers on a shift. My last ride-along flashed through my mind. I had been travelling with two male officers on a late night patrol. We were in a part of the city where crime was fairly common so police patrols were frequent. We came across a young male walking along the sidewalk. He seemed to be weaving a bit as he walked, so the officers pulled over and talked with the person. I got out of the back seat of the vehicle to listen and observe as the officers interviewed the young man as to where he was going, what had he been doing out in the middle of the night, and was he in possession of any alcohol? In a few minutes of talking with the young fellow, the officers were satisfied that he was not in illegal possession of alcohol, was not drunk, that he had been visiting with friends and that he was now on his way home. The officers asked him to show them the contents of his pockets. He pulled out a wallet, lighter, a few coins, a handkerchief—and a marijuana roach. One officer reached out, took the roach, saying, "You don't need this shit," and crumpled up the roach and let it slip through his fingers. Then he dropped it into the gutter along the roadside. The young man shrugged his shoulders and headed for home. The officers and I returned to the cruiser. As we pulled away from the curb, the officer who wrecked the roach commented, "Not everyone needs to be charged." Our patrol resumed, uneventfully, for the last hour or so of the shift.

I STOOD QUIETLY in Ron's room for what seemed like an eternity, thoughts racing through my head. What would I do? What should I do? What is the right thing to do? He was young but what would the police, prosecutor and judge decide if they knew what I knew? The possibility of Ron receiving a prison sentence for all the stolen property kept nagging at me. He was now doing very well at school, getting along well at home, and had distanced himself from his former accomplices; yet if I reported the matter to police, no doubt there would be a lot more charges and the distinct possibility of a prison sentence. He had made positive changes in his life since being placed on probation; I feared those positive moves would be jeopardized if he was to face many new charges.

The fact that Ron admitted his involvement in the items that filled his bedroom impressed me. I interpreted this as his way of dealing with his conscience. He clearly knew he did something wrong and he "fessed up." He took a huge risk in telling me, and I wondered if this might be his way of reaching out for help.

Eventually, I said to Ron, "I'll come back in a week's time.

This stuff better be gone." I didn't say the words in an angry manner. I tried to be rather matter of fact. I did not intend to threaten him. I just wanted to respond in a constructive, helpful way to his question, "What should I do with all this stuff?" With that, I left the house and returned to the office in an emotional turmoil—had I done the right thing?

As a new and young probation officer with limited life experience and even less professional experience, I was fortunate to work with several men who had served many years with a national police agency, then retired, and came back into the workforce as probation officers. These guys had a great deal of life and professional experience and they were prepared to take young guys, such as myself, under their wings and help us learn our jobs. They did not usually tell us exactly what to do but made sure that we had all the information we needed to make an informed decision.

I spoke with one of these sages, outlined my work with Ron, informed him about Fred, and presented my dilemma—had I done the right thing with Ron? He listened carefully and asked a few clarifying questions; then paused and seemed to be deep in thought. Then he said, "Doug, if you still honestly believe in what you said to Ron about getting rid of that stuff, then that is probably a good answer. It is a tough call, but you probably did the right thing."

I felt much better, believing that I made the right call and that a trusted colleague, who was not my supervisor and who had no ambitions to move up in the probation hierarchy, supported the decision I had made.

A WEEK LATER, I was standing in Ron's bedroom in the basement of the family home. It was neat, clean, well organized—and no evidence of stolen property anywhere to be seen. He had obviously gotten rid of the stolen items.

I felt I did not really need to know how he did it or when he did it. He had turned his life in a better direction, a sort of out-with-the-old-and-in-with-the-new situation. Now, it was my turn to make a comment. I said, "Good job. Now, how is school going? Still working part-time? Things OK here at home? See much of you old buddies?" I hoped this was a clear signal to him that we were moving on, and that I was not going to do anything that would see him face a lot more charges.

Over the next nine months, I had regular monthly contact with Ron. I sometimes spoke with his mom and informally checked on his performance at the school through a contact I had with the school counsellor—no formal questioning other than, "How is Ron doing?"

Ron had done well at turning his life around. Maybe it would be more accurate to say that he adjusted his life a bit, enough to head in another direction, one in which criminal behaviour was not an option. Tensions were less at home. He completed high school. He developed a new circle of friends. He continued to work part-time in the family business and he was considering his options—continue with the family business, take post-secondary training such as business or maybe even working in a new field altogether. He had lots of choices and I believed he had a lot to offer his family, friends and the community.

There had been no further charges against Ron, either for new offences or for ones dating back to that year or so that he had gone on a crime spree.

Three years after Ron completed probation, he called and made an appointment to see me. He was in the process of applying for a pardon (now called a record suspension). I happily provided a letter to him in support of his application. The effect of a pardon is to remove and set aside his criminal record from the police record database so that searches will not show that he has a criminal record.

Many years later, I learned that Ron was vice-president

in the family business and was, like his parents, taking a leadership role in the community through service clubs, charities and business organizations.

I still smile to myself when I think of Ron. I believe I had a hand in helping him turn out to be a very good citizen. One of the key decisions I made was to keep him from potentially facing more criminal charges. Yes, that decision was controversial; but I made it in good faith and I had the backing of a colleague I very much admired and respected and whose judgment I trusted completely. I believe I did the right thing with Ron. However, I also believe I did the right thing with Fred. Both cases are to me a source of both personal and professional satisfaction. These are examples of good correctional service that protected the public, in both cases, and gave an offender, Ron, the opportunity and support at the right time when he needed it.

I never heard anything more about Fred—maybe the penitentiary experience opened his eyes to the error of his ways.

Ron never contacted me again—there was no need to. I am okay with that. There are many people in our communities like Ron who realized they needed to "smarten up" and went on to become outstanding citizens.

Over the years, I admit to having fleeting thoughts about stopping in at the family business and having a quick visit with Ron. I dismissed these thoughts every time they crossed my mind—he does not need his former PO checking on him, yet again, even on a friendly social call. Ron is on his own and is doing fine! That is good enough for me.

CHAPTER 3

PETER: A BROKEN HEART

T HE PROBATION ORDER for Peter contained the usual conditions such as stay within the jurisdiction of the court, keep the peace and be of good behaviour, and report to a probation officer once a month or as required, plus a condition that sometimes appears— refrain from consuming alcohol. The period of probation was for one year.

The restriction on alcohol alerted me that it was likely a real problem for Peter and was probably involved with his behaviour that landed him in trouble with the law.

I looked at the charges listed on the probation order. He had been convicted of criminal offences in the city related to causing a disturbance, willful damage of property, assault causing bodily harm and assaulting a peace officer.

"Here is an interesting case for you," my colleague from the court house said. "Peter is from a northern community, pretty isolated, and he has been ordered to reside at a high-needs care centre for men outside the city. He is to be under close medical supervision." When I asked my colleague to go on, he explained, "Peter caused a big ruckus a week ago, and there was a lot of pressure on the prosecuting attorney to throw the book at him, you know, send him away to jail for a while. But I talked to the judge and told him I thought probation was a better sentence. Here's the centre director's card. He is expecting a call from whoever will be Peter's probation officer."

I had heard of the men's centre before but had never been there. I had a rough idea where it was, so I looked forward to the trip to see Peter. I referred to the centre director's business card, called him, and set up an appointment to meet with Peter the following week.

On the drive to the centre, I pondered the details of the offences—a lot of damage had occurred and two people were injured, one being a police officer. Yes, there must have been quite a ruckus.

I pulled into the designated parking area at the centre from where I could see through the trees the shimmering water of a large lake. The centre was comprised of a large main building and about twenty small cabins. Trees about the height of the cabins dotted the landscape. There were paths between the cabins and the main building and lots of grassed space along the paths and beside the cabins. It struck me as a peaceful, serene and quiet place, away from the hustle and bustle of the city and within walking distance of a large lake.

I went into the main building, explained that I had an appointment to see Peter, and asked for the director. A staff member said the director was busy, but that I could go over to Cabin 12 to see Peter. Off I went along a path leading to Cabin 12. My knock on the door was responded to by a man's gruff voice growling, "Come in."

I opened the screen door then the inner door, "Peter?"

"Yeah?"

"Hi. I'm Doug, the probation officer. How are you doing?"

"This place sucks but I gotta stay here—no choice. The government says so."

I closed the door behind me, "Can I join you at the table?"

"Sure, why not?"

My eyes gradually adjusted to the dim light in the cabin. The windows were small and the ceiling lights did not generate a lot of light. I could, however, make out Peter sitting at a table, on a metal chair. Another grey metal chair seemed to be waiting for me to join him at the table. Peter had greying hair, was unshaven for a few days and looked about sixty years of age, with a solid, muscular build.

"Okay if I sit down?"

"Sure," Peter said.

"Okay," I started, "I will go over the probation order and then I have a bunch of questions to ask you for a report that will go on your file back at my office in the city."

"No need to talk about that stuff again. Lots of guys have told me what it is, and I don't need you to repeat that stuff. I know what I done and where I am at. I just wanna know when I can go back home to my own cabin."

"Well," I said, "How about we start by you going over what happened?"

> Well, my doctor back home said I have some kind of a disease, something in my brain—I don't remem-ber what he said it was—but I had to go to the city to see a specialist. So, I cleaned up my little place out in the bush, headed into town, stayed with my brother overnight and then in the morning caught the bus to the city, took until evening to get there. I didn't know where to go so I went down to one of those cheap hotels downtown 'cause that was all I could afford. I went to the café in the hotel for supper, then to the bar for a few drinks, ya know, for a night cap.

Peter continued:

> Ya know, I didn't know anyone in the city. It was a bit scary in the bar by myself, but I am used to being on my own. At home, I live in a cabin year round and hunt, fish and trap fur; sometimes do odd jobs and labourer stuff—make an okay living but I ain't rich. Don't get many visitors, just other trappers once in

a while, and my brother. In the bar, this one big guy came up to me and said he'd buy me a beer. 'Okay,' I said. He was from out of the city too, he said, somewhere, and I got to thinking after a while he was looking for something more than a beer. I said he better go and leave me alone but he didn't. I told him to fuck off and he didn't. By this time, I'm pretty pumped. He is trying to touch me, so I haul off and punch him good, in the face. He fights back—he is strong. I guess the beer kicked in, and I knocked him down and put the boots to him. He grabs my leg and we fall down, punching and kicking. The chairs and little tables were flying all over the place. The bar keeper yells at us to quit, but I keep pounding on this guy—I'm getting my wind now. 'Bang, bang,' I hit the guy and he is out like a light. Now another bar keeper and two cops show up. They try to grab me, but I am really going now and I punch that one cop in the face. So he gets out of the way and I turn and fall down, kinda black out. That other cop gets the cuffs on me I guess, 'cause I wake up later in police cells—no idea how I got there."

Peter pauses and I wait for him to continue.

Then I go to court. A guy from the Salvation Army seen me and so did a doctor, but not the doctor I came to see in the city. The judge puts over my case. I have almost no money, just a bus ticket home. In a few days it was like that so, I said guilty to the charges and said I just want to go back home in the bush.

The judge says I can't go home to my cabin just yet—I gotta go to this seniors' place 'cause the government is paying for me to stay there until I get better. I said, 'Okay, for a while'.

So here I am. I got some pills to take—they keep

me calm and I can't drink which is okay 'cause I hardly ever drink at home. You can't be drunk and live in the bush, too much can go wrong. I guess in the city, too. They say I gotta stay here until I settle down, then maybe I can go home. The food here is good but some of the other guys are bossy and get on my nerves. At least I got my own little place here—I come back here when I want to.

I now had a pretty good idea what happened and why Peter is on probation. For the next half hour, I took over the interview, finding out that he did not have a criminal record, learning that he grew up in the bush up north, that he lived for many years on his own and that he felt very uncomfortable in the city, even at the centre. These were places quite foreign to him.

I CAME TO THE CENTRE three times over the next three months to see Peter, as per the condition on his probation order. I had two phone conversations with the director of the centre who said Peter was not eating much and seemed depressed and withdrawn. He had been diagnosed with a brain disorder for which he now took pills. If he drank alcohol, the disorder would quickly degenerate into violence.

When I visited Peter, I steered the conversation to his life back home in the bush. He seemed to relax and open up to me a bit more each visit. He would talk about trapping fur, preparing it for sale, then taking it to town to sell it. Some years, fur prices were good and he had money to spend; other years, fur prices were low so he watched his expenses very carefully. "I could be a nice guy with money to spend or I could be a real miser," he explained with a grin.

He would bring out a scrap book that his brother had mailed to him. Peter would slowly turn the pages and tell me about the contents. Pictures of wild animals, his brother, his log cabin and the bush which sheltered him and provided everything he needed.

Peter's stories took me back to my childhood where I grew up in a small town on the edge of a large river valley. I'd spend countless days with a friend or two in the bush and along the river, watching birds and animals, exploring game trails and tending small campfires to warm food and keep us warm over night as we camped in brush bivouacs.

I, too, was concerned about Peter's deteriorating condition. He liked my visits—it seemed to brighten his day a bit but he kept saying that he could not wait to get back to his cabin in the bush. I was not sure that he could look after himself, living alone in isolation yet he was not thriving at the centre. The director would not authorize Peter's return to the north just yet—he was concerned with his safety, but the director also knew Peter was very unhappy with the present circumstances.

I received a phone call one day from the director—Peter had died during the previous night. His personal effects would be sent to his brother.

I closed the file on Peter and sent a letter to the judge who had placed him on probation.

My guess is that Peter died of a broken heart.

CHAPTER 4

ELAINE: IS STEALING THE SAME AS EXCHANGING?

ELAINE SHOWED UP at the probation office right after being placed on probation for eight months on a charge of "Theft Under" for shoplifting. She was assigned to my caseload; and, as I happened to not have any appointments for an hour or so, I agreed to see her right away.

The receptionist showed her to my office. We shook hands, introduced ourselves, and Elaine settled nervously in a chair located across the desk from where I was seated. She hesitantly looked around my office, pausing to notice the pictures, cartoons, coat rack, desktop phone, metal desk, two chairs and bulletin board—a bland but functional government office. She was nervous and anxious, as most people are when they first meet their probation officer.

I started the meeting by going over the Probation Order with her, making sure she understood the legalities:

- The judge had suspended the passing of the sentence and she would not be sentenced for eight months, providing there were no further charges and providing that she complied with the conditions of the probation order.
- She had to remain in the jurisdiction of the Court.
- She was required to report once a month or as required to a probation officer.
- She had to report any change in address or employment to a probation officer.

- If she successfully completed the period of probation, she would still have a criminal record but the
probation would be over and she would not be sentenced on the shoplifting charge.

She indicated she understood what being on probation
involved and that she had no intention of "screwing it up."

I LED HER THROUGH a series of questions in order to get
a picture of who she was and what kind of a person she
was. Here is the picture that emerged. Elaine was nineteen
years old and living at home with her parents, a younger
brother and a younger sister. Her siblings were in junior
high school. She and her siblings got along fairly well, especially now that she was working—they saw her as mature
and 'all grown up'. She said she had a good upbringing, with
no major problems or traumas. Elaine said she was in good
health and was not experiencing any health problems. She
had her own room in the basement of the home, which
was a four bedroom bungalow in the city's east end. She
pays nominal rent to her parents so she becomes comfortable setting aside money for rent as part of her learning to
become independent. She buys her own clothes and pays
for her own entertainment and transportation. Her mother
classifies herself as a homemaker but she also does work
part-time as a babysitter for families in the community. Her
father worked for many years in a nearby industrial plant,
often working shift work.

Elaine finished grade eleven in school, which she
said she enjoyed, then went to work as a receptionist in a
local hotel. She indicated she became bored with school
so decided to take a year off and go to work. She enjoyed
the work at the hotel, meeting with guests as they checked
in, arranging payment details and directing them to their

room. She also enjoyed dealing with a wide range of people who came to the hotel to attend business luncheons, meetings, conferences and other gatherings. She said she got along well with staff and management. Her hours of work were from 9 a.m. to 5 p.m., with one hour for lunch. She was undecided as to how long she would continue working at the hotel but, for now, it was a great job. Her plans for the future included finishing high school and getting a place of her own.

She did not have a steady boyfriend but did date from time to time. She said she was in no rush to get married, as she might continue her education at the university or a career college. Elaine enjoyed a variety of sports, liked to read, and visited regularly with aunts, uncles, cousins and grandparents. Elaine said she had a small circle of girlfriends, some of whom she went to school with, some from the neighbourhood and some colleagues from work. She said her parents did not know about her being charged, going to court, or being placed on probation. Elaine claimed she did not have a previous criminal record, nor had she shoplifted before. She said she was now very embarrassed by her legal difficulties.

So far, the picture that was developing was of a well-established young woman who was pro-social in her attitudes and behaviour. I wondered how the picture would change as we got into a discussion of the crime she committed—shoplifting a bra.

"So, Elaine," I said. "Let's talk about what you are charged with? Tell me what happened."

"Well," she replied,

I went shopping at a department store in the shopping centre near my house. I wanted to get a new bra and they were on sale, so I bought one and took it home. When I tried it on, it did not fit very well—it was too small—so I decided to take it back to the store and get another one; this time, one that fit. The next day, during my lunch break, I went back to the store. There were lots of shoppers around and not too many staff and I was feeling a bit rushed to get back to work, so I put the bra in its package back in the bin where I bought it from and then picked out the next size up—I figured that would fit okay.

I went down the aisle and out the entrance of the store into the main hallway of the mall. A security officer came running up behind me and yelled at me to stop. He came rushing up at me and demanded to see the bra. I showed it to him. He took it. He said he saw me take it out of the bin and walk out of the store without paying for it. The guy didn't let me talk; he did all the talking. He called the city police.

Two officers came. They wrote down what the security guy said then wrote me a ticket to go to court. I was pretty scared so I just shut up. When I came to court and the clerk asked me how I plead, I said, 'Guilty'. I did take a bra without paying for it. I was pretty embarrassed in front of all those people in the courtroom, so I just shut up. The judge asked if I had anything to say and I said, 'No'. What could I say? The security guy said it all. I did it. And here I am.

I thought about how to respond to her explanation. I asked, "Elaine, you say that you exchanged one bra for another, right?"

"Right."

"How come you didn't take the first bra to customer service and ask them for a refund to get a bigger one?" I asked.

"Well," she replied, "I know that is what I should have done but I was running out of time on my lunch break."

"So the department store is not really out a bra. You paid

for one, returned it; then took another one, right? You paid for one, right, but just not the one you wanted?" I asked.

"Yes," she said.

"The problem is that you did not do the return in the regular way so it looks like you were stealing. Do you understand that?" I asked.

"Oh yeah," Elaine replied. "I sure do now!"

I replied:

Based on what you have told me, there is some doubt that you legally stole the bra. As I understand our criminal law, to be guilty of theft, you have to actually steal the bra or deprive the rightful owner of it; and, at the same time, you have to intend to steal it. In my mind, exchanging the bra is something different than stealing it. You took the bra but your intention was to exchange it, not steal it. So, I recommend that you contact a lawyer and tell them just like you told me. I think there is a chance here for you to get off on this charge and not have a criminal record. But there is no guarantee this will happen. Do you understand this?

"Yes," she said.

"OK," I said. You are still on probation until another judge says otherwise. Let's set up a reporting schedule that you will be expected to follow. Are you okay with that?"

"Yes," said Elaine.

We agreed that Elaine would report in person the first Tuesday of every month during her lunch break. She could catch a bus downtown to my office, meet with me, then catch a bus that would drop her off across the street from the hotel, in time to return to work. She followed this schedule flawlessly for four months. She reported no changes in her circumstances at all. She brought her pay stubs from work as proof of her employment. That way, I did not have to contact her employer by phone or in person to confirm her employment. I decided not to contact her parents; she was old enough to be on her own, and I could not see any point in possibly upsetting family relationships. I decided that the picture she painted for me was an accurate one—an honest one. I had no information or suspicions that called her story into question.

One day into the fifth month of her probation, I saw Elaine's name on the court docket. I notified my colleague who spent his day representing the probation service in court. Later in the day, he reported to me that she appeared with her lawyer to request a change of plea. The judge granted the application and a trial date was set for six months time. That would be after Elaine had completed her probation.

Since she was not a problematic case, I discussed with my supervisor the possibility of having Elaine report by phone each month for the remaining three months on her probation. We agreed to this and I informed Elaine. She was pleased and she completed her probation this way, with no changes in her circumstances and no further charges.

PROBATION OFFICERS, with the help of their supervisor, develop (either officially or unofficially) a caseload management plan as a way to streamline and prioritize their workload as there is a great deal of work to be done and the time available to do it is limited. They review the number of cases assigned to them, the type of cases under their supervision, whether it be drug offence, sexual offence, property crime, violence, addictions, mental health issues, special needs, extent of criminal record, gang affiliation, among other things. This plan helps the probation officer determine where best to focus his or her attention, so the needs of the offender and the conditions ordered by the court receive the required attention. It is based on the reality that not every case is the same and not every offender has the same needs, so it is reasonable that the probation officer's time be tailored and targeted so that high needs cases receive far more attention than low needs cases. Some cases presented unique approaches, like probationers who lived or worked in isolated, rural locations. I had several cases where roads were often impassible or they were simply non-existent, so the client used his employer's telecommunication equipment to report monthly to me. Normally, I would drive to see the client if there were difficulties for the client to come to my office. I had other cases where clients were working in the Middle East at a remote oil well site and reported to me via a personal letter every month while they were away from the city.

For me, the "low-needs" cases were enjoyable to deal with—these most often were people who made a mistake, then smartened up and moved on with no repetition of the criminal behaviour. However, many cases were "high needs" and a lot of work was required in an attempt to help the probationers change their behaviour so that no more offences were committed. These were tough cases to deal with, a real challenge. In my experience, our success with high-needs cases was limited; but it was exceedingly gratifying when these clients made notable headway towards a law-abiding lifestyle. We often referred our probationers to other professionals like psychologists, therapists, health educators, counsellors and other helpers with specialized skills and knowledge that we believed would help the client. Sometimes, these referrals were met with appreciation and cooperation; on other occasions, the referral was met with hostility and non-compliance. Sometimes, the courts would make accessing professional services as a condition of the probation order. Sometimes, this was helpful in getting specialized services for a client; sometimes the client's resistance and refusal led to new charges for breaching the conditions of their probation order.

About this time, I had Tim, a young fellow, on probation for stealing his father's car. The family dynamics were messy and disintegrating quickly, and I was on the receiving end of a stream of complaints from dad about Tim and from Tim about dad. Mom was trying to keep the family together but she felt the family dynamics deteriorating and slipping through her fingers. Dad was well known in the city, and he was convinced something horrible like suicide or murder could happen unless Tim received professional help. In consulting with my colleagues and supervisor, the idea of a psychiatric assessment came up. This appealed to me so I took steps to have Tim committed to a mental hospital through a court order by the judge who had placed Tim on probation. Tim was arrested and hospitalized for 30 days. Upon his release, I went to visit him at his home. He seemed more settled than before. He was going to stay with his mom, now that his dad had moved out. He obtained a job in the automotive industry—he loved his car and took exceptional care of it. He finished his probation. In hindsight, I wondered if dad should have been committed for a psychiatric assessment as well—it eventually became clear to me that dad was as much or more of the problem than Tim. Who is "high needs" in these situations—the parent or the child?

In terms of Elaine, I checked the court docket on the day of her trial. She was found not guilty. I was pleased to see this outcome—I think it reflected the reality of her situation. I felt comfortable with my role in outlining an option she most likely would not have thought about on her own.

Elaine may not have been an astute consumer in that she did not go about making the exchange in the usual way; but, in my mind, she was not a criminal in the usual sense of the word. The criminal justice system eventually confirmed this. It was rare in my experience as a probation officer to run across innocent people. Every once in awhile, someone would claim they were innocent; but they could not offer circumstances or explanations that convincingly supported their assertions. When Elaine was given the time to fully explain the circumstances, she presented a plausible explanation in a forthright manner. She clearly did not make the best decision when she exchanged the bra, but I am comfortable with the ultimate decision by a court that she did not make a criminal decision.

In my view, she did not deserve to have a criminal record for the rest of her life or until she obtained a pardon/record suspension—the record would not be a valid reflection of her conduct. I did not see her name in court ever again so I can assume she continued to live in a pro-social manner.

CHAPTER 5

BARRY: MORE OF A NUISANCE THAN A RISK

B ARRY CAME TO BE on my caseload when he was transferred from another probation officer who had resigned
to take another job. A quick look at his file revealed Barry
had been in court a lot. He was twenty-one years old, with
little education, no trades training, and a troubled upbringing in foster homes and group homes. He'd reported regularly to his former probation officer and was cooperative
and pleasant. There was no mention in the file of personal
characteristics, such as personal cleanliness.

The receptionist called my office and said, with a
chuckle, "Barry is here to see you. Shall I send him down
to you?"

"Sure," I said.

I heard someone stomping down the hallway to my
office. Barry poked his head in the open door and greeted
me, "Hi, Mr. Heckbert. I'm Barry."

"Hi, Barry. Come in and sit down."

He appeared not to have shaved in a month or so. Barry
wore thick glasses with black frames that rested cock-eyed
on the bridge of his nose—one arm of the frame was much
higher on one side of his head that the other arm. His beard
was scruffy and patchy, his black hair unkempt and sticking
up in places, and he reeked! Barry smelled of body odor,
unwashed clothes, and horrible breath. It was hard to take,
especially when he closed the door as he sat down on a chair
just across the desk and leaned forward to speak with me.

"You can call me Doug, if you like," I said, trying not to be too obvious in pulling back from him.

"Nope," he said. "You are an official so I gotta call you by your last name. I learned that in one of the foster homes, but I ran away."

"Where are you living now?"

"With my friend John."

"What is the address?"

"I dunno—in the west end just off the main road—some avenue near that bar," he explained.

I leaned forward. "What is John's last name?" I asked, getting a bit suspicious.

"I dunno," said Barry. "I met him at work. We got along good, he needed a roomy and I needed a place to stay. But I quit that job at the car wash 'cause it was cold working outside in winter getting the cars ready to get washed."

"Are you still living with John?"

"Yeah, he is a good guy."

I looked through the file and found Barry's criminal record: A dozen or so convictions for theft, shoplifting, breaking into vehicles, businesses and residences, breach of probation, possession of stolen property, and illegal possession of liquor. He was usually fined but did receive two short jail sentences of 10 days and 30 days.

"Barry," I said, "your file shows you have quite a few charges and you have even been sent to jail twice. What is going on? You don't even know where you are living or who you are living with."

He looked at me puzzled. "Yeah, the jail wasn't bad—three squares a day, guys I knew there, got dried out and cleaned up; it was okay. I can show you where I live, Mr. Heckbert, and you can meet John. Some of those charges were a long time ago, maybe a year. I don't go around stealing like I used to way back then."

"Your last trip to court was for stealing cash out of

cars—you'd smash a window, steal cash and tapes," I pointed out. "And you'd B and E houses and businesses to steal liquor, clothes, anything of value you could carry away with you. Are you a professional thief or are you just a pest?"

Barry laughed at that question, "I never thought of that before. I just took stuff I need to get by."

I wondered how long I should keep interviewing him. My small office was pretty rank by this time, and Barry did not seem in a hurry to leave.

"Mr. Heckbert, you are my PO and I gotta see you. I know that—the judge even told me to see a PO. You know, I used to be on the streets, couch surfing, sleeping in cars and old buildings but now I got a room with John so I think I'm doing good. I got along good with Mr. Brown, the other PO, until he got another job so I'm gonna spend time with you. You can help me with lots of stuff I don't know about so I can come see you lots!"

I tried to keep a straight face at his last comment. I wondered how I would address the personal cleanliness issue but decided now was not the time.

"Well, Barry," I replied, "how about you come back next week with the exact address written down on a piece of paper and write down John's last name, too. I want to know if you are back working and what you do in your spare time. Okay?"

"Sure, Mr. Heckbert, we can sure do that. I like you. See you next week."

Barry got up, opened the door and a wave of fresh air wafted in my direction. No doubt a wave of foul air poured into the hallway. Another probation officer passed by the doorway on the way to his office, stopped quickly and looked in at me. "You okay?" he asked. "Sure," I responded. "Barry likes me and he'll be back next week."

"Lucky you," grinned my colleague, as he turned and headed down the hall to his office.

For the next five months, Barry faithfully reported once a month as required and more often if he had some news for me—like, he had a girlfriend or wondered about something—like if his criminal record would ever disappear.

One time, he came in to see me without an appointment, just showing up unannounced at the reception area of the office. I was working on a pre-sentence report at the time, writing down the information I had obtained in an interview with a wife regarding her husband who was writing bad cheques by the dozen. Nevertheless, I told the receptionist that I could see Barry; so he wandered down the hallway to my office. This time, his odour was not an issue—that was a relief! He settled himself in the chair and announced that some slime-bag had taken his good winter coat. He was pretty mad about whoever had the gall to steal from him—what an inconvenience that was! He said he did not know who might have committed this crime but made it clear he was upset by the theft.

I listened attentively and nodded my head as he explained the impact that the crime had on him, and I let him vent. He finished by saying that if he ever found out who did it, he would "beat 'em up real good."

I then asked Barry if he ever thought about the people he stole from—might they have similar reactions to him stealing from them? Barry looked blankly at me and showed no reaction. I asked him if he thought anyone who he stole from would want to beat him up; again he looked at me as if he were puzzled by the question. It dawned on me that maybe he'd never had to deal with that type of question before—that he had never been confronted with the consequences of his own criminal actions on others. Now he was the victim, but I was not sure he saw any connection with his behaviour and other people's reactions.

This reminded me of a similar situation that had recently occurred with another client who had been placed on probation for stealing a pick-up truck loaded with tools and other small equipment. He came to me asking what he could do about being sued by an insurance company for the truck and tools. He blurted out that the statement of claim included on the list of insurable items a set of Ping golf clubs, an expensive golf pull cart and a box of top-of-the-line golf balls. He stated emphatically that while he did steal the truck and tools, there were no golf clubs, cart or balls in the truck at the time. He wondered what to do. I suggested he contact the police service to see what their report listed as missing as well as speak with a lawyer who might be able to help in the matter. The client finished his probation before I heard anything further about the golf equipment. This incident got me reflecting on people's honesty/dishonesty. Yes, there are people who get caught doing illegal things, but there seems to also be people who take advantage of others but don't get caught. Might there be a fine line between those who get caught and those who don't?

On another visit, when Barry wondered when his criminal record would go away, I launched in on a discussion of a "pardon" what it was and how it worked. I explained that after about five years, if he had no further convictions, he could apply to have his criminal record removed from its regular place in the police data-base and set aside. If he were to be granted a pardon, but then was convicted of committing another crime, his old criminal record could be brought back and used against him in subsequent criminal matters as well as impact his travel, employment, and volunteer opportunities. I spoke about the waiting periods, the reports he would have to file, the records of conviction he would have to get and so on. At this point, his eyes glazed over from too much information. I doubt if Barry ever followed through with a pardon application. He, like so many others with a criminal record, become overwhelmed with the process; and, I suspect, he just gave up on the matter.

Barry reported regularly about once or twice a month while he was on probation. He was transient and unsettled, moving from job to job, residence to residence. One time, he proudly announced he had a steady girlfriend, they had known each other for nearly a month! And he said he was really in love. Barry wondered if I wanted to meet his new girlfriend?

I said, "Oh, not right now; how about next month?"

Barry was okay with that.

When Barry reported next month, he explained that he didn't have the girlfriend now, that she wasn't his type and they couldn't get along.

I gave a subtle sigh of relief. Good choice, Barry. I thought to myself that he was not ready for the responsibilities and obligations that went with having a girlfriend, much less more long-term considerations like children.

He bounced from one low-skilled job to another, stayed with John or other friends until they had arguments; then off he would go to live with a new friend. Barry's name did not show up on the court docket during the time he was on probation and so, as far as I could tell, he was abiding by the condition on his probation order to keep the peace and be of good behaviour—that is, no more charges.

ONE INVESTIGATIVE ACTIVITY that probation officers do regularly is home visits—where they go to a client's residence to meet with them and /or their family. Usually, these visits are booked in advance but not always. With Barry, I had trouble getting phone numbers for where he lived. Over time, he became better at giving me his address but remembering a phone number was not one of his strengths. On two occasions, when I started to get a bit suspicious as to Barry's whereabouts, I stopped at one of his last known addresses when I was in the west end of the city, working on other presentence reports. The first time, no one was home at a rundown house with junk scattered all over the lawn. A few days later, I went to the address of a walk-up apartment where Barry had at one point said he lived. A young man answered the door and said that yes, Barry did live there but that today he was at work with their roommate, John. I thanked the fellow and left, being somewhat more satisfied that Barry was being honest with me.

In the past, most of his crimes had involved stealing small items like cash, tools, clothing and food. It seemed like he took something when he was out of money. He knew where he could fence the stolen goods, even though he would only get about ten percent of the actual value of the stolen goods. So far as I could tell, he never used force to get what he wanted—he simply stole what he figured he needed.

About six months after he completed his probation, there was a knock on the front door of my home around 6:30 p.m. At that time, we lived in a small, single-family bungalow in a suburban community just outside the city. My wife and I had finished supper and were cleaning up the dishes and putting away the washed plates, glasses, and cutlery. I went to the door and opened it. To my surprise, there was Barry, standing on the landing of the stairway.

I opened the screen door. "Hi Barry," I exclaimed. "What brings you all the way out here?"

"Well hi, Mr. Heckbert. What are you doing here?"

"Well, I live here, Barry."

"Oh, that's nice, Mr. Heckbert. Hey, do you want to buy some potatoes?"

I looked out to the road and there was a small, beat up, rusty and battered pickup truck with what looked like big sacks of something in the box. Two figures were scrunched in the front seat.

"Oh," I said, "I don't think so. We always grow our own potatoes and vegetables. But thanks, anyways, Barry."

Barry replied, "Well okay, Mr. Heckbert. Thanks. See you." He turned and bounded down the steps towards the truck. "That's Mr. Heckbert. He don't want no potatoes!" he bellowed to those in the truck. I wondered if his friends/business associates in the truck could hear him—I'm sure my neighbours could if they were outside.

"See you, Barry!" I called out after him.

I decided not to call the police to report suspicious potato merchants. I figured the police had better things to do than to deal with Barry. He was more of a nuisance than a serious criminal; and they would likely lay additional charges, given his criminal record. What good would that do, I wondered? I doubt neither Barry nor his friends had a business or peddler's license—this probably never even occurred to any of them. After this potato fencing incident, I never saw or heard from Barry again.

CHAPTER 6

MARY: A FIVE-DOLLAR HOOKER

I CAME TO KNOW ABOUT MARY in early February. The Probation Order that my supervisor handed to me indicated that she had been placed on probation for three months by the judge on two charges of "being a common prostitute." (Today, being a sex worker is not a criminal offence, but some activities such as communication of sexual services remain classified as criminal conduct). The main condition on the order was that she report once a month or as required to a probation officer. There were other conditions, too, as usual, such as keep the peace, be of good behaviour, remain within the jurisdiction of the court, and report any changes of address or employment. As my supervisor handed the Order over to me, he grinned and commented, "Mary. Placed on probation for hooking. No fine, no jail time. She must be really something!" 'Hooking' was a slang term we'd use back in the day for sex work, practiced, of course, by a 'hooker'.

I took the order and sauntered over to the window overlooking the main downtown avenue in the city. Light snow was falling, with traffic moving slowing along this main thoroughfare. There were two hookers working the street across from the building that housed the probation office and a number of other government services. Seeing sex workers had become a non-event for me and the other probation officers in the office. They were present daily from noon right on through the day, into the evening, and well into the wee-small-hours. Some of the women were gorgeous; some were plain; some were old and some were new at it.

I wondered how Mary would fit into the scenario I saw across the street. How old was she? What did she look like? Was she an oldster or was she new at it?

I glanced at the probation order. The date of occurrence for the offences was mid-December, the year before, about six weeks previously. I noticed that there was an address and phone number written by hand on the order and I recognized the writing as belonging to one of my colleagues who had spent most of his day at the court house. He would have seen her and quickly gone over the conditions with her. It was now my job to interview her to gather information for the Social History, which included a detailed picture of her employment, education, family circumstances, health and criminal history. I was also expected to develop a case plan as to how she would complete her three months on probation.

I didn't have a chance to work on Mary's case right away as I had other more serious (so I thought) cases at the time involving break and enter, assault causing bodily harm, possession of drugs for the purpose of trafficking, and theft. Somehow, in my mind, writing up a Social History of a hooker on probation for three months didn't qualify as urgent, but a few days later, when my schedule was less hectic from doing pre-sentence reports and supervising my caseload, I gave Mary a call. I wondered why she had not come to the office, as most new probationers did, and this was my chance to find out.

I called the number written on the probation order. No answer. A few hours later, I called again and still no answer. Okay, I thought, she's away from home for the day. I called again the next day. No answer. I called several times a day for the rest of the week and still no answer.

"How else to locate her," I wondered to myself, but, I

decided to try one more time—my patience was wearing thin. How much more time would I have to spend tracking her down? I called and a female voice came on the line. "Hello?" I asked if this was Mary and I heard a mumbled "Yes." In an authoritative voice, I introduced myself and said, "Mary, it's time to go over the terms of your probation order. Can you come to the office?"

After a pause, she replied, "No."

"Oh," I said. "It usually happens that a person on probation such as yourself comes to the office for the first meeting."

"I can't," she said, after another short pause. "I got kids. They're little. Two of 'em."

"They can come along with you, if you wish." I said. But then there was nothing but a long pause. "Okay," I added. "How about if I come to your place?"

"Do you have to?" she asked, her voice trembling. She sounded worried about something.

"Well, it boils down to either you come here or I come to your place. What will it be?" I asked.

Another pause, again, quite long.

"Mary?" I asked.

"What?" she said.

"What'll it be, here or your place?"

After short pause she dejectedly muttered, "Oh fine, you can come here."

MARY WAS CLEARLY UPSET but we managed to set up a time to meet later that week, Friday at two in the afternoon. When Friday rolled around, I was ready to interview Mary. My objective was to gather information for a Social History about Mary's family, employment and educational history, as well as information about her health, future plans and, of course, the crime. "What type of hooker was she?"

I wondered. "Why had the judge placed her on probation rather than fine her or give her a prison sentence?"

The address I had for Mary was in the central part of the city, not far from what was commonly considered to be the inner city. I reached the address after a ten-minute drive from the office. The street was tree-lined with tall elms and the sidewalks were cracked and uneven. Snow banks lined the streets and the sidewalks. Caragana hedges were common along that street, and the tangled branches of a caragana bush pretty well hid the house I was looking for. A ramshackle fence leaned against the hedge. As I pushed the gate aside, I could see foot-deep snow drifts silhouetting bottles, boxes, other garbage and a few toys, including a child's small, rusted, three-wheeled pedal bike. The veranda on the front of the house had rickety wooden stairs leading up from the sidewalk to a dilapidated screen door with holes and tears in the screen. I entered the veranda and knocked on the front door. As I waited, I became aware of the musty smell of the residence, including periodic whiffs of what I took to be dirty diapers and garbage.

The front door creaked slowly as it opened a bit.

"Yes?" came a women's weak voice from behind the door.

"Hi," I said. "I'm Doug; here to see Mary."

I waited for the door to open up or to be invited in but that never happened. Standing there on the veranda, not quite sure what to do next, I wondered what things were like inside the house. I could see that it was gloomy inside and I could not recognize anything in the poor light. Rather than just stand there, though, I slowly pushed the front door open, entered the house, and looked around. As my eyes adjusted to the dim light, I gradually made out the form of a short, heavy-set person about five feet tall standing about ten feet away, in the middle of the front room.

"Mary?" I enquired.

"Yah," came her reply.

I moved forward and extended my hand, expecting her to take it in a handshake. She kept her hands at her sides. Turning, she said, "Come to the kitchen. The kids are asleep." As I followed her toward the kitchen, I saw that the windows in the front room were covered with tattered curtains, thus accounting for the gloomy interior; and there was a shabby chesterfield, two dilapidated stuffed chairs and a small dark-brown wooden coffee table in the front room. There was clothing lying all over the floor plus a teddy bear and a doll. Odours in the room were even more pronounced than what I had smelled out on the veranda.

The kitchen was a brighter room but also smelly. It was small and I could see down a hallway to where three closed doors were evident. A white painted table with four scuffed chairs dominated the room. Looking over at Mary, I confirmed that she was short—5 feet tall, no more. And she was heavy. I remember struggling to estimate her weight. I concluded she was not just heavy—she was obese. Likely over three hundred pounds. Her round face was framed by cropped hair. Her skin was fleshy and mottled and she had big round dark circles around her eyes. My conclusion, based on a few glances at her was that she was not the most gorgeous sex worker I had ever seen.

"Sit down?" asked Mary.

"Sure," I replied, taking a seat at the table and looking around the kitchen at the dishes stacked in the sink and piled on the stove. I noted whiffs of onions and other foods and the distinctive smell of rotting garbage. Mary seated herself across the table from me. When she moved, her dress, which hung like a large sack from her shoulders, wiggled as her body rolled and jiggled.

"Thanks for meeting with me, Mary. I am here to go over your probation order with you, to make sure you understand the conditions that apply to you for the next three months— more like two months, now. I also have to compile a report called a Social History which tells all about you, things like where you live, your work, your education, health, that sort of thing. Okay?"

"Yah," she responded.

"Can we start with your living arrangements?" I asked. The training I had about interviewing suggested starting interviews with topics like this one as it was relatively easy, familiar and generally non-controversial. In practice, I had become comfortable leaving questions about the offence to be covered later in the interview, once I had established a bit of trust with the interviewee.

I took out a note pad and pen, placed them on the table and leaned back with the intention of letting her speak first. A tense silence settled over the room.

"Okay, Mary, I'll start with some questions. I'll make notes in this book—you can see the notes at any time. I will use my notes to type up the official report back at the office. You will get a copy of that report, okay?"

"Sure," she mumbled.

"Tell me how long you have lived here, and where did you live before this place?"

Mary took her time, then replied, "About six months here, in the fall. Before that we lived in the west end for about a year."

"Okay," I said. "Who lives here?"

Again, Mary took her time. "Me and the two kids. Johnny is six months, Celia is two years. Paul is at work. He said he'd be home about now. He is busy."

"So, Paul is your husband?" I asked.

"Yah, common law. We've been together about two years."

"Okay, do you have a job and what have you done in the past?" I enquired.

"I got no job now," she mumbled.

"So, you are the one who looks after the kids and the house, a house wife?"

"Yah."

"A domestic engineer?" I grinned, hoping to add some levity that might help our struggling conversation.

"A what?"

"Nothing." There were only a few words in my notebook.

"What about before you became a housewife and started having kids? What did you work at?"

Mary lowered her head and quietly said, "Not much. I worked a bit in a factory and a restaurant."

More silence.

"Then you met Paul, fell in love with him and you moved in together?"

"Yah."

"Mary, how old are you now?"

"Twenty-two."

"Twenty two?" I said, and wrote it down. My emotional reaction was that she looked weary and in poor health. I wondered if my facial expressions and tone of voice hid my shock at learning her age.

"Yah," she said.

Another silence occurred. I suspected this was going to be a very long interview without a lot of insightful information.

As I waited, either for Mary to offer a comment or for inspiration that I could think of an effective leading question, there were heavy footsteps on the porch and the front door opened.

"Mary!" a man's voice hollered.

Mary looked relieved and said, "Paul!" and looked at me.

She and I sat there, waiting for Paul. He stomped his way through the front room and entered the kitchen. "Paul," he said, extending his right hand to me. "Doug," I replied, extending my right hand as I pulled out my business card from my shirt pocket. Paul examined the card, looked me up and down, and sat down at the kitchen table. I estimated he was six feet tall, about 220 pounds, in pretty good physical shape and about 35 years old. He was wearing denim jeans, jean jacket, plaid shirt, and work boots.

"Ok," Paul said, "where are we at?"

I filled him in on the process I had to follow and stressed that I needed information to paint a word picture of Mary.

"You want information from me about these things?" Paul asked.

"Sure," I said.

"Okay, here goes," he sighed and proceeded to tell me how Mary had grown up with her mom and dad and two older sisters in a small town outside of the city that was also his own home town. The family moved into the city so Mary could go to school but that didn't go well so she went to work.

"We started living together about two years ago," he continued. "She looks after the bills, house and kids, and I bring home the bacon." Then with professional zeal, he explained. "My business keeps me busy. You seen my delivery trucks around the city? Pick-ups, cargo vans, cube trucks with a big PL on the side? Big green letters on white?" I nodded as I did recall seeing vehicles as he described from time to time in the city. "Deliver all over the city, sometimes way out of town. I'm getting a good reputation."

Mary sat quietly through this part of the interview.

Paul shook his head and added, "You know, I got no idea what happens to the money I give her. She gets enough to look after all the food, clothes, rent, baby stuff—you know, everything. I work hard to bring it in but she pisses it away."

Mary started to fidget on her chair. She blurted out, "Wait, you don't give me that much money. Sure not enough for Christmas, too."

"Oh, bullshit!" exploded Paul. "Is that why you did the guys in the alley? To make Christmas money?"

That was it. The big reveal. The offence part of the Social History ramped up fast. I thought to myself, "Where is this going now and how's it all going to end up?"

"Yah, that's why," replied Mary in a quiet but firm tone of voice. "Yah," she repeated.

Nobody spoke for what seemed a long time to me. I had learned to be patient with periods of silence where people seemed to think about what they had said and maybe what they were going to say next.

A baby started fussing and crying softly, breaking the silence. Mary, Paul, and I sat in the kitchen, each wondering who would say what next. The baby started howling.

Mary struggled to her feet saying, "I'll get him." We watched her shuffled down the hall into the bedroom and that's when Paul blurted out, "Well, that's what she did. Two guys in the back alley while I was at work. Five bucks she charged –five bucks each. If she needed more money, all she had to do was ask."

Mary emerged from the bedroom with the little one, still softly whimpering. She made her way back to the kitchen. "I gotta get a bottle for him," she said, pulling open the door of the refrigerator. I decided right there that the interview had come to an end. I pushed my chair away from the table and stood up. "Well. I'm going to leave now. I need more information but now is not a good time, is it? We'll talk some more later, okay?"

"Sure," replied Mary and Paul in unison.

I had a feeling that I needed to bring some kind of closure to the interview, partly for me but especially for Mary. I could escape back to the office, then go home for the weekend but Mary would have to deal with two kids all day, every day, as well as deal with Paul who honestly seemed to think that he was doing a fine job as the breadwinner of the family. Obviously, there was tension on a number of levels between Mary and Paul.

"Mary," I said. "Do you realize you committed two criminal offences, two crimes?"

"Yah," she said quietly, looking down toward the floor.

"Will you promise me that this won't happen again?" I asked her, looking then directly at Paul. I was hoping that he got the hint about money.

"Yah," replied Mary. "Sure."

"I'll be in touch."

I gathered up my notebook, pulled on my jacket and headed for the living room, then outside and down the stairs. I got in my car and drove away.

I NEVER DID FORMALLY COMPLETE Mary's Social History. In the week following the first and only interview with her, I went to the police station and put in a request, as usual, to review a copy of the police report. This way, I would obtain detailed information about the offences. The clerk indicated the report was not available. This was rather unusual, but I had to accept that fact.

Over the next month, I phoned the number I had for Mary once a week, but there was no answer. One day, I drove past the house and decided to stop in unannounced. No one came to the door. I sometimes saw Paul's work vehicles around the city.

In discussions with my supervisor, we decided not to take any action against Mary for failing to report as required to a probation officer. What was the point? Her name did not appear again on the court docket so we knew she had not been charged with any offences while on probation. When her three month period of probation ended, we closed the file. We reflected on the options the sentence judge had faced in this case: a fine, imprisonment, or a suspended sentence with probation. The first two were impractical, leaving probation as the only viable option. Although Mary did not comply with the condition to report to a probation officer, what would be gained by charging her with a breach of probation? Take her back to court for sentencing? Extend the period of probation? Why would she do anything different on a new probation order?

In Mary's case, there were a host of other issues: child care, money management, spousal relations, future plans. It was enough to get a promise from Mary not to do this again.

Given that sex work was a crime at that time and the sentence options were a term of imprisonment, a fine, or a suspended sentence with probation Mary's case raised a number of perplexing questions for me. She was clearly not a suitable candidate for prison. What would happen to the kids if she was sent away? Most likely, child welfare authorities would become involved. Maybe Paul could take time off work to look after the kids, but then what would happen to his business?

Mary could obviously not just pay a fine. I had seen in several other cases where a convicted sex worker had asked the judge for time to pay a fine. The judge had always smiled slightly and replied, "No." Giving a hooker time to pay was just an invitation for her to go and turn another trick so she could pay the fine for the previous trick. Not a good idea.

As it happened Mary did not turn out to be an ideal candidate for probation. She was so overwhelmed with her life circumstances that following the conditions in a probation order were of no real concern to her. She was poverty stricken, with little hope of ever changing that situation.

This is where alternatives to going to court could be most helpful. In my view, Mary needed a host of life-skills development opportunities that she obviously missed as she grew up. I fully supported the changes that eventually removed the offence of being a sex worker from the criminal law. That made a lot of sense to me. Community-based programs that focus on prevention, intervention and support have a more positive impact on people like Mary than using criminal sanctions. Still, aspects of sex work remain criminalized in many jurisdictions. Is that the most practical response to this behaviour? What other responses might we consider?

CHAPTER 7

DRUNKS, NUDITY, AND OTHER DYNAMICS IN THE COURTROOM

IN THE EARLY PART of my career, it was an offence for a person to be inebriated or drunk in a public place contrary to provisions of the Liquor Act. I came to understand that for many years, this was a well-established way to deal with the problem of drunks on the city's streets. Police officers on patrol would stop someone on the street who appeared to be intoxicated and would determine if they had a place to go, such as a residence or shelter. If not, police tended to arrest the person—mostly men—and escort them to the downtown police station where they were housed in the "drunk tank." This was a room with some metal bunk beds for men, with a separate room for the few women arrested for being drunk in a public place, who were drunk and/or vomiting, with no other criminal involvement. The room also had a few cells for men who were belligerent or combative. Needless to say, the "drunk tank" was not a very nice place to have to stay (or work, for that matter). As the night wore on, more drunks would be thrown in the tank. It was noisy and foul-smelling, with at times more than a dozen men usually wearing ragged and dirty clothes, soiled with human waste and vomit, jammed into a cramped space. They were expected to be sober enough by the morning for an appearance in court, charged with being drunk in a public place.

When I was assigned to work at the courthouse as the court contact/liaison person for the probation service, I had a small office down a narrow hallway away from the main hallway that led to the four courtrooms. Nearby to my office were the offices of the judges and the prosecuting attorneys. This arrangement worked very well for me as I had access to the judges and prosecutors when needed. I could also use my office for interviewing people like social workers, court workers, lawyers, and agency representatives from organizations such as the Salvation Army who often came to the courthouse. From time to time, I interviewed parents in my office when they needed a private spot to talk to me about their son or daughter who was appearing in court. However, I used my office mainly to write brief reports, make notes, and place phone calls back to the probation office.

When courts were in session, I spent most of my time in the hallway talking to, or looking for, people like lawyers, accused persons, and court clerks in the adjoining courtrooms. In the main, and busiest, courtroom, dubbed Docket Court, I had inherited a favoured spot in the courtroom, thanks to the influence of my predecessor, Ernie. This spot was comprised of a chair and tiny wooden desk situated right at the front of the courtroom and off to the immediate right of the raised dais reserved for His Honour, the Judge. (Her Honours were yet to be appointed to the judiciary). This way, if the presiding judge wanted further information about an accused person appearing before him, all the judge had to do was turn his head and quietly direct me to interview the person in question, whether they were in custody or in the courtroom. I could leave the area, conduct an interview; then conveniently report to the judge what I learned when I returned to my chair and desk.

Inside the courtroom, there was a low, wooden fence-like barrier that stretched across the room. This barrier served as a divider between persons who had some official business in court—such as court officials and accused

persons when their name was called for them to appear—
and other persons who would be in court to observe. About
one third of the room was for officials while the remaining
two thirds was for spectators and other members of the
public, all seated on wooden benches.

From my desk, situated at the front of the courtroom, I
had a bird's-eye view of the whole room. I could see people
entering and leaving the back of the courtroom through
two large doors, watching them pause and look around
for someone already seated that they knew, such as a their
buddy, or a co-accused; or for someone to avoid, such as a
parent or a victim.

There was a wide range of people who entered the
courtroom. Some were well-dressed, for example women
with high-heeled footwear. Others wore jeans, a sweatshirt
and running shoes. Some men wore a suit and tie with pol-
ished shoes; others wore ragged jeans, t-shirts and tattered
runners. A few mothers would bring infants or young children, but a courtroom is not an easy place to attend to kids.
A general sense of quiet fell over the courtroom as people
found their place. Rarely did a clerk or judge have to raise
their voice to ask those in attendance to be quiet. Often,
several young adults would enter the courtroom crowded
together, then worm their way along one of the wooden
benches to find a spot where they could sit together. This
demographic seemed to have a harder time sitting still and
keeping quiet.

DURING MY TENURE at the courthouse, the court dealt
with a full range of offences, ranging from extremely serious, such as murder, drug trafficking, and conspiracy, to
less serious, such as bad cheques, assaults, and routine
impaired driving. Also dealt with were offences having to do with public disorder such as prostitution and

public drunkenness. Needless to say, some people seemed ashamed to be appearing in court, some were angry and argumentative, and some did not seem to care all that much about being there at all. Some were well-spoken and articulate; some were withdrawn and uncommunicative. Some appeared to be dealing with addictions and/or mental health issues. Most cases took only a matter of minutes, with many adjournments to a later date to continue the matter.

Those of us working around the courthouse never knew what would happen from one day to the next. This made for an interesting workplace. Concerns regarding security were dealt with by court officials and temporarily assigned police officers. This was a far cry from the massive security presence nowadays in all urban centers featuring cameras, empty-your-pockets-and remove-your-belt routines, security scanners, metal detectors, and cursory briefcase and purse inspections, in addition to dozens of security-oriented staff posted at entrances to a courthouse and located strategically throughout the building.

WHEN I WORKED at the courthouse, there were few disturbances and no imminent threats that I was aware of. The disturbances usually amounted to angry people objecting loudly to being remanded in custody or protesting vigorously when additional charges were laid. There were only a few times when some people appeared to be under the influence of drugs or alcohol and were escorted out of the building—they would have to wait until later to find out what happened to their friend or colleague in court that day.

Court officials tried to maintain an air of solemnity throughout the proceedings. References were made in legal terms, such as indictment, adjournment, waiver, and information. Individuals appearing in court on criminal matters were addressed as Mr., Mrs., or Miss, not their first name. Judges were referred to by other court officials as Your Honour, although some accused referred to the judge as Your Highness or Your Majesty. That comment always brought smiles and a few quiet chuckles from other court officials. It looked like that judge would try hard not to let a slight grin cross his face.

There was a general sense of tension in the air. This is not surprising, given the issues at stake. Judges have a great deal of authority, including lawfully depriving an accused of their liberty and freedom by remanding an accused into custody, sentencing a person to a term of imprisonment, revoking bail, levying a fine, convicting an accused so they have a criminal record for life, and other forms of adjudication. Generally, I find that people in general do not look forward to their day in court. Yes, a day in court can prove one's innocence; but, most of the time, most people do not like going to court—there is a lot to lose.

A journalist from a local newspaper spent much of his morning in the courthouse, checking dockets to see who was appearing in which courtroom, speaking to prosecutors and defence lawyers, and sitting in court when sentencing was taking place, looking for facts and catchy comments that might appear in articles for his crime beat. Members of the public tended not to line up to be interviewed by the journalist—no doubt the last thing they wanted was their name appearing in the paper the next day.

There were, however, a few people I had on probation over the years that took considerable pride in producing newspaper clippings of what a reporter had written about them and/or their criminal behaviour. These were generally young adults, and they seemed rather proud of their story as it appeared in the newspaper. Sadly, as I got to know these folks, they did not have much else in their lives that they (or others, such as parents) could be proud of that warranted a column or two of good news in the local paper. I found it rather sad that their criminal conduct seemed to be such a noteworthy event in their lives. Maybe if they had participated in sports, work, school, or volunteered, they would have been more likely to avoid getting a criminal record and public recognition for criminal behaviour.

To my far left, on the other side of the judge, was a passage door to the hallway through which court clerks entered and left the courtroom, arms laden with files containing all the paperwork needed to process each case. The clerks scurried in and out of the courtroom quickly and quietly. The information they carried enabled the court process to function with efficiency and effectiveness. In my view, the judges, lawyers, and prosecutors may have thought that they ran the court; but I came to value the crucial role of the clerk of the court's staff in keeping track of charges, future court appearances, and decisions made by various officials. The clerk's office could also claim that they ran the court. I went out of my way to get on and stay on the "good side" of all the clerks, court reporters, and filing clerks. Working collaboratively with them made my job that much easier and enjoyable.

Lawyers, articling students, and court workers entered the courtroom through the main doors and made their way to the front of the room where they made their presence known to the clerk of the court and indicated which accused they were appearing for. There was a confident superiority about the veteran lawyers—this process was not new to them. After reporting to the clerk, they would jostle for a place to sit on a long wooden bench with one of their colleagues and wait for their client to be called by the clerk. Student lawyers, new to the profession, tended to be a bit more tentative and hesitant as they checked in with the clerk and reviewed their notes to make sure they had the right client in the right courtroom on the right day and time. They too would sit on the long wooden bench, waiting for their case to be called.

AN INTERESTING DYNAMIC in the main courtroom occurred in the front row of the public section occupied by self-appointed observers—up to six or eight men seated quietly on the wooden bench. Some of them would line up in the hallway ten minutes or so before the courtroom doors were unlocked and opened, just so they could be among the first into the main courtroom and then hustle their way to the front row to get a good seat. Then, after court convened, they would speak quietly among themselves about the sentences, adjournments and other court matters, expressing their pleasure or displeasure with the decision. They did not interfere much with the goings on in court—they just made their views known with nodding or shaking heads, either in agreement or against, and quiet, short comments such as, "You bet," "No way," "Aaah," or "No good." Many court personnel got quite a kick out of the "peanut gallery," and on many occasions they brought a smile to my face with their comments and insights.

As mentioned, when I was seated at my desk to the right of His Honour, I had a terrific view of the entire courtroom—the front of the courtroom where the officials such as the judge, prosecutor, and the clerk of the court worked, where accused persons stood to hear the charges against them and the lawyers awaiting their case to be called while seated on a long wooden bench; and the gallery beyond where the accused, not in custody awaited their turn before the judge, and family and friends who waited to see what would happen.

When accused persons heard their name called, they moved from the public gallery to a position in front of the judge. Accused persons, who had been arrested before court day, had that morning been moved from the police holding cells to a secure narrow rectangular room beside the main courtroom. A locked door controlled by a uniformed police officer was the only access that persons in custody had to the courtroom.

When an accused in custody was called by the clerk, the police officer opened the door slightly and shouted the person's name. The person would work their way through the others in custody and present themselves to the officer, who would then fully open the door and indicate to the accused to step forward into the courtroom. The door would then be slammed shut behind the accused and the court proceedings in that particular case would commence.

For persons charged with public intoxication, the clerk of the court would call out all the names of those so charged. This was done at the first of the docket, or list of persons appearing in court. All would be in custody and the police officer would unlock the door to the holding room and call out the names again. The door would open wide and the "drunks" would shuffle their way out of the holding room and cluster together—right beside me! Over time, I eventually became accustomed to the sight of disheveled, foul-smelling men close at hand. As a rule, the clerk of the court would read out the charge, "You stand jointly charged with being intoxicated in a public place, contrary to the provisions of the Liquor Act. How do you plead?" As a rule, too, there would be a muffled, group response that sounded like, "Guilty" caroling from all the accused. The judge would then declare, "You are each hereby sentenced to time in custody."

The police officer would then open the door to the holding room, the accused would shuffle, more quickly this time, back into the holding room. Then the door would slam shut behind them. The court process would then begin for accused with lawyers, accused in custody, and finally accused waiting in the public gallery.

I will never forget the day that dealing with drunks took a rather strange turn. It started out as usual. The clerk called out about a dozen names. The police officer controlling the holding room door opened the door slightly and repeated the names, then fully opened the door so the dozen tattered, dirty and smelly accused shuffled their way to a spot close to my desk. The holding room door slammed shut and a hush descended over the courtroom. The clerk read out the charge and the accused jointly entered a muffled, garbled plea of guilty. Then one voice rang out loud and clear, "Not guilty." The judge turned quickly to face the group and said, "Who is not guilty?" The group morphed and then spit out one of the members. I had a quick look at a male of about age 50 in ragged and torn clothes—his pants torn so much so that his genitals were plainly visible from the tear that extended from his stomach to his knees. I noted that he was "well hung." The man turned from facing the judge and me, and then faced the public gallery, which roared with laughter. He was in full view of everyone in the courtroom and everyone was in stitches! "I am not guilty," he loudly declared. I heard his plea and I am sure the other court officials heard it, but I doubt that the audience in the gallery could hear his declaration above the laughter.

The prosecutor was quick to speak, "Charge withdrawn, Your Honour." The judge was quick to speak decisively, "Time in custody for the rest of you."

The police officer was quick to open the door to the holding room to hustle the whole group out of the courtroom and back into the secure area.

Those in the courtroom were not so quick to stop laughing and all the members of the "peanut gallery" smiled and vigorously nodded their heads in approval with the delivery of justice that played out right before their eyes that day.

While this case was humorous, not all cases are light hearted. One day in the fall, while I was in court and scanning the docket of who was to appear that day, I saw a name that I recognized. While this is not usual in a large community, meeting people with a recognizable name can happen. The person was charged with trespassing at night and indecent exposure. These were serious charges and I was curious to see if the person in custody was in fact someone I knew personally. When the clerk called out the name, the police officer manning the door between the lock-up area and the courtroom opened the door, and out shuffled Bruce, a friend from university days. An additional twist in the case for me is that Bruce's father worked in the justice system in a public, high profile position.

He looked scared and his eyes darted around the courtroom. Our eyes soon met as I was seated about three meters from where he stood. His eyes and head drooped as he looked away. The clerk read out the two charges and a hush fell over the courtroom. I suspect the onlookers were anticipating a guilty plea followed by the "juicy details" of the crimes. Bruce listened to the charges, then reserved his plea and the case was adjourned for seven days. The prosecutor and the judge briefly discussed bail, which would release him from custody until his next court appearance. Bail was granted and Bruce returned to the lock-up, to be released from custody a few hours later.

I met Bruce a week later, just before he was to appear in court again. I steered him to my office and we sat down. I briefly explained that I was now a probation officer that worked at the court house and I asked, "Do you want to tell me what happened?"

"Sure," he replied,

I had been at the football game with some friends and we had a few beers. Our team (a community-owned professional team) won so we were pretty happy. I grabbed a bus to head home. It was about 11 at night. As we travelled along, I suddenly had to pee real bad. I tried to hold it but the pressure mounted so I hopped off the bus and headed for a yard surrounded by bushes. I sure did not want to pee in public on the sidewalk. I scooted off the sidewalk and darted into the yard. I peed for what felt like a very long time, then headed back to the sidewalk. Just as I was walking away, a city police car drove up. Two officers jumped out and started interrogating me. I just told them what happened. They said I was under arrest for trespassing by night, being a peeping tom and for exposing myself to the lady in the basement suite of the house in the yard. I recalled seeing a house but I didn't see any person. She said someone was exposing themselves outside her basement window, by the bushes. I guess she could see me but I had no idea anyone was there. I guess she called the cops who arrived real quick—like, within a minute or two.

"What are you planning to do now?" I asked.

"I'm going to get a lawyer," replied Bruce.

I told him that was a good decision, wished him well, and escorted him to his courtroom. Over the next few months, he dutifully appeared in court as required. Eventually, all charges were withdrawn by the prosecutor, who obviously concluded there was little chance of a conviction should the matter go to trial.

I NEVER SAW Bruce again. His story is a good example of how easily people can get themselves into difficult situations, without realizing the precariousness of their circumstances. What looked criminal was not actually so—stupid, maybe; a poor decision, for sure. I believe the court system eventually came to a reasonable and effective solution to a human dilemma—what are you going to do when "ya really gotta go bad, real bad?"

CHAPTER 8

BLEACH, COATHANGERS AND OTHER CASES THAT IMPACTED ME

MANY OF US—yes, us, commit crimes but do not get caught. So far I have shared stories of people who were on my probation caseload and had committed crimes. In many ways, they were ordinary people who broke the law and just happened to get caught. People in this book who I have called Mary, Barry, Ron, Sally, Peter, and Elaine really stand out for this reason. I will always remember them.

However, they are not the only ones I remember. There are many others. Each of the following cases illustrates ways my views, opinions, and perspectives about criminal justice, and society in general, changed as a result of working with the people involved. It was cases like these that led me to the questions: Are there other ways, maybe better ways, to deal with this behaviour or this person other than getting the police involved, laying charges, and having them appear in court? Are there ways to adopt new ways to deal with crime and people who commit crime, with less reliance on traditional punitive measures?

THERESA and AGNES

Theresa and Agnes were placed on probation on one charge each of attempting to procure an abortion. From a legal perspective, to attempt an offence is as much a crime as actually committing an offense. This was at a time when no aspect of abortion was lawful unless the woman's life was in danger. There were no abortion clinics and very little public discussion about the issue other than statements that abortion was a serious crime.

When they both appeared in my office right after their court the first thing I did was review their conditions of probation. I then began taking down notes with an intention to gather the basics needed to create their files, then see them individually at a later date to get more details. I just got started the interview, getting their names, addresses and phone numbers, when Theresa blurted out,

> Look, we are neighbours, friends, married, and both have children. When we found out that we were both pregnant and due at about the same time, we both decided we did not want any more kids. This is not something to talk about openly or even with a doctor or our husbands so we decided to help each other have an abortion.

There was a long pause, as she seemed to be searching for words and I was waiting to hear what was coming next.

She continued, "So we used coat hangers and bleach on each other."

I was stunned.

I had been involved in a few discussions with friends on the topic of abortion, and I had heard about "back-alley butchers," but this was my first up-close-and-personal exposure to real people who had real experiences with illegal abortion. This reality really hit home because these ladies could have easily been my friends or neighbours. They seemed to be ordinary people, yet here they were, in my office, charged with a serious crime.

I wondered how the police officers who conducted the initial investigation felt about this crime and other women who had or attempted to have abortions. I wondered how the judge who sentenced the ladies to probation felt about the crime and these people. Were these criminal justice officials as stunned as I was? Maybe they had more experience than I did on this matter? Or maybe not?

I concluded the interview at that point, saying that I would be in touch later with each of them.

Both ladies completed their probation successfully.

I struggled with the issues raised in this case for many years. Was there a balance somewhere between a woman's right to choose and the state's need to protect its citizens? I eventually concluded that this matter was mainly a personal health issue, not a public safety issue.

In my view, Theresa and Agnes were ordinary people who would have had their personal needs better met by health professionals than by criminal justice personnel. By defining abortion as a criminal matter, ordinary people became criminals. Abortion is now mainly dealt with as a personal health issue but there is a vocal segment in the population highly opposed to this approach. I shudder to think of the various pressures on our elected officials to deal with this issue. My hope is that these officials will not redefine abortion as a public safety/crime matter, thus creating a new batch of criminals.

ALLEN

Allen, an Indigenous man of about fifty years of age, grew up in a community north east of the city. He racked up dozens of arrests for public intoxication, illegal possession of liquor, and shoplifting which landed him many fines and a dozen or so short prison sentences. He served a lot of time in jail, as well, for non-payment of fines. A judge asked me one day to prepare a pre-sentence report regarding Allen, with the view to exploring the possibility of the court trying again to convince Allen to sober up. When I broached the idea of sobriety with Allen, he blurted out defiantly,

Why the hell would I quit now, just because a judge ordered me to? I will quit when I am damn ready to quit and not before. You, the cops and the judge are just wasting your time trying to get me to sober up. I ain't hurting nobody but myself!"

Years later, I met Allen when he was working for a treatment centre in the city. He looked much younger than when I did the pre-sentence report for the Court so I presumed he was sober now, and living a healthier lifestyle. His job? A driver who met people from out-of-town coming to the city for treatment, and he made sure they got to the treatment centre as planned. I concluded he found a reason to quit drinking and was now making an important contribution to the community.

I often wondered if the criminal justice system needed to show more patience and understanding of persons with serious drug and alcohol problems. Might there be non-punitive approaches to substance abuse that would have better outcomes? How many people caught up in the criminal justice system just need more time to smarten up? Is the justice system being realistic in thinking there are quick fixes via incarceration for substance abuse and addictions?

EDWARD

"We have to find something new for this guy or he's going to die."

These were the words spoken by my colleague who worked at the court house as he handed me a probation order for Ed. My colleague continued, "He's got a long record. Nothing seems to work in getting him cleaned up. It seems he has the potential to do better but he's not living up to that. Good luck with this one."

I was looking forward to working with Ed to see if

we could find some way to get through to him about his drug use/abuse. I had known a few guys at university who were users but so far as I knew, their use was nowhere near that of my new client. I spoke to a few co-workers and read a few articles about drug use/abuse, hoping to learn more about the topic.

A few days later, Ed came into the office to see me. He was about 35 years old, but he looked a lot older— haggard and unhealthy. He was pleasant with me but it soon became evident he and I had very little in common. He acknowledged his extensive drug use that led to charges of possession of drugs, possession for the purposes of trafficking, and trafficking a variety of drugs, theft, possession of stolen property, and break and enter. He served sentences of fines, probation, jail terms and terms of imprisonment in penitentiaries. There were a few treatment programs scattered throughout his life so far but clearly nothing to date had helped him refrain from heavy drug use. As he was leaving my office, I commented that I would try to find some new resources that might help him. Ed offered guarded support for this but it seemed he was not as optimistic as I was.

Two days later, I read in the local paper that Ed had died in a rooming house from a heroin overdose. My colleague's prophesy had become a reality. I realized my optimism had overshadowed Ed's struggles with drugs. This was hard for me to accept. I had not helped him one little bit.

Maybe, I thought, drug use/abuse should be seen mainly as a health issue, not a crime issue. Maybe treatment programs would be a better way than lots of court appearances and prison sentences. Maybe drug counselors would be better than probation officers in helping to turn around the lives of drug addicts.

ELIZABETH and SHARON

Elizabeth and Sharon were placed on probation for one charge each of theft—shoplifting. They were sisters, about thirty years of age, and each was married. They were from a town south-east of the city and often came to the city to go shopping. They were employed in the town as sales clerks and they volunteered at a local church in Sunday school with young children. They related how they drifted into shoplifting and found this to be exciting and exhilarating, so much so that they had a regular schedule of "going shopping in the city." They knew it was wrong but they talked themselves into believing it was fun with minimal chances of being caught.

They completed their probation without incident, reporting regularly that they continued living in the town with their families, working steadily, and staying out of trouble.

I often wondered if they were truly as naïve as they seemed. I also wondered how many other women found shoplifting to be a challenge, something fun and exciting, in an otherwise law-abiding lifestyle? How many adults in general did a bit of stealing from time to time? Could their lives be so boring that theft was an attractive notion?

TOMMY

It was a quiet Friday afternoon in the probation office and most of my colleagues were away, either in training sessions off site or doing home visits meeting with clients, or with clients' employers, teachers, or friends. I was assigned to be the Duty Officer for the afternoon which meant that I was to deal with any cases that came into the office, either in person or phone calls related to clients.

My phone rang. The receptionist said, "Hi Doug. We have a walk-in case from out east. Can you see him?"

"Sure," I said.

"Okay, I'll bring him to your office with his probation order."

A minute or so later, the receptionist arrived with a man in his mid-twenties tagging along behind her. I instantly recognized him and he recognized me. The receptionist introduced us, gave me a file folder with papers in it, and then returned to the main reception area.

Tom and I stared at each other for a few seconds, then I said, "Sit down, bud." Tom settled stiffly into a chair in front of my desk. "This will be a bit awkward," I said, "but we can deal with it." Tom and I had been very good friends in high school and in our first year at university. We had hunted ducks together in high school and acted in high school plays. At university, we drank beer and socialized and attended a few clubs and bars for an evening's entertainment. He was on probation on a charge of possession of an offensive weapon. I reviewed the conditions with him. He fully understood what they were and what a year's probation would look like.

He explained that in a major city in the country, he had been a regular pot and LSD user. He outlined how he was continually hassled, even bullied and beat up, for being a user, in the community and at work, so he decided to defend himself by buying and carrying a machete. Tom said the weapon worked well. Most people left him alone when they saw he was armed. In one incident, though, where Tom waved the machete in self-defence, the police were called and he was charged. Tom said he came back to near where he grew up in the hopes that he could avoid being hassled so much.

In cases where a probation officer personally knows a client, especially when the relationship was a friendship, we would arrange for the supervision to be handled by another probation officer. I told Tom he would not be seeing me as his probation officer and that his new PO would call him soon.

I referred the matter to our senior probation officer who assigned another probation officer to supervise Tom. Once, during the time that Tom was on probation at our office, I looked at his file. He was working steadily and there were no new charges.

Years later, at a high school reunion, Tom and I met again. We had a good visit without any reference to his criminal past. I wonder how Tom is doing now. Might there be others with whom I was good friends and they, too, got into trouble with the law to some extent? Are there people who I now consider friends but I don't know about their criminal convictions? How ordinary would these folks be?

DANIELLE

Danielle was on probation for break, enter, and theft from her foster parents' home. She had been apprehended from her mother by child welfare authorities when young and had lived at that particular foster home for several years, after having bounced around from many other foster homes and group homes. There was a hard crust to Danielle. She was initially distant with me, uncommunicative, and seemed to only tolerate me if we absolutely had to talk. Eventually, she warmed up to me and seemed more settled. She was living by herself in a small suite in the central part of the city and was working as a server in a diner.

At one visit in my office, she surprised me by inviting my wife and me to a party on the next Saturday at her place. She asked that we bring some snacks and said that two other couples were coming. She commented that this would be the first party she hosted without drugs or alcohol. I normally did not socialize with clients but made an exception in Danielle's case—she did not have many pro-social friends.

Her place was spotless when we arrived. The other couples arrived about the same time: a police officer and his wife, and a social worker and his wife. The officer had been involved in investigating Danielle for the break and enter that landed her on probation, the social worker had been one of her child welfare workers in the past. We were all a bit uneasy at first but were all impressed that Danielle seemed to be making a concerted effort to lead a pro-social life.

At her next appointment, she brought a man to meet me. This was her new boyfriend, Wally, and he was about six years older than her. I detested him from the first time he opened his mouth. He was patronizing towards me and misogynistic toward Danielle. He said that he worked at selling used cars. I feared he would not be a good influence on her, despite her efforts to live constructively. Danielle said she adored Wally. "Yeah, right," I thought.

A week later, I saw Danielle's name in docket court. She had been arrested, charged with prostitution and would appear again in two weeks time. I asked my colleague who worked at the court house to find out what he could do about the charge. He got back to me later with the story that Wally had been pimping her out of a café not far from where she worked. This confirmed my suspicion that he was a bad influence on her. When I confronted her about the charge, Danielle swore she was not guilty and that Wally was helping her out as a friend. She was eventually convicted at trial and paid a fine. She was finished probation by this time so I lost contact with her.

Several years later, I went to introduce myself to a new neighbour in the community where I lived and both Danielle and I were rather startled when she came to her door to greet me. She invited me for a coffee and filled me in on her family and her new job in sales. For about six months, I saw her name in ads in the community newspaper; then she disappeared. I later heard from a colleague that she had been charged with trafficking and possession of drugs.

That was the last I heard about Danielle. She had been making headway in overcoming the instability of her early years then hooked up with Wally, who dragged her back down. She seemed to briefly rebound with a new husband and a good job in a new community then something happened to facilitate her returning to drugs.

Years later, I thought I recognized Danielle at a funeral service of a friend, a former drug user, but she disappeared from the hall before I could track her down.

I have always wondered what happened to Danielle, a person with plenty of potential to do well but without sufficient support to fulfill this potential. She was vulnerable but did not see herself as being preyed upon. I find this is a very typical feature of many people who get into trouble with the law. Sad but true.

DONALD

I met Don as I prepared a pre-sentence report for the Court about him on a dozen or so charges of writing bad cheques. He was age 34, born and raised in the city, graduated from a local high school, married his high school sweetheart, fathered two children and had a stable employment history. At the time, he owned a small business selling office equipment. He was placed on probation for twelve months, was ordered to report monthly to me, and to make restitution of about $1,000 to repay the bad cheques. Within a month, more bad cheques were reported to police by friends, business colleagues, his church, and his parents. The parents told police they'd had enough of this over the past year and were now turning to the police and the courts for help.

When Don and I met, he had no explanation for the new charges other than to explain that business was slow and he had a family to look after. According to his wife, he was a good husband and father except for money management skills. She had taken over looking after the family finances but the bad cheques kept on coming. Don was placed on probation on two additional occasions. His wife was becoming more and more concerned, but she could offer no insight into his behaviour. I spent hours with Don and with his wife, together and separately, trying to get some idea why all this was happening and what might be done. No insights.

I enjoy curling during the winter months and one of my team mates was in the business machine industry as a sales rep. Over drinks after the games, we would socialize for an hour or so and he sometimes mentioned Don— with disgust! My teammate concluded Don was a scumbag who took advantage of people for no obvious reason. I never let on that I knew Don, but, to be sociable and aware of my professional interest in what information people had about Don, I listened and encouraged him to talk about Don.

More new charges led to Don being sentenced to prison for six months so that ended his probation. For most of the time he was on probation, new charges kept coming up. Some were from the past and some involved recent cheques that bounced.

I saw Don about a year later. He was serving a new one-year term of imprisonment. He looked haggard, much older and quite listless.

I never figured out why he went off the rails as he did. No one else had any idea why this was happening or what to do. This has gnawed at my conscience for a long time. What more could I have done to help him and to protect the public from his persuasive manner of bilking a lot of money from friends, family and acquaintances by writing bum cheques?

MR. LEE

Mr. Lee was placed on probation on a charge of swearing to a false document. The address that was on the probation order was on the route that I took most days to drive to and from work. I decided I would stop in on my way home.

As I drove up to the address, I recognized it was a corner grocery store where I had once stopped in the past to buy a pop and snacks. I recalled that an elderly Asian couple ran the store, which served local residents with non-perishable goods and a few fresh items like milk, apples, and oranges. The store, located about ten blocks from a major shopping centre, was run down—in need of window and door repairs, and a fresh coat of paint. I entered the store, wondering if I would recognize the couple. An older Asian man was stocking some selves with canned goods and a woman was at the checkout. There appeared to be no one else in the store at that time. Was this them?

I asked the woman if I could see Mr. Lee. I included the man's first name that was on the probation order. She replied in broken, heavily accented English, "Go see man," and she pointed awkwardly to the man stocking shelves down the aisle, watching our conversation. As I made my way over to him, he retreated to the end of the aisle and then went to the far corner of the store. I followed him. When he could retreat no further and when I ambled up to him, I asked if he was Mr. Lee. He nodded his head and mumbled a heavily accented, "Yes."

I introduced myself and pulled out a copy of the probation order from a file folder. I held up the order so he could see it and said, "Is this you, charged with swearing to a false document?" He glanced at the order, looked to the lady at the checkout, nodded his head and again mumbled, "Yes."

I asked the man if he had time to go over the order, to make sure he understood it. It was hard for me to be sure of his responses, due to what appeared to be limited knowledge of English. I thought I heard him say he was too busy to continue to meet with me, he had a store to run. I gave him my business card and said I would stop in next week. By now, there were other people in the store.

One of my concerns was: Did he really understand the probation order? It would have been explained to him at the court house but many people just want to get out of court, so they will say they understand when they don't. Another concern had to do with his understanding of English. Would he or I need an interpreter?

Back at the office, I raised my concerns with my supervisor and other staff. The conclusion I came to, based on comments from my colleagues, was not to worry about his understanding of the order and that an interpreter was not needed at this point.

I checked with the clerk's office to find out who the police officer was who was involved with the case. I then contacted the officer, making an appointment at his office. He outlined the offence this way:

> Mr. Lee is from a large family, with siblings in Canada, the United States, and China. Canadian Immigration officials contacted us when they suspected sworn immigration documents contained false information related to Mr. Lee. He had submitted a sworn document listing his siblings, including a sister who had passed away.
>
> When this document was compared to other documents, it was noted that the sister was very much alive. When asked about the apparent discrepancy, Mr. Lee explained to police that his sister had married a non-Chinese man and, in doing so,

she had violated Chinese culture. She had, in his mind, died by marrying outside her culture and he treated her as being dead; thus the false document. Mr. Lee had a lawyer throughout the court process so he very well understood the probation order. He does not speak English very well but he does understand enough to run his store with his wife. He is not a security concern to us and he keeps his nose clean, other than this incident.

With this information, plus input from my colleagues, I decided to see Mr. Lee at his store again rather than direct him to come to my office. I stopped at his store every six weeks or so and always had a brief conversation with him. He would answer with a "yes" or "no," indicating there were no changes in his address or employment. He was living within the law, he had no problems and that everything was fine. He never asked me for information about anything and he did not volunteer information, just answered the questions, briefly. I did not see his name on a court docket and the police never called me. I concluded he completed the period of probation successfully.

This is one of those cases where the judge could have fined him or sent him to prison or put him on probation. The latter sentence seemed to be a reasonable choice, given the principles of sentencing such as denunciation, deterrence, protection of society, helping offenders, and holding offenders responsible for their behaviour. I doubt he could afford to pay a fine without jeopardizing his business. And what would be the point of a prison sentence?

X

MRS. SMITH

When I was assigned to complete a pre-sentence report on a young adult named Billy Smith, I wondered if he was related to the Smiths who lived west of the city in a residential acreage subdivision. Several young adults from this family had been on probation in the past few years. Billy was in custody, pending the report that the judge would use to assist in determining a sentence. I searched the closed files and sure enough, Billy was listed as the youngest member of the Smith family.

I made an appointment to see his mother and I drove to an acreage address. Driving up the driveway, I noted a run-down bungalow with a detached garage, also badly needing repair, and a yard full of junk—old cars, wrecked cars, rusted ride-on mowers, piles of lumber, and a huge pile of full garbage bags.

A haggard woman of about forty answered my knock on the door. We introduced ourselves, and I learned she was Billy's mother. She invited me to the kitchen, waved her arm and said, "Take a seat at the table; I'll get you a coffee." I was reluctant to sit at the table because it was covered with four large, bulging, smelly garbage bags. "Where would I place my coffee cup?" I wondered.

There was no other place to sit in the kitchen. Mrs. Smith must have read my mind. "Sit here," she directed, as she used her right forearm to sweep away two of the bags off the table and onto the floor with a thump. The two bags left a large, thick smear of what I concluded was garbage juice on the table. Mrs. Smith grabbed a dish cloth from the sink, swished it on to the table and wiped the juice stains, trying to make them disappear. "There," she exclaimed. "That's better, eh? You want cream or sugar?"

It was tough getting past the smell and filth in the house and yard. I started asking my standard set of questions to gather information about the accused and their family. At one point, Mrs. Smith blurted out, "Ya know, I don't know what's wrong. My husband is in the penitentiary for a bunch of thefts, the three older boys are all in jail for who knows what, and now Billy is in trouble. What's going on? I have tried my best and look what I get, more and more trouble. What's wrong?"

I simply did not have an answer for her. Where would I start?

I vaguely remember finishing the interview and returning to the office. I felt my skin crawling for the rest of the day. The hot shower I had when I returned home helped somewhat. I later made contact with Billy in custody plus one of his teachers and a former employer and reviewed the closed files of his siblings to get information as requested by the judge. I recall learning that the local family services agency had become involved with the family but eventually withdrew their involvement due to a lack of cooperation from Mrs. Smith.

I am sure the court would have suspended the passing of sentence on Billy and released him from custody on a probation order. I am sure the judge, too, wondered what was wrong. I am sure Billy did not stay out of trouble for very long.

Would it be fair or reasonable to expect a judge to craft a sentence that would fix what was wrong in this family? In my view, the family and its individual members needed the involvement of far more intensive interventions from the community than just the criminal justice system. The community seemed quick to call the cops when many other services were so badly needed.

X

RALPH

The probation order stated that Ralph was placed on probation for a period of one year for a charge of assault causing bodily harm. The usual conditions applied, except one infrequently used condition: not to have contact with the victim. This is a serious charge, used when serious injury was inflicted on the victim.

When I met with Ralph to gather information for the case plan, he painted a picture of himself as a stable, hard-working family man, involved in immigrant community events. As I found out more about his involvement in these events, I wondered if perhaps I had met him, as my wife and I were frequently invited to some of these same events by friends from that community. I had to be careful not to disclose to Ralph too much of our personal information or any information about our friends.

When we discussed the charge, Ralph stressed that he was wrongly convicted of injuring his wife. "She fell down," he stated emphatically, "her injuries were not my fault." As a probation officer, I quickly learned not to get involved in arguing with clients. What was of paramount importance was sticking to the facts, and the facts were clearly stated on the probation order.

To get a better idea of what had happened, I contacted the victim, who invited me to her home. I learned her story of years of abuse from her husband, culminating in a severe beating where he used his fists and boots. She showed me photographs of her face, taken right after the assault, which was black and blue with several long cuts closed by stitches. Her face was swollen to the point where her lips were split and bruised and they were puffed open, unable to fully close. Her eyes were completely swollen shut, with little evidence of sockets. Her entire head was swollen, including her ears. She said she thought she was going to die. She said she was terrified that Ralph would now stalk her and "finish me off."

I decided not talk to Ralph about the assault—I could not see anything constructive coming from such discussions as he would continue to deny his guilt. When he reported to me once a month as required, I ensured we discussed where he was living and that he was still working at the same place as he had for many years. I always stressed the "no contact" conditions, and would interrogate Ralph as to any of his actions which might bring him into contact with his wife, either on purpose or inadvertently.

I wanted to be sure that he did not drift into contact with her through meeting with their children or with mutual friends. I always reinforced the fact that if he broke one of the conditions of the probation order, he could be charged with the new offence of breaching the probation order and, in all likelihood, he would be returned to court for sentencing on the original charge of assault causing bodily harm. If that happened, I stressed it was unlikely that he would get more probation or be assessed a heavy fine. He would most probably be sent to jail.

I worried about what he might do but there were no further charges. He completed probation and I never heard of him again.

TONY

Tony was twenty-five years old when he was placed on probation for four months on one charge of assault causing bodily harm. This is a fairly serious offence, in that someone he assaulted was quite badly injured.

After gathering information about his childhood, family, education, employment, training, health, and personal interests, I asked Tony about what happened that resulted in him being charged, appearing in court and placed on probation.

"Well," he began,

Let me tell you what happened. I'm still pretty mad about this; embarrassed, too. On a Saturday, I finished my shift working on heavy equipment and I got paid; so I cashed my cheque, went to my apartment and got cleaned up real good, then headed to the local bar to eat and have a few drinks. Maybe pick up a woman and who knows what might happen, know what I mean? I was eating a burger and kept looking at this good-looking chick and she was eyeing me up so I bought her a drink. She moved to my table, and I bought us some more drinks. I think she was kinda hot on me and I kept the booze flowing. It was getting late and it was dark outside so I said to her, "Let's go for a drive." She said okay so I paid the bill and out we went to my truck.

She got in, sitting right up beside me. I put my arm around her, pulled her close and gave her a kiss. She kissed me back—lots of tongue! So, now we were getting worked up, ya know. I figured I could go further with her so I felt her face, then her neck. She said she liked that. So, I kept going, feeling her breasts through her shirt. I slid my hand under her shirt to her bra. Then I got under the bra and felt her breasts, pretty nice, eh? Small but nice. She moaned a bit, like she was enjoying this so I kept going, down into her pants. I then pulled down her pants past her knees and went inside her panties, heading down there, you know what I mean. Then she spread her legs and I reached for her, you know, private parts, and guess what? It was a big cock and balls! No shit—she was a he!

Well, I jerked my hand outta there real fast, grabbed him and started punching him in the face. I opened my door, jumped out of the truck and pulled him out, throwing him on the ground. I leaned over and kept hitting him. That son of a bitch! No way was I gonna be with a man—I only like women. Then I kicked him real good—son of a bitch! He got up crying, saying he was sorry and took off, stumbling out of the parking lot, and headed for the bar. I got back in the truck and just sat there for a while, trying to calm down.

Then a cop car pulled into the parking lot and two cops got out, checking trucks. They came to mine. They asked for ID and asked what I was doing there. There was blood on the seat and back window and on my hands and jacket. So, they arrested me, took me to the police cells downtown, and I stayed in there until court on Monday. I pleaded guilty in court. The prosecutor read out that I beat up a guy pretty bad in the parking lot. "Ya, I did that." The judge asked me if I had anything to say—I said, " No."

No way was I going to say what really happened, what with all those people in court watching and listening. Now, I kinda feel silly. She looked like a woman, sounded like a woman, smelled like a woman, felt like a woman....until I got to her crotch; and all of a sudden, she's a man. Holy shit, that is hard to take!"

I wanted to smile, even laugh, when I heard Tony's explanation; but I controlled my reaction as much as possible. We focused on his case plan to complete probation. Tony had only just started his job, and he spent a fair bit of money on alcohol that night so he did not have much money.

I could see why the judge did not fine him. Sentencing

him to prison did not seem to be a good option as he had a job and did not have a criminal record. He had caused significant harm to the victim but was that somewhat understandable? What might the victim have been thinking as Tony "made his moves" on him (her)? Who wouldn't be upset and angry under these circumstances? But, did the victim deserve such a beating? Might this be an example of what many judges say is the toughest part of their job—sentencing? What would you do if you had to determine a sentence for Tony? How would you react if a male friend told you that what happened to Tony had also happened to him?

PART II

CONTEMPORARY CASES

INTRODUCTION TO PART II

CONTEMPORARY CASES

IN PART I of this book, the stories are about people I supervised on probation or met when I worked as a probation officer. Their crimes and circumstances, and how I dealt with these folks, were written about in a general way. In Part II, however, I have chosen a different approach in writing about people who commit crime. I have selected some contemporary cases that were recently involved in the criminal justice system. In sourcing these stories, I drew upon my experience as a probation officer, parole officer, prison caseworker, staff trainer, instructor, and researcher to recall colleagues whom I knew would have interesting stories to share. I approached correctional officials and told them about the book I was writing. Some were supportive of the project and were willing to refer cases to me.

Most of the cases referred to me were individuals who had initially lived a fairly ordinary, stable life, then something happened and they spiralled downward into crime. Then, after a while, these individuals made a decision to turn their lives around and return to a more normal lifestyle. This is the general profile of many criminals.

I also received some referrals from friends who knew that I was working on a book and they referred people to me who they knew from work or from family circles.

I ended up selecting stories that bear a resemblance thematically to the story themes and individuals I wrote about in Part I. With the cooperation of selected offenders and correctional officials, I am presenting a more detailed picture of people of a more contemporary era who have committed crime. No doubt the reader will see similarities and differences between the folks in Parts I and II. The folks in Part II tend to be in more serious trouble over a longer period of time than those in Part I and, in my view, their road to normalcy is remarkable, considering the challenges they have overcome. These are mostly stories of hope. This is one of the differences I noticed about the people who I wrote about in Part I; they were not so entrenched in criminality as the folks in Part II.

To gather these stories in Part II, I met with prospective candidates who had been referred to me. At the initial meeting, I outlined the purpose of the book. I explained that I would interview them, digitally record the interview on a recorder, transcribe the interview, then review the transcript of the interview to gather information about their early years, their criminal lifestyle, and their road back to normalcy. I explained that there would likely be three interviews, with each interview lasting up to two hours. I went on to say that we would meet wherever they feel most comfortable. It turned out we sometimes met in their homes. We sometimes met in a quiet room or quiet space in the public library and in a boardroom of a society dedicated to crime prevention in the community. In some cases, we connected via FaceTime on our cell phones, due to the Covid-19 pandemic. The people I interviewed were cooperative. Some communicated effortlessly and provided significant information and insights into their situations. These folks could have spoken with me for days as they had plenty to say and made a point of being as thorough as they could. Other respondents were quiet and more reserved; they needed to be prodded by my questions. Their responses tended to be shorter and more to-the-point.

During all these interviews, there were some snickers and some good laughs, and some quiet moments when the person seemed to be really thinking deeply about their response. At other times, some were near tears and their voices trembled with emotion. For many, recalling and talking about a chaotic time in their lives was not an easy thing to do. Throughout the interviews, I shared a bit of information about myself from time to time, in order to show that we were taking part in a conversation, not just a simple question-and-answer exchange.

In presenting their stories, I used their words and phrases wherever possible, although I did tone down the swearing. At other times, I used their descriptions to guide me as I told the more general parts of their stories. With some, I was granted access to their confidential file, so I used some of this information to round out their account of things that had happened in their lives.

With the cases in this Part, you will notice a pattern similar to the cases in Part I, with one notable difference—most cases in Part II are more serious. In Part II, the chapters about Jessica, Brandon, Juanito, and Richard describe people who were reasonably stable, then became involved in crime. However, it took Juanito nearly four years before he smartened up. He came very close to serving a substantial prison sentence. Richard received a long prison sentence late in life and has recently been released to the community; time will tell how successful he is in the return to normalcy. Paul had a troubled youth. He avoided lengthy prison terms but it took him ten years to get his life on track. Joseph as well had a troubled youth, and he served a substantial prison term. He is well on track to normalcy when he completes his sentence before too long. Ryan had a normal childhood but his teen years were in turmoil, paving the way for fifteen years of dealing drugs and doing "pen time" before he decided to get clean. Paula's whole life was one of turmoil, anger and upset, with her ending up many times in prison before she found a way to live normally. Sadly, these profiles where the person experiences significant instability are what we now typically deal with in the justice system. They are all too common, too normal, in my view. Sadly, these are the circumstances where prevention did not come to play an effective role. The profiles do not surprise me, but it may shock and disturb some readers who do not know about the life stories and realities of many members of the community, other than the snippets about the crime they hear from the media.

Several cases in Part II are about people on parole, also known as parolees. Although there are differences in actual law, policy, and practice in the various parole jurisdictions across the country, a general description is that parole is a type of conditional release from prison. There are three types of parole in my jurisdiction—day parole, full parole, and statutory release. A parolee serves a portion of their sentence of imprisonment in the community under the supervision of a parole officer and subject to conditions. Some conditions are general, like reporting to a parole officer and some conditions are specific to the parolee, such as refraining from the use of alcohol or non-medical drugs. Most inmates become eligible for release on full parole after they have served a portion of their sentence, commonly one third.

For example, an accused person sentenced to a three-year term of imprisonment would be eligible for release on full parole after serving one year of that sentence in custody. Just because one is eligible for parole does not mean they will automatically be granted parole. The inmate has to apply to a parole board for release on full parole. The parole authority then orders an extensive investigation into the offender and the offence. Generally, a parole-granting authority denies far more applications than it approves. Only those inmates whose risk to the public is deemed to be manageable will be granted full parole.

Any inmate released on full parole is subject to numerous conditions which are designed to manage the parolee's behaviour in order to protect the public and also to assist in their positive adjustment to the community. Most full parolees reside at home in the community, under the supervision of a parole officer. In cases where the home environment is not suitable, the parolee may live in a halfway house until other suitable housing can be obtained. In my example, the parole certificate allowing the inmate to be lawfully absent from a specific prison would be in effect for two years. If all goes well, the offender will be deemed to have satisfactorily served the sentence upon successful completion of the two years on parole. If the full parole is revoked due to violations of the conditions or the commission of new offences, the parolee is returned to the prison and a new date for the completion of their sentence is calculated.

In some cases, an inmate can be released on day parole, prior to being released on full parole. Inmates are eligible for day parole after they have served one-sixth of their sentence. Day parolees spend their day in the community, working or attending educational or training programs and then return to an institution or halfway house in the evening. The idea behind day parole is that the offender needs to gradually adjust from living in an institution to living in a less structured yet supervised setting such as a halfway house and, if that adjustment is satisfactory, could then go to full parole in the community. The role of a parole officer in day and full parole cases is two-fold:

1. Closely monitor the behaviour of the parolee, ensuring that the parolee is complying with all the conditions of their release and is living a law-abiding lifestyle.
2. Help the parolee to deal with circumstances arising from living in the community, such as friends, finances, use of spare time, interpersonal relations,

employment, training, travel, use of drugs and alcohol, and health which might turn out to be harmful to the parolee's successful reintegration into the community.

In some jurisdictions, there is another form of parole or conditional release known as statutory release after the inmate has served two-thirds of their sentence. In these cases, the inmate did not apply for parole or was denied parole by the parole board. If the inmate was not a serious behavioural problem in the institution, they can be released to serve the final one third of their sentence under supervision by a parole officer in the community rather than being detained until the end of their sentence. The role of the parole officer in these cases is the same as for other types of parole: Protect the public by ensuring the offender is abiding by the conditions of release and help the offender adapt to the community and live a pro-social lifestyle.

I HAVE SEEN MAJOR CHANGES in the criminal justice system over my forty-year career. For one thing, there is more specialization. When I worked around courts, there was one court that heard all types of cases but today, courts are divided into Drug Courts, Domestic Violence Courts, Traffic Courts, Small Debt Courts, Indigenous Courts, and Mental Health Courts. There have been changes, too, in police, prosecutor, and defence counsel roles, and the varying roles in correctional services, with each formulating specialized approaches to their duties.

Another change I have noticed is that addiction and mental health issues are more prevalent now than before. These issues were certainly present when I was working in the field, but not to the extent they are now. Since this represents a change in the wider society, those working in criminal justice have had to adapt to new realities. Over the years, the justice system has made other changes such as adopting diversion and alternative measures programs to steer some accused away from the regular court system. As well, the inclusion of conditional and absolute discharges are examples of changes by the justice system to deal more efficiently with low risk, less serious offenders.

THE NEWS MEDIA AND SOCIAL MEDIA has always tended to focus on details of high profile, dramatic, shocking, horrific, and notorious crimes. Information gleaned in this way is often incomplete and sometime outright incorrect. Stories are usually covered in a sensational way when police make announcements related to arresting and charging, but unlike what you read in this book, rarely do the media offer any substantive followup about the lives and recovery patterns of the perpetrators. Information about the person outside of, or after their criminal involvement seldom receives much attention. I focus instead on the people who commit crimes and the circumstances in their lives that might have led them down this road. There are many success stories, but these rarely become known to the public. Once again, as I urged readers in the preface of this book, get comfortable, relax, and read about some of the people I came to know in the latter part of my career—crimes that would not have been heard about in the media.

CHAPTER 9

JESSICA: GUILTY WITH AN EXPLANATION

I HAVE ALWAYS ENJOYED being around courtrooms, so much so that when I had some spare time on my hands, I would pop into a local court house and sit in the docket court (court of first appearance) to see the action. At times it can be pretty boring, such as when the court process is in discussions to find a common time for the offender, victim, police officers, other evidence providers, and lawyers to hold a trial. It amazed me how often police officers changed their family holiday plans to accommodate trial dates. It also amazed me how long it could take to find a courtroom in which to hold a trial—in some cases it could be the better part of a year before a courtroom would be available for the time expected for the trial.

At other times, being in court was exciting and real life drama was playing out before my eyes. One day, I had a class of eight students, all older adults, sitting in the front row of the public gallery. They had heard me talk about court processes and issues in previous classes and everyone was patiently waiting for the court to start at 9:30 that morning. Court staff were getting their files and papers organized, people were slowly filtering into the public seating area, and lawyers were talking to court clerks and prosecutors about the cases and clients they were representing.

The class and I were seated on the right hand side of the public gallery, as close as we could get to the part of the courtroom reserved for officials and the accused. We had a perfect spot to see and hear what was going on in the courtroom. A lawyer came into the room, headed over to the prosecutor and steered the prosecutor away from his table to a point right in front of our class. They began discussing a case in quiet, subdued tones. The lawyer pointed out some circumstances of his client and some of the details surrounding the charge. The prosecutor replied by pointing out some of the details of the alleged offence from the victim's perspective. For about a minute, these officials discussed case issues back and forth. The lawyer then summarized the discussions, "We can go to trial and see what happens down the line or I can plead guilty today to the reduced charge and we are done with the matter, case resolved. What will it be?" The prosecuting attorney thought for a few seconds, then said, "I'll reduce the charge."

One of the students sitting beside me jabbed me in the ribs with an elbow and whispered in my ear, "That's plea bargaining, isn't it? What we talked about in the last class?"

"Yes," I whispered back. "We'll discuss this more in the next class."

We did talk about plea bargaining and case resolution in the next class. Having been in court and seeing what actually goes on set the stage for a wonderful, informed discussion about fascinating issues that can swirl around in a courtroom. At least the students had a much better understanding of what is meant by plea bargaining and its role in coming to a suitable and practical resolution of a criminal charge. There were still some negative opinions about the idea of plea bargaining, but now the students could take part in informed discussion.

On another day, I stopped into the court house and found my way into the courtroom where accused persons appeared in court by way of a summons, rather than being arrested and held in custody. Shortly, the handling of cases got underway. Names were called, people from the public gallery moved into position in front of the judge, the charge was read, the accused indicated what they wanted to do, and a sentence would be handed down if the plea was guilty.

What follows is a detailed account of one defendant:

"Jessica Brown," droned the clerk of the court.

A young woman about twenty-five years of age, seated on a bench, stood up and slowly made her way from the public gallery, taking a position standing directly in front of the judge.

"Are you Jessica Brown?" enquired the clerk.

"Yes," came a hesitant and trembling reply.

Jessica had light brown hair, a fair complexion, weighed about 150 pounds and was five-foot-five inches in height. She was dressed in a white blouse and blue jeans with running shoes.

"Jessica Brown, you stand charged that on or about July 5th, you did unlawfully steal meat of a value of $38.99 from [XYZ] Foods, contrary to the Criminal Code. How do you plead to this charge?"

After what seemed a long time, but actually it was only five or ten seconds, she said, "Guilty" in a quiet and trembling voice.

"Guilty," pronounced the judge, confirming for the official record what had just been decided.

In a few cases over the years, I have seen an accused person say, "Guilty" and then quickly add a comment like: "But I didn't do it," or "With an explanation," or "But only a little bit," or "Yeah, but another guy is more guilty than me." When a judge hears comments like these which tend to mitigate the concept of guilt, they quickly interject, saying something like, "Okay, please don't make any further comments. I direct that the plea be recorded as not guilty and the matter be set over to determine a trial date." In criminal law, an accused is either guilty or not guilty. These are absolute terms. One cannot be partially guilty or a little bit guilty.

In some settings, such as where I taught courses about criminal justice, I have used an analogy to pregnancy—one is either pregnant or not; one cannot be a little bit pregnant or only partially pregnant. The idea of an accused offering an explanation comes later in the criminal justice process and can be an important aspect in a case, but such an explanation does not come into play when the accused pleads guilty. Like pregnancy, one is either guilty, or not.

THE PROSECUTOR IN JESSICA'S CASE rose slowly to his feet, holding a sheaf of papers in his hands. The prosecuting attorney spoke:

> Your Honour, on July 5th, store security at the food store in question observed a female take a roast of beef wrapped with plastic film in a foam tray from a meat display case and place the item in question under a light blue jacket she was wearing. The time was 11:47 a.m. She wandered along some of the other aisles then departed the store into the main hallway in the mall. Store security stopped her in the mall and directed that she show them what was under her jacket. She pulled out the roast. She admitted to taking the roast. Store security called the police who charged her with one count of "Theft Under"—shoplifting—and summonsed her to appear in court on this date.

The judge looked curiously at Jessica and asked, "Do you have anything to say for yourself?"

"No," she murmured.

"Any record?" asked the judge, directing the question to the prosecuting attorney.

The prosecutor thumbed through his file, then said, "No record, Your Honour."

The judge again turned to Jessica, "How come this happened?"

Jessica stood there, looking downtrodden and defeated; she was trembling.

In the spring, I come out here to the city from the east coast. There was more work here, and I heard you could get a good job here fast and do good. I couldn't find a job and I got sick so I was scrimping by. I told everyone back home I was doing good and how good it was here in the city. Then my mom phoned and she said she would be out to visit me the next week—you know, to celebrate my doing good. I just could not let my mom come all the way out here and see me, really, so I took the meat so I could at least make a nice meal for her and show her that I was doing good.

"Any reference to this in the police report?" the judge asked.

The prosecutor again thumbed through his file, "No, sir."

The judge looked back at Jessica, "Have you done this before?"

"No, sir, I never stole nothing before," she said quietly, her gaze towards the floor. "I am really embarrassed by this now."

"Are you working?" asked the judge.

"I get a few hours a day at a car wash. I'm still kinda sick," she explained.

Said the judge,

Okay, there is no point in fining you or sending you to jail. You don't need to be on probation. Therefore, I am directing that you receive an absolute discharge— the case is over and done with right now; nothing further for you to do. You will not have a criminal record. Now, get out of here and don't come back into a courtroom again—clear?

"Yes, sir." This time, her voice sounded stronger and she spoke clearly. "This won't ever happen again!"

"Good," said the judge. "Away you go."

And away she went, heading purposefully with her head held high, down the aisle in the public gallery and out the doors of the courtroom to the hallway. The street was now only one flight of stairs and one main entrance away.

My guess is that she virtually flew down the stairs and out the entrance, heading for home, feeling very relieved that her ordeal was over.

CHAPTER 10

PAUL: A TEN-YEAR JOURNEY TO NORMALCY

As I DRIVE to Paul's address to meet him for the first time, I enter a newly developed residential area in the city. Real estate signs dot the boulevards, and four open house sales centres cluster around the intersection of Paul's street and the main road winding through the subdivision. Newer SUVs and pickup trucks fill the driveways. Paul's address reveals a nicely finished duplex, built about two years ago, with two driveways accessing garages that front both residences. All homes along the street are either single family homes or duplexes. Signs along the main through-road direct locals and visitors to the nearby shopping complex and refer to schools, parks, playgrounds, transit stops, an off-leash dog park, and a health centre. An additional sign says a recreation centre is scheduled to appear in the area sometime in the future. This area is a far cry from the places that Paul used to live—at emergency shelters, in cars, and on the street.

Paul buzzes me in and I wait for him in the foyer of his home for a few minutes. I can see into the kitchen and then past the kitchen to the grassy backyard. A child's ball and some stacked chairs rest on the wooden deck overlooking a fenced backyard. He comes down a set of stairs and extends his right hand. "Sorry I'm late," he explains, "I was working out." His face is flushed and he is breathing faster than normal. He asks, "Coffee or water?"

I opt for water and we sit at the kitchen table. He pours us both a glass of water.

A few days earlier, I'd spoken with Paul on the phone,

explaining that I was writing a book and securing his permission to be interviewed and to tell his story. Now, he is
eyeing me carefully and thoughtfully. He is calm and serene,
albeit a bit distant. I wait to see if he has any questions or
comments; he seems to be waiting for me to speak first.

I decide to break the ice and again review the idea of
my book. He listens attentively, comments that the book is
a good idea, and he agrees to be interviewed to tell his story.
He seems interested in the process and does not express
either excitement or concern about doing so. He utters a
matter-of-fact statement, "Let's do this!"

PAUL'S EARLIEST MEMORIES of his family are vague. He lived
in the city with his parents and sister in what he described as
a normal family—two parents working at well-paying jobs,
family outings and going to school. Then his parents separated and divorced, and his mom moved away to another
city in another part of the country. Paul now experienced
a new family—his dad, a step-mom and her three children.
They continued to live in the same city.

He relates that when he was thirteen years old:

> My older sister and I were acting out, rebelling, upset
> about the divorce. We both were kicked out [of dad's
> place] to go live with our mother. I left one toxic
> environment for a worse environment. I had a lot of
> resentment. Our family was utter chaos—no parent-
> ing, no structure.

He continued:

> My mom had mental health issues—she suffered from
> depression. I felt I was all on my own with no friends.
> I was in grade nine in school. There was no parent

figure to look after me at the time. When we were left alone, we would throw massive parties and sometimes they would get pretty disastrous, like fire extinguishers being blown all over the place. My sister was not into the drugs as I was but we could pretty well do anything we wanted. We had the place to ourselves just about every weekend, totally trashed the house at massive parties every weekend. One time, a guy came to buy some weed but when he got it, he just left without paying so my sister's friend smashed a bottle on his head. Then there was an all-out brawl and the guy and his friends were beaten to a pulp. There were bottles flying, punching, kicking. The neighbours called the cops. Later, we actually got the guy to pay for the weed—double the price. This is an example of the craziness that happened.

I started smoking weed and cigarettes, and I made friends this way. I drank lots of alcohol on the weekends. I sold weed to have my own habit. I was skipping school and failing my courses; I didn't put in any effort. My mom couldn't handle me, and she didn't seem to care about me; she would be away for days at a time to be with her boyfriend. Often, I would take off for a few days, not tell her where I was going, to party with friends. One time, mom phoned the cops on me because she thought I was a missing person.

This had gone on for about two and a half years. At age sixteen, Paul's parents eventually decided it would be best if he moved back to live with his dad, who wasn't happy with the way Paul's life was going.

According to Paul:

My dad was trying to fix me, get me on the right track, and I didn't want any part of it! I just wanted to rebel and do what I wanted to. I was really upset and I rebelled; I missed my friends. My dad was strict; he had me working part-time as well as going to school. I still used alcohol and weed. I was angry at the situation I was in and would not listen to anyone. I did not like my step-mom. I worked in a restaurant part-time but I still skipped school a lot. I was still angry. I stole things from vehicles—some money. My dad was trying to help me with social workers and mentors but I wanted to move out on my own. Finally, my dad had enough and he kicked me out for good at age seventeen. He pretty well had enough of me, I guess.

It was a pretty dramatic step for me, going from having a certain lifestyle, clothes and food, going out to restaurants, to living in a shelter in the city and working part-time at a restaurant. I made friends with people in the shelter; they had some rough stories themselves. That's where I got involved with more serious drugs such as acid, mushrooms, and crack cocaine.

Others there were heavily into crystal meth. Nine to five during the weekdays we used to all get together to get out of the shelter to look for jobs. There was a curfew at the shelter; but on the weekends we'd all go to a nearby avenue, walk around and panhandle and have fun, pretty much. We'd break into places and vandalize; do drugs and smoke weed and drink. I was working at the time so I had a sort of income. We broke into a bus one time and found a wallet with a credit card. Someone used it to buy alcohol, a fair bit of alcohol. We bought some spiced rum and a friend said he could chug it. We kinda dared him to chug it and he did chug it—a 26 ouncer—and he ran out somewhere and then just passed out. It ended up the ambulance came, and he had his stomach pumped. It looked like he was dead for a while because of the rush of the alcohol. After that, we all just relaxed in the bus shelter with some booze. The cops came and asked whose alcohol it was and we said no one, so they just poured out the booze—40 ounces of whiskey. That would have lasted us a couple of days. I was pretty quiet at the time, and it was lucky I didn't get into crystal meth 'cause that was a pretty serious drug. I was more into alcohol and weed. There was a time that I got into crack cocaine; that was pretty crazy. One time, we met a guy who was doing a lot of crack and we were doing errands for him, like getting him stuff at the grocery store and taking it to his house. He wanted us to buy him porn magazines, but we were just too young to buy. Eventually we left.

Paul was better behaved for a while but went back to his old behaviours. He ended up getting kicked out of the shelter because of his drinking, getting high, and fighting.

I kept getting kicked out of each shelter because of being drunk or high or not following curfew. At one halfway house, I was play-fighting with a girl. She damaged the wall and we both got kicked out. I pretty well got kicked out or banned from all the resources in the city. There were some programs at the shelters, but I never went to any 'cause I was working at a restaurant. The shelter was just a place to eat and sleep. I pretty well wore out my welcome. I stayed in other places but was using again so I got kicked out. Housekeeping smelled weed and reported me. At first, I denied it to the manager but eventually confessed.

Whenever Paul cashed his cheque from work, he went on a drug binge. For a while, he lived on the street. The streets scared Paul. He struggled to find places to sleep other than on a bus or light rail transit. He slept in waiting rooms. He never knew what to expect or what would happen. He learned about sex workers, drugs, and the street lifestyle. This was all new to Paul. He explained:

> When I lived out on the street, we used to stay up all night and then ride the light rail transit during the day, trying to sleep. Sometimes I got caught for riding without a ticket. I would try to sleep at the university in a lab but eventually security would catch me.
>
> When I lived on the streets, that is when I got into the more serious drugs—acid and crack cocaine. I would stay up all night then sleep on the transit during the day. One time, a used clothing store had a furniture drop-off area and I slept there on a couch. I kept getting woken up by customers asking was I dead or passed out? That was annoying. To kill time during the day, I used to sneak into movies and spend all day in there; it was a place to stay. Security would eventually pick up on us.
>
> It's mostly a kind of fog. One time, I shoplifted some food. The cops came and I was arrested. I told them I had no place to stay. It was kinda funny. The cop drove me to a halfway house but the manager said, 'Oh no, you can't come here', 'cause I had been there before and got kicked out. The cop eventually just dropped me off downtown.

I THINK PAUL DOWNPLAYED what it was really like to live on the streets. His comments sparked my recollection of what others told me about the streets. Several young adults that I supervised on probation told me about their twist on the crime of "dine and dash." Instead of eating a meal in a restaurant then fleeing before paying the bill, some street-wise people had the courage, or were desperate enough, to enter a restaurant and wander around looking for a table where the diners had left the table, then sit down and clean up any food and/or scraps left on the plates before a server came to remove the dishes. One young man proudly told me how he sometimes obtained food.

> Yeah, you know, when I lived on the streets, I was dirty, dressed real scruffy and didn't shower so I didn't smell so good. If I was desperate or high, I would see a table with an extra place, a vacant place, then go and just sit down in that spot at the table, right with the others already there. Those people would get right pissed off and mostly they would scramble right out of there, real fast. So I would finish their meals real quick and leave before the server came around.

In keeping with life on the streets, I read powerful memoirs by Jessie Thistle and Yasuko Thanh that document their lives (see Reference page). Here are common activities and vocabulary about life on the streets:

- Begging. Sitting on a street and asking for spare change; extending a hand to a passer-by. Most people avoided eye-contact, did not make a donation and just walked on; a few passers-by kicked at the extended hand.
- Couch surfing. Staying for free with friends or acquaintances in a house or apartment; moving frequently when wearing out a welcome.
- Starving. No regular meals, sometimes going several days without any food.
- Stealing. Snacks, food, liquor, clothing; sell new

clothing to get a few dollars.

- Staying in emergency shelters where theft of possessions is a problem. Sleeping with boots on to prevent theft of the boots—not always effective.
- Curling up in bus shelters and sleeping as long as possible until awakened by someone who objected to your presence.
- Sleeping in shopping malls during the day.
- Sleeping in staircases at the top of apartment buildings or parking lots at night, using whatever extra clothes you have for a pillow.
- No baths or showers for weeks.
- Short-term jobs with temporary job agencies, sometimes not paid at all, where the agency cut is about 50%; cheque cashing agencies charge about 50% as well.
- Flashback memories of better times such as birthdays and family gatherings.
- Silent tears and crying.
- Feeling close to death; people you know keep disappearing.
- Feeling helpless and utterly alone.
- Giving up and blaming others.
- Come to expect something for doing nothing.

Eventually, Paul went to a three-month drug and alcohol residential rehab program followed by a stay in a halfway house. He was in and out of treatment and halfway houses, using for a while then cleaning up, using, then getting kicked out. He was angry and frustrated. He turned eighteen during this time and tried an adult shelter in the city, but Paul found this experience frustrating so he left.

He soon started using regularly again and his dad would not have him back in the family home. So Paul, at age eighteen, went back to live with his mom. She still wasn't able to handle him, so he lived in an adult shelter again for a while. Shelter residents could sleep there but were required to be out of the shelter during the day; so Paul spent the day time hanging out with friends, using drugs and alcohol and, in his words, "Getting ready for the day."

> This involved bumming around the city, drinking, and jacking people—you know, trying to take valuables from them. I ended up getting charged with one charge of robbery and some assaults, then had to deal with police, go to court, and face a lot of jail time. The robbery wasn't planned out very much—it was something to do at the time, I guess, kinda spontaneous. We were drinking and doing drugs. For some reason, I thought it would be a good idea! It was pretty scary for me. I was placed on probation for two years and wasn't supposed to hang around with other criminals. Being on probation was a pain in the ass; I had to go see the probation officer every month. I had to prove to him that I was looking for work. It went pretty smoothly, I only got picked up once for being drunk. Mom still couldn't handle me but she convinced me to go live with her boyfriend so she could come to visit me. That turned out to be a really awkward situation.
>
> I figured this was getting out of hand, getting pretty crazy; so I got a job at a restaurant as a cook. (I had lots of experience at this and was pretty good at it.) I started back in school—adult upgrading. I was doing okay for a while. But then I got back into my old habits—the wrong friends, using weed. Then I lost my ambition to go to school. My mom broke up with her boyfriend so I had to move out.
>
> Mom set me up in an apartment. It was cheap rent, but in a bad area. I quit school, kept working, started buying and selling weed, drinking and using

other drugs—just working and partying. I was on my own and my mom was helping me out with rent—pretty good deal.

Paul eventually got his own apartment and kept up the lifestyle of working and partying for several years.

I spent six days in jail because of drinking. This was a real wake-up call for me. I was in a big dorm, not an individual cell. It was hard for me. I got to know everyone in there. This was not the planned route that I wanted, and it leads to nowhere. There were bunk beds with twenty or thirty other people. It was pretty much hell. One time, somebody stole my mattress. Another time, somebody put peanut butter on my sheets so I woke up with it all over my face. It was more like practical jokes, nothing really serious. The issue was that you were stuck in that dorm pretty well all day. That was depressing. You watch TV, eat at your bed. I was so isolated, stuck in the dorm all the time.

At twenty-three, I realized I wasn't going anywhere. Mom raised the idea of me getting a trade and living with my sister and brother-in-law. This now sounded pretty good so I moved back to the city to get a fresh start. I got a job in construction. There was drug testing at work so I quit drugs but drank pretty heavy all weekend. I was going to school for my apprenticeship.

Then I got my own apartment, kept on drinking heavily, ate in restaurants, and gave up on my schooling. I got kicked out of the apartment so I went to live with a house full of college girls. I was spending all my money on take-out food and booze; now I needed to take out pay-day loans. Then I met the lady who currently is my wife. We started dating and we clicked.

We moved in together and I cleaned up a bit for her. When she got pregnant I started to smarten up. I went back to school and finally passed with pretty good grades. I quit smoking cigarettes and quit drugs; but, for some reason, it was very hard to quit alcohol.

I was involved with AA in my earlier years when I was twenty or so, but I really never stuck with it. It wasn't until Christmas 2017, when I was thirty-two, that I finally was able to quit drinking. I basically did this on my own. I admitted I had a problem with alcohol and I wanted to make a severe effort to quit drinking. My wife urged me to get into a nutrition program, lose some weight, take care of my body, and get healthier. This is when I started my path to improve.

I asked him if it was tough to get over his addictions. He nodded thoughtfully and said:

It took me a long while to get through my addictions, and alcohol was a big one for me. I don't drink anymore and I feel a lot better—I lost 80 pounds. I now work out at home every day and follow a strict nutrition regime. We bought a house so things are good. We now have three kids. It was a long journey for me—about ten years from when I was 14 to 24 years, battling addiction.

There was a time in my life when I was living in another city and was charged. I realized this was going not the way I want. I want to have a wife, I want to have kids, I want to have money. I didn't have much education at the time. I realized that if I joined a trade, I didn't need a high school diploma. You just write an equivalency exam; if you pass that exam, you are basically good to go. Now I'm making good money as a journeyman in the trades. For me, it was a willingness to work—it is hard work, you are outside, you have to be good at problem solving, be intelligent with the issues that come up on the job.

Right now, I work away from home and stay in work camps—home for two weeks, away for two. I've worked at shut downs, new construction, various projects. These usually last from six months to a year; then you move on to the next project, the next employer. There is not too much work in the city right now so you have to go where the work is—up north.

My wife is working part-time right now in health care. She helped me with my addiction and straightened me out. I was working on my apprenticeship, she was working on her education, and we had a child. Eventually, I got my apprenticeship done, she got her education, and we had more kids. We moved from apartments to a townhouse, to a house in another community then we moved here. It's a nice area, close to movie theatres, parks, and stores. It's really good, location wise. I fell in love with the area the first time I came here, and it's reasonably priced, it's affordable.

Now, the three kids keep me busy. We do activities like go to the library and to the park. It's best to keep the kids active like going swimming. It takes a lot of work to eat healthy and work out, prepare my meals from scratch, shopping. We eat healthy instead of ordering take out or fast food or eating in restaurants—that's expensive and high in calories. I enjoy playing video games.

Exercise is a big thing for me. My wife and I like to watch movies or play cards or exercise together. Since I've quit alcohol, I've been really active with the kids, more active around the house.

Paul's face cracked a bit of a smile:

> I still have that temptation to drink. If we're going
> to have alcohol in the house, it's got to be locked
> up in a liquor cabinet; my wife is the only one who
> knows where the key is. My brother came over one
> day and saw the locked liquor cabinet. 'Oh', he said,
> 'is that locked for the kids? 'No', I said, 'that's for me!'
> The honest truth is that I am an alcoholic, and I just
> don't want that temptation. To remove that tempta-
> tion just makes it easier for me not to drink it. For
> me, having the cabinet locked helps my temptation.
>
> Overall for me, it's a life of change. I feel a lot
> better, more energetic, not as angry. I have to be
> proactive—deal with the temptations, stresses,
> emotions. I used to deal with it by drinking. It is
> interesting to try to learn how to deal with different
> types of situations. When I'm sober, I actually deal
> with things better.
>
> I am applying for a pardon and an entry waiver
> so I can volunteer, do things with the kids, and travel.

Paul also said he sat on the board of directors of a
charity dedicated to assisting youth who abuse drugs and
alcohol.

Quietly, he concludes, "It was quite the journey. I
pretty well had to learn everything on my own, quitting
drinking and recovery. Everything is good now; I think I
have returned to normal."

I FIND THERE IS A QUIET CONFIDENCE in how Paul com-
municates. The confidence, in my view, is well founded
and I share his confidence.

Paul is a perfect example of how hard it is to get away

from dependency on street drugs and alcohol. It took him ten years to recover. Some people expect an addict to "get over it" in a short period of time and that is a very unrealistic expectation, in my view. Patience, faith, and support would seem to be more helpful to those in recovery than orders ("Quit drinking!") or punitive responses (jail time instead of treatment).

CHAPTER 11

JUANITO: SIR, YOU ARE LOOKING AT 42 MONTHS IMPRISONMENT

I HAVE LONG BEEN an admirer and supporter of drug courts, where serious drug-abusing offenders turn their lives around to become esteemed law-abiding citizens. Their journey to normalcy is remarkable in that an estimated seventy percent of drug court graduates do not return to the chaos and dysfunction that so inflicted their lives and the lives of their family and community for so many years. This low rate of recidivism is rare in the criminal justice system and is a testimony to the effectiveness of the community, police, courts, and correctional services working together to give new knowledge and opportunities to drug-abusing men and women of any age who commit crime. But, like Juanito, the subject of this chapter, they are up against a tough decision. The decision he faced? Given that he was facing a long term of imprisonment, would he instead consider a single day in jail plus go through and complete a thirteen-month drug treatment program? What follows is Juanito's story about choices he made, woven through time.

JUANITO SAT IN THE WAITING AREA of his lawyer's office in a ten-storey office building, wondering how long he would have to wait to actually meet the lawyer. Thumbing his way through a magazine, he felt his stress level rise; he was getting hot, feeling very anxious and nervous. Others waiting in the same area also seemed anxious, not surprising given what was at stake when you need a lawyer in a serious criminal matter. This was a legal aid appointment and Juanito had heard lots of negative, put-down comments about legal aid lawyers. He was hoping that these comments would not apply to his lawyer. He was hoping for a good lawyer because he was in criminal court facing three counts of trafficking in a controlled substance, two of which related to the drug fentanyl, and a host of other charges related to the chaotic life he had led for the past few years. Conviction on charges of trafficking in drugs like fentanyl carries with it the possibility of imprisonment for life. Depending on the circumstances in each case, there could be a minimum sentence of imprisonment as well.

For Juanito, this was a big deal. He had a lot riding on this meeting—like his freedom for a long time. The receptionist led him down a long hallway of doors to the office of his lawyer. He seated himself in front of the lawyer's desk, and looked out over the city through tall windows. After some chat about the weather and local sports teams, the lawyer got straight to the point.

"I had a conversation with the prosecutor," said the lawyer. "She is adamant that there will be no more remands; she wants to resolve the matter soon." The lawyer reviewed the disclosure (an outline of the evidence to be used by the prosecuting attorney in the case) with Juanito.

"Sir, you are looking at a grand total of three and a half years in a penitentiary if you plead guilty at your next court appearance. We could go to trial and see what happens, but they do have you with the sales. What would you like to do?"

Juanito sat in a stunned silence, his mind racing. He thought to himself, "Based on the disclosure, it was pretty horrible what I had done and what I looked like on paper."

"Do you want a few days to think about it?" enquired the lawyer.

"Sure," replied Juanito and he left the lawyer's office in turmoil, his mind racing. He knew he was going off to prison, which is what he already thought would happen the whole time anyway, but hadn't realized it would be for so long.

He recalled hearing something about a drug court when he was at a treatment centre the year before. If he successfully completed the drug court program, he would be sentenced to one day in custody which would actually be the last day he appeared in court. What a choice: Prison? Or the year-long drug court program?

After leaving the lawyer's office, he contacted a friend, a former dealer who had since graduated from drug court, who suggested that Juanito call them. He gave Juanito the drug court manager's phone number.

JUANITO WAS BORN in South America, in a county known for a turbulent political past. His family consisted of his parents, a brother, and a sister. They had lived in a small coastal fishing village. His dad worked in sales and his mother was a stay-at-home mom. Juanito says he grew up in very close-knit family that was very religious, so these values and practices influenced much of his early life. His dad dreamed of having more opportunity than those available in that country, so the parents explored different options to move for better opportunities.

The family decided to go to North America, living for a year in a city where they had relatives, then later moving to the present city where there were also a host of aunts, uncles, and cousins. Juanito recalls a close extended family, strongly influenced by their religion.

Family and church was all I knew, right? Life was good! I remember a sign in the city that welcomed immigrants and newcomers to the community— that felt good to see that! I went to kindergarten and school to grade five in that community. Everything was good—a church-going kid, close family where I did what the family wanted. I wasn't bullied; I was in a good place.

A few years later, the family returned to their country-of-origin for a year in the hopes that opportunities had improved there but that did not work out so they came back to the city. Juanito did not want to leave his country-of-origin. He loved being with his cousins, was popular in school, and doing well. But he had to leave to be with his family.

Juanito started to notice changes upon his return to the city. He started to be rebellious when he was placed in grade seven and he started to get into fights at school. He felt like he was a nobody. As an adolescent, he was beginning to feel shame for some of the sexual urges he felt and some of the sexual thoughts he had that were contrary to the teachings of the church. Juanito explains:

I started to feel evil and to think I was a horrible person. My parents at the time were property managers, looking after some condos. One time, I took a set of keys and entered a few condos, just looking around, curious. I got caught in one lady's place. I was charged for mischief as a young offender, and I got one hundred hours of community service. A church leader talked to me; I was super ashamed of what I did.

That was the first time I felt that I was different and that I wasn't connected to my family. I was put into a more restricted routine and was watched more carefully by my parents, and I felt like I wasn't meeting

their expectations. The older I got, the further disconnected I got from the church that my family belonged
to and from my family as well.

Juanito continued in school, playing sports there and
through the church. He was good at soccer and football. He
did not get into trouble when he played sports, but he was
not allowed to go to the team parties. He was beginning to
feel that he did not fit in. He said he felt lost.

When he was seventeen years old, he continued feeling
disconnected from his family and church. He lost interest in
the church, in its teachings and in its expectations for young
men. After graduating from high school, he started work as
a cook in a restaurant and this is where he saw illegal drugs
for the first time. He knew a bit about drugs before but he
had been pretty sheltered from their impact. Juanito continued to be exposed to the drug world through colleagues
at work and now at sporting events. It seemed everyone he
knew was using, so he eventually did cocaine, alcohol, and
weed. He met people who used extensively but also main-
tained a job. Juanito's drug use gradually increased, even as
he was employed.

I started hanging out with these guys, and I felt alien-
ated from my family and the church. I felt like a puppet, hanging out with the guys and sort of getting
involved more and more. I saw myself as becoming a
gangster—that was pretty cool. The lifestyle was fun.
I was fascinated by it. Now I was starting to feel like I
fit in. Now, people were calling me to buy drugs and
there were girls around all the time.

By now, my dad figured out what I was up to. I
couldn't deny it, so he changed the lock on the door
of the family home and kicked me out. I got bitter
about that, and it solidified my new role in life. I felt

my family had turned its back on me. Much later, I realized my dad was just trying to protect the family, especially my younger sister, from me and my friends. Getting kicked out solidified my image of a bad guy.

My life went downhill fast after that from the age of eighteen to age twenty-four. I was with my new friends 24/7 and would go long periods of time without seeing my family. I experienced a lot of the ugliest things that life has from my addiction, and my life was going to get worse as time went on, but the shock to my system was the complete 360 degrees my life went and how naive I was about the world I had entered.

Juanito subsequently started selling drugs. He enjoyed the money he could make. He quickly learned to go with the flow in his new lifestyle which also gave him a sense of being his own person; a sense of purpose. He liked being a rebel. He accepted the lifestyle—the violence, drug use, weapons, dealing, working on and off, and getting high. Always getting high.

Once I got addicted, it was all a game—stealing and using. It was pretty bad when I got to the point of robbing an old lady in a mall. I tried to take her purse but she held on real tight. I knocked her over and didn't even care what happened to her. I was always trying to get high; to make a dollar. I had no idea how twisted my thinking and behaviours had gotten; to me, it was the new normal. I would jump to conclusions on a regular basis, leading me to behave—basing my actions on a conclusion that I had made up in my mind to be true when in reality it couldn't have been further from the truth. I was an all-or-nothing thinker. I felt I was a bad person; therefore, nothing I could possibly do would be good, so I might as well continue on the path I was on.

When he was nineteen, he met a young woman and they became close, eventually living together. She condoned his drug use, even as it continued into addiction. This relationship lasted for eight years, with a number of ups and downs, including break-ups and reconciliations. The woman became pregnant and had a baby. This was a wake-up call for Juanito, who caught a glimpse of new purpose now because of the child in his life. His family learned about the baby, and his dad pressured him to get some help. So, after years of using and dealing, Juanito decided to go to a treatment centre. He confessed his addiction but continued to use drugs and alcohol and was soon kicked out of the treatment centre. His continued substance abuse and a charge of impaired driving contributed to a final break-up with his girlfriend.

To me, the lifestyle became more addictive than the drugs. In my addiction, I was very much a thief. Everything became a game—using, stealing, lying, cheating. It was interesting to see how ingenious I became just to get myself some drugs. I became proud of how I did things, even with all the core beliefs and morals I had from before.

I got good at wearing masks. I had trouble talking to girls but not when I was high—then I had power and a false sense of respect. I found a new family, even though it was dysfunctional. It was nice to see homies around, people you would see every day and come to rely on, even if it wasn't to good ends. I got involved doing thefts and dealing outside the city. Lots of drinking and drugging in the city, too. I dealt in bars and wherever I was. I even got into buying and selling handguns. I would sometimes have no place to stay. My parents took me in from time to time but I didn't follow their rules, so out I would go.

One of the biggest shocks to me was when I started selling drugs and getting into that lifestyle was that I had never before seen that side of this world, you know? It was interesting because I stopped going to church where this belief in God was instilled, and it wasn't until I had experienced a lot of the ugly stuff on this earth that I really re-affirmed my belief in God. I definitely believed in evil, this darkness. A lot of the things I would see or do I wasn't okay with, but it seemed I wanted to be a part of it—I didn't want to be alone. The first thing that gave me a sour note was all the violence. I hung out a lot with Bobby—his dad was a pimp and his mom a prostitute. There was a lot of violence in his upbringing and you could see it by the way he was now.

Looking back now, there was a lot of just taking advantage of other people. There is always an agenda, you know? We're gonna rob this guy or rough him up— just to intimidate people. I turned into a menace. I liked the rep that it gave me. I remember walking around, enjoying when people looked at me then looked away real quick. I enjoyed having the power that came with being bad. As a kid growing up, I learned there were consequences to being bad but now I learned there were no real consequences. I felt like a bad-ass. I wore it. I knew I had to play this role so I started wearing it. I enjoyed it.

I'd always be wearing these masks—show different sides of me to different people. I didn't have any inter-action with my family, my spouse at the time, or friends from back-in-the-day who were trying to help as they could see that I was in a bad place. I was swallowed up by my addiction and that was all that I was at the time. I couldn't control my anger or my emotions. I'd always be running from stuff and wouldn't face anything. I took out my anger and frustrations on people who were vulnerable and who I could exploit.

At this point I asked him if there were things he regretted and would have changed.

Yeah, there are definitely things I'm not proud of. In my addictions early on, it was all like a party. The women who were around; it was always for sex. With using drugs and selling drugs, I wasn't interested in meeting new people—just in partying.

I felt I was in control. For a while, I felt like a real man especially when I had a job working on the rigs and being their drug dealer as well. I was intrigued by the power and the lifestyle that came with selling drugs; but, most of all, I loved this acceptance. Knowing what I know now, I realize that I was a naïve boy in a world I knew nothing about and I was just getting taken advantage of. I learned a lot of lessons the hard way.

The more and more that I was consumed by my addiction, it became like a movie, Disney-like, a production—hanging out with homies, smoking weed all day, having a barbecue, drinking beers, going to the club at night. My life became unmanageable.

I used an alternative measures program and community services to work off the impaired driving fine. I would diligently go every day to the program, then sell drugs at night. I felt comfortable with this, like a gangster—calls coming in, regular customers, the money coming in and I felt successful.

That life was pure chaos. In a span of two months,

I was shot at, went into houses with the sketchiest of people, using, selling—a kind of a robot. It was all about the drugs and I was literally a block from my parents' house. It was crazy.

It was like a roller coaster. I lost the power of choice—I couldn't stop using, no matter what. I got into chaos situations real quickly. The only person that communicated with me was my dad and he saved me a few times; three times took me out of bad situations, took me back home once, rented a room for me on two occasions, bought my groceries, gave me a little bit of money. I liked the regular people, the quietness, birds singing—yet I always fucked up the situation by going back to dealing. I thought I had to keep my options open. When I was using, I was good at making commitments but then not following up.

Within a year, Juanito was facing three trafficking charges for selling fentanyl and cocaine to undercover police officers, possession of cocaine for the purposes of trafficking, and three charges related to the proceeds of crime, in addition to theft and breaches of probation charges. Also at this time, he learned he was under investigation by police for possible charges of manslaughter because one of his suspected clients had died from an apparent overdose of fentanyl. In short, he was now in very deep shit.

I wasn't selling anymore, just using. I didn't trust people any more but I was using with people I didn't know, getting high all the time. I was homeless, couch-surfing for two months before I decided to sober up. At the time, I was disconnected and full of anger. I wasn't doing anything for my probation officer.

One time, when I was in custody in a remand centre for two months, I thought, 'Wow, this is an evil place, like, it is really sickening.' This is when I first realized how much worse life can get. But what really was odd about the situation was how quickly I became comfortable in there. To me, that just means I am evil, too. Up to now, I just thought selling drugs was normal, not really terrible—I was just providing a service. I had a moment of clarity real quick because I wanted to be out of there, especially when I had my daughter on my mind.

But two months prior to sobering up, I was at a drug house in the city, preparing a package to go back into the remand centre. You know, I never put anything in my bum before but little did I know that you can put an ounce of meth in there, a half ounce of shatter, a half bale of tobacco and some guy wants you to stick a lighter in there, too. I'm not putting a lighter in my butt. Are you crazy? Yeah, there's a cubby hole back there; I never knew that!

I was in custody on remand for four months on three charges of trafficking. When I raised enough money for bail and got out, I didn't know what to do. I went back couch-surfing—it was hell. But I knew I had to get into treatment so I went to a treatment centre. More importantly, I decided to quit drinking.

The first staff member that I met at the treatment centre gave me the love of the AA Big Book. I could feel his passion for it but I didn't believe any of it at first. I had to call in every day until I got accepted. A few days later, I got the call that I had been accepted so I went and just started going through the motions, doing whatever they said. I went to meetings—AA and NA (Narcotics Anonymous). I met people who were faking it and others who were loving and caring. I felt so alone but someone recognized me and called me by name. I couldn't understand how or why he would do that, but that impressed me. I think he saw the hurt in my eyes—that touched me.

I've come to believe that the Big Book saved me. The things it covers—all those things we experience in addiction—can change. It talks about fear. It took me ten months to realize I did not have to fear things—recognize it, accept it, but question it. The Big Book's promise to me about fear came true; I just couldn't believe it! Now I see the little miracles every day and it's really cool that I get to be part of it.

For three months at the treatment centre, I just did what they said, whatever they asked me to do; that was the first time I was accountable. This gave me purpose, some responsibility. My parents could see I was changing, so they agreed for me to see my daughter at their place. A friend at the centre told me about drug court so I told my lawyer and I got accepted within a month. My probation officer could see what I was doing—all the changes. When a friend died of an overdose involving fentanyl, I now took it as a message—before, I would just use. Now, my perspective was changing. I came to understand the Big Book's teachings of acceptance and being obsessed with alcohol.

JUANITO HAD BEEN IN DEEP CHAOS for more than three years when he was faced with the big decision: be sentenced up to three and a half years imprisonment or apply to take part in the drug court treatment program. After making a call to the manager of the drug court program, Juanito put down the phone, his mind reeling and whirling. He wondered what he had just gotten himself into. Could he actually do drug court and only get a sentence of one day's imprisonment? As it worked out, Juanito was selected to take part in the program and he threw himself whole-heartedly into it for the next thirteen months.

I was granted access to Juanito's drug court file which described his thirteen months in the drug court program. He attended court sessions every week where his conduct and attitude was reviewed by program staff, in open court, and presided over by a judge. Over that time he consistently provided clean random urine samples, attended hundreds of recovery meetings, and volunteered hundreds of hours with community agencies. Programs he completed included first aid, parenting, meal planning, and Big Book study.

AT JUANITO'S DRUG COURT GRADUATION, the courtroom was packed. It was a noisy place, with people talking excitedly and loudly about sobriety and recovery, visiting with friends, wishing each other well, hugging, and in general celebrating their journey to normalcy. There were about sixty people in attendance, comprised of those currently in the program, some accused in custody who were granted permission to observe the proceedings (people who had expressed interest in the drug court program while in custody), a handful of drug court grads, friends and family, including Juanito's six year daughter who followed him everywhere he went in the courtroom, at times clutching his leg and holding on to his hand.

A gowned Clerk of the Court emerged from a door in the corner of the courtroom and announced, "All rise. Court is now in session. Please ensure your cell phones are turned off." Gradually, people quieted down and order was established in the courtroom.

The manager of the program rose from her chair in

front of the judge. "Your Honour," she said proudly, "today we are celebrating the achievements and graduation of Juanito. Juanito, will you take the stand?"

Juanito slowly walked to the witness stand next to the judge's dais from where he had been standing in the courtroom beside his father. Program staff, including the prosecutor, legal aid lawyer, probation officer, program manager, other drug court staff, previous grads and community agency representatives, approached Juanito and, one by one, reported on the remarkable progress he had made over the past year. Reference was made to the sanctions he received for failing to disclose part-time employment and failure to attend volunteer hours on one day. Reference was also made to the rewards he received, such as curfew extensions, gift cards, an Achievement Award certificate, and reductions in the number of recovery meetings and court appearances, all in response to his ongoing progress in the program and his self-motivation.

A hush descended over the courtroom as Juanito's mother, father, and sister came forward to speak. His dad spoke quietly about the hurt their family experienced when Juanito was out of control. He then spoke about the pride and love their family now feels, given all the positive changes Juanito has made. Juanito's younger sister spoke of her joy at seeing him return to normalcy. Juanito's daughter repeatedly hugged her dad.

When all the accolades were finished, the judge confirmed a sentence of one day imprisonment, to be served by the day's appearance in court. She then rose from her chair on the judge's dais, descended a few stairs to the witness stand then gave Juanito a large framed certificate and a big hug. Juanito and the judge quietly exchanged smiles, a warm hand shake and a thank you to each other.

Everyone in the courtroom stood at attention, cheered and applauded. Tears were evident in many eyes.

Juanito is now steadily employed as a Peer Support Worker with a health authority in the city, has reconnected with his family, is active in leisure activities such as sports, watching television with family and friends, gardening, hiking, spending time with his girlfriend and is working toward having his six-year-old daughter for a sleep-over at his residence. He continues to attend recovery meetings and has become involved at the international level with recovery associations.

> I don't question where my life, my path, has taken me. Some things weren't so necessary to go through but with most things, I think they were."
>
> The strength and self-esteem gained from partaking in drug court is something I truly value and am grateful for. I see it as a blessing in my recovery to have gotten picked and accepted into this program. I had three and a half years I was looking at in prison time wiped away with a program that not only allowed me to not go to prison but gave me all sorts of programming that has supplemented my recovery and made me a better man today.
>
> Now I can see how much I have changed—my debts are paid, my job is fulfilling, family connections are growing. I see the miracles we do at work every day and it's really cool. I've seen so much misery and regret; I can't justify it. Before, I always had so much fear so I would use. I now can't justify throwing my life away. I have found the recipe that works for me.
>
> It's amazing how much energy you get from natural highs in life.

In my view, Juanito has made remarkable changes in his life in the past four years. He is confident that his days of chaos are behind him. I share this view as well. It will be exciting to see what this remarkable man will achieve in the future, knowing how he came from an immigrant family, descended into years of drug abuse, crime and chaos, then emerged as a new man well on his way to normalcy.

CHAPTER 12

RICHARD: BITTER OR BETTER

*"When there is nothing left, you got two choices—
you will turn bitter or you will turn and get better."*

RICHARD PLEADED GUILTY to six charges related to child pornography: accessing, possessing, and making available images of a sexual nature of a child. He entered the guilty plea six months after he was charged and arrested: a relatively short time period considering the seriousness of these charges. He told me the following:

> From the moment I was arrested, I admitted, 'Yes, I pleaded guilty, true, true. Yes, I did this.' I never tried to argue any of it. Obviously I was totally caught. I wanted to get it behind me so why fight it. I'm still not denying it. I did not intend it but that is splitting hairs. I just want to deal with it and move on. That is my intention.
>
> There was a sense of relief when I got caught. I never felt like, "Damn!" It was kind of like, now I can start dealing with it. There must have been some part of me that wants it, now we can start working on it.

At the time of sentence, Richard, sixty years of age, appeared via closed circuit television from a distant remand facility rather than appear in open court in the community, several hours from the city. His lawyer entered guilty pleas on his behalf, and Richard was sentenced to a total of ten years imprisonment. The judge credited his six months of pre-trial custody prior to conviction, so that shortened the remaining time to be served to nine and a half years. The sentences were to be served concurrently rather than consecutively. Most sentences in criminal matters are handed out in this manner.

The reaction of most people from most communities to this type of crime is one of revulsion and condemnation. This view is also reflected in the length of sentence issued by the court; in Richard's case, this is a very long sentence, a tough sentence. The focus of the sentence seems in this case to be primarily on the protection of the public and holding the accused accountable, less so on helping the offender.

After an initial reaction of revulsion and condemnation, some community members will wonder: How did this happen? Is the offender really such a monster, a low-life? What lies ahead for the accused?

This chapter takes you through a journey with Richard and at the end of the chapter, you will no doubt reach your own conclusions to the questions I have presented. You may well have more.

IN HIS OWN WORDS, Richard outlined his early years:

> Well, my dad died when I was just a baby. And then after that, my mom raised us in a little one-room log cabin with a dirt floor. It was out in the bush, literally. No water, power, sewer, phone, vehicle—like nothing. Mom had a big garden, she raised chickens, and we had a couple of goats for a while. I did lots of hunting, fishing, and trapping. I went trapping with an uncle when I was ten years old and when I was sixteen, he wasn't in good health so I took over the trap-line for about ten years. Other than going to school, I had no contact with anybody other than my family. There were no sleepovers or visiting next door, just a few

get-togethers with relatives. People would count it as a very rough childhood. We had nothing, but I look at it as it done me great. You learn how to just rely on yourself. You don't get upset at things or worry. I know how to stretch dollars and save pennies. I'm sure by most standards, I had a very different childhood from most people, but I would hate to say I was hard done by. Without a dad and all these things, to me, you can't miss something if you never had it. I never had it so I never missed it. To me, that was normal life. And that's a good thing. There were no jobs for mom— nothing. There was no way she could work; she had no transportation. She raised me and my brothers. She got a widow's allowance from the government of $40 a month for years and years. It went up to $80 a month when we were all in high school.

Richard went on to talk about school, then going out into the adult world and working:

A bus went by every day so that's how I got to school. I finished grade eleven, and then I quit. I never failed a grade but I never got good grades—I just didn't study. I was not overly interested in school. There was, by then, a sawmill in the community. I went felling trees with a chain saw at first, and then I went to work inside the mill, got married, continued working in the mill. And then when that kinda fizzled out, I worked on an oil rig, worked on the railway, and then I got going in some businesses. I did some landscaping for a while; then we bought the store, and we ran that for seven years. About half of my adult life was working in mills and the railway. The other half was running a business of one sort or another. I've always been steadily employed, one way or another, at a variety of jobs. I've worked a lot in forestry, running heavy equipment, driving truck. I got my Class 1 licence when I was fifty-eight years old so I could drive bigger trucks.

Everybody said I was crazy not to get my grade twelve, but to this day I am okay with it. I got enough education so that if something interests me, I can learn to do it and do it fairly well. To me, I never did see the point of getting more education. I was never turned down from a job for not having grade twelve. I never got fired from a job. I did get laid off a couple of times when things got slow or the mill shut down, so I'd go try something else."

Now, Richard turned his attention to getting married and his family:

I was twenty-five when I got married. Actually, it was kinda neat. I lived north of town, and she lived south of town, about fifteen miles apart. We never knew the other one ever existed, and she was quite a few years younger than me. I had no idea who she was. We got hooked up on a blind date and then we got married. We have two children.

My marriage was quite good. Well, actually, I am still married. It'll be forty-two years this summer. I think we did a lot of damage to the kids when we took over that store. It was a booming business, eventually. In two years, we got the gross sales up over two million dollars a year; but we were married to the store, working sixteen- or seventeen-hour days, seven days a week for seven years. Unfortunately, our kids got shoved aside and they watched us run around like chickens with our heads cut off.

A guy was going to open another store in the

area, and we realized there was not enough business there for that. Normally competition is good; but, if that other store got up and running, it would have been a race to see who starves out who first. So, we thought if the area wants convenience store hours, we'll give it to them. We were open early in the morning, and we closed late at night. We plowed all the revenue back into the store, renovating, new services, that sort of thing. It was taking all our time and all our money. And we did shut down that other store. We turned our store into an extremely profitable business that serviced a big area, but we had no time for the kids. I'm sure there was a lot of damage there. There was no neglect or abandoning but the TV was there as a baby-sitter. The store was a big success business-wise, but it did not do our kids any good at all.

We just burned out and that's when we sold it. Just, life is too short. So, you can see we made a super success of it; but, in hind sight, I'd never do it again. Once we sold the store, we decided to try a few other small businesses; and then we got into logistics and delivery. I injured my leg and it didn't heal very well so driving was all I could physically do. We eventually got other delivery contracts in the region; and that's what I did, a driver, until I was arrested. My wife is still running that business, with other drivers.

At this point in our conversation, Richard began to talk about the offences that led to his arrest, conviction and sentencing:

The six charges—it started with the store, for sure. There was so much stress. My sex life and my marriage went totally down the tube. There was so much pressure. It just started out with mainstream pornography which is addictive; and, one degree at a time, it just got more. You do something that you're slightly uncomfortable with, let it sit for long enough, and now you can just push it. I think it is shocking what most of us are capable of. It wasn't a clear-cut thing when it started. It was a little degree at a time. I justified it in my own mind that it was just a little bit more, there was nobody involved and it went slowly, slowly… that's how it went. That's the best I can explain.

At this point in our interview, Richard was holding his hands in a prayer-like manner, palm to palm. As he was explaining how his use of pornography slowly expanded, he moved his hands slowly apart, inch by inch, with palms facing each other, physically reflecting the words he was using.

I was downloading child pornography. I had no interest in sharing, in distributing to others—it was for my own use. There was a file sharing program on the computer and when you are downloading, it goes into a file that is available to anyone else using that same file sharing program software. While it's downloading, they can access it. As soon as it was downloaded, I put it in another file. I was not into making child pornography or distributing child pornography. But others could access it, and they were getting it off my computer, so now that is where you get the distribution.

At the end, I did take a picture of a child so that was the making child pornography charge. I'm not trying to justify what I did, but I was using the child pornography I got off the internet for my own use. Because of the way it went through that file sharing program, I'm distributing child pornography. If you look at my charges, it looks like I was producing and distributing, but I wasn't making a living off it. I was not selling it. I never once talked to the people I was file sharing with. That wasn't what I wanted.

I'm not trying to justify what I did; I'm not trying to minimize it. Absolutely no other kids involved. Over a one month period, I think and three times, after that—for a two year period. I understand the seriousness, but I wasn't trying to make a buck—to make a living out of it. The only computer I used was the one for our personal use and part for the business, after hours and late at night. Pornography was a relief from the stress of the business. I pushed the envelope a bit and then a bit more. I slowly justified it a little degree at a time that this isn't really hurting nobody and it was just— *(he trailed off)*

My wife was stressed out. I wish in hindsight I had confronted my wife; there had to be a happy medium. We had zero sex life for the last ten years of our marriage. I wasn't into getting a divorce or whatever. I thought this was just the easiest way. I'd gotten into a total rut of being a workaholic. Child pornography was a way for me to relieve my stress. I chose to go down that road rather than confront my wife in the right way and get it sorted out. I'm not sorry it come out in the end. I'm happy it all come out 'cause, yes, I have got my life turned around. Let's say, if I hadn't got caught, I should have gone and voluntarily reported and said, 'Help me, I want to get this all behind me and straightened out and get my life turned around,' but that didn't happen. That's what is sad. So, in hindsight, the saddest part was that when it all come out, it really hurt my family."

The child pornography on my computer had been on there for close to ten years. That picture of the child was there for over a month, month and a half time slot. The stuff was on my computer and how I got

caught was half the time with file sharing. You didn't
even know it was downloaded until you looked at it. I
was downloading a video off of there; and that's when
the detective got onto that, and they got a copy of it
and that's where the warrant got issued—that's where
it all come out.

Richard became somewhat philosophical, speculating
what might have happened if he had known how to reach
out and ask for help:

Even before I got caught, what if I coulda went and got
help? And I don't mean get off scot-free; if I'd gone to
somebody and said, 'Hey, I'm kinda down the wrong
path. I want help.' To me, you'd encourage others to
ask for help, then happily go on with the rest of your
life. Where is the incentive to come and ask for help?
Are you never cured? I have a bit of a struggle with
that. Why isn't there help before you get charged? The
help is not there. It seems they can help you after you
are charged and got a record for life but you're not
gonna get the help until that happens. It counts for
something if somebody says, 'I want you to help me,'
rather than, 'Oh shit, I got caught.'

Richard served the majority of his sentence, about six
and one-half years, in a medium-security penitentiary.

I started in the work training program. Cabinet work
always interested me. I got on there; and then because
of health issues, they took me off the work program,
so I just read and wrote. I was three years in medium
security and because I didn't work, I was three years
in a cell. I never got bored. I did watch a little TV,
very little. I just read and wrote. I got fired up about

Christianity when I was in the medium security section. Then I was transferred to the minimum security complex in the institution and became a chapel clerk, and that really opened up things for me. I lived in one of the fifteen houses, ten guys to a house. I spent all day, every day there as the chapel clerk.

I had an office in a separate building in the minimum complex, with a coffee pot, chairs, books, and music that people wanted, so people would come and visit, and I could help people. I went there early in the morning and come back to my house late at night. I had total freedom there. And because I put in the hours and did as much as I did there, I came and went as I wanted. I came home to eat and sleep, that's it. At the office, I had more freedom; anyone could come and see me.

I had no visitors my total time at the institution— no family or friends. I got used to being on my own. Actually, one pastor from a town near the city did come to see me, and he got me hooked up with the church I go to now.

My leg was very buggered up. I also had prostate cancer and an enlarged prostate. I knew I had the cancer all the time I was in the institution. I never got involved with the inmate committee, or recreation.

I learned how much I got caught up in things such as work, owning a house, a vehicle, a skidoo. I never realized how that stuff ties you down, and you become a slave to your things, your stuff. And it costs you big money to protect it, maintain it, insure it, and you are spending most of your life guarding your little treasures which all crumble away. I learned I can be actually happier and totally content with the stress gone out of my life because I'm not tied down with things now. Do I get bitter or better—that's the only two choices I have. I'm still floored how I enjoy life more, now that I don't have a house, vehicle, and skidoo.

It all boils down to I realize I didn't need all the stuff I had. God is enough, more than enough. I think my life is now proof you can live a very satisfying useful life with nothing. That's what I think got drove home to me. I didn't realize how stressful all that stuff was until it was gone. I just can't believe how I've never been happier. I just don't want a vehicle again."

Most of the time during our interviews, Richard described the things he did in his life and the things that happened to him. He did not often express negative opinions about his experiences. He did, however, have an opinion about health care in the prison. He said, "There is no health care in prison. They keep you alive because there is too much paperwork if you die in prison." Along this line, he also had comments about programs. "I'll never understand why I never got into any programs. Most other people in the institution are made to take programs. I tried to get in on them, and I got refused." Richard also had made comments about his lawyer and the court system. "My lawyer? That was a total mistake. I never tried to deny anything. Lawyers and the justice system don't like that. There are too many dollars to be made when you fight every charge and fight every sentence. I pleaded guilty, so they have no interest in me. To me, it is a racket."

AS HE WAS APPROACHING RELEASE from the penitentiary, staff at the institution turned their attention to preparing Richard for release into the community. While in custody, he had not applied for an early conditional release on parole. He had been of good behaviour in the institution and had earned remission, also known as "good time." For Richard, this amounted to about three years so he was released on statutory release, a form of parole, under the supervision of a parole officer for the duration of the sentence—the three year period. In order to increase the chances of a successful reintegration into the community, he was transferred to a halfway house in the city. Richard notes:

> At the halfway house, I had no pension in place and no idea where I would stay, so they let me stay until my statutory release, which helped me 'cause it was November before I got the pensions in place. Otherwise, I would have been out on the street with no place to live.
>
> I had no programs there, which I was okay with. With what my faith in God did for me and by what I learned in the institution by helping these people with their programs, I see where I went horribly wrong. I know there is no cure for a pedophile and you're branded for life; that's okay with me. I know I can manage my risk, with my faith in God and I see how I hurt my family, so there's no way ever—I simply will not go down that road.

Here he was on day parole, free to go into the community during the day but had to return to the house in the evening. While at the house, the focus was on arranging suitable accommodation and exploring ways to support himself in the community. For younger residents in the halfway house, they would focus on getting a job lined up and finding a suitable place to live upon their eventual full release. For Richard, the focus was on getting his pensions identified and in place so he could support himself if he was unable to find employment or could not work due to health issues. As well, he looked for and found suitable accommodation with a friend in a condo. He said:

After I got out of the penitentiary, I would have liked to have gone back home but the drivers that worked for my wife said if she had anything to do with me, they would quit. She was put between a rock and a hard place. She would have had trouble finding other drivers, and therefore lose the contracts; and I doubt I would find another job. So, I said don't worry, we'll work it out down the road. She pretty near had a nervous breakdown, having to turn her back on me. What choice did she have?

She was blind-sided by the whole thing and that is so unfair. I can see people mad at me, but at her? She is being punished, making her an outcast. Since my arrest, the kids want nothing to do with me, so I have never seen them since then. I don't know why our kids are doing that to her. I can live with the hate that people are going to show toward me, but I feel real bad for what they have done to her.

My wife and I phone every two or three days to talk; things are good between us. I am fortunate enough that she is forgiving enough to see that the change in me is real and that she is willing to give me another chance. She is basing that on what I am now—not what I did. Most people won't do that, unfortunately. They brand you, put a label on you, and that's it for life.

Now, I'm fortunate. I'm drawing my old age pension so I don't need to go find work, and I'm living with a friend so I don't need to go looking for housing. If I was younger, it could be tough with a record to find work or a place to live. I can see if you are kicked out of work or housing due to your record, what choice is there but to go back to jail—at least there, you eat and have a roof over your head.

Richard is convinced his faith has played a crucial role in his life since his arrest.

My faith—I can't say enough what that's done for me. I had my faith for thirty years before my arrest but it was a whole different level completely. I called myself a Christian then and I believed in God, but I wasn't living it. I was going through little motions, going to church and other things a Christian is supposed to do, but there was no personal relationship with God. There was hollowness—an empty shell. In the church in the community, I could see fine-looking people sitting there in church but the rest of the time, their life showed no difference. There was a real disconnect between what they were claiming and what they were living—and that was me, too.

That's why I say that in some ways, the whole thing of my arrest and imprisonment is one of the best things to happen to me. I'm not saying I'm glad I did what I did, and I'll always regret what I have done to hurt my family, but it changed my life—for the good. There are a lot of people living hollow lives—they just haven't been caught yet. It's an empty, hollow life for them. I feel my life now is close to stress free. I feel like I have a purpose. I think I have a lot to offer to a lot of people but, if it were to come out about my record of what I did, I'd be gone so fast my head would spin. I know I need to prove myself; and I need to gain people's trust, to my wife on down. I understand that and I don't struggle with that but I hope I get a chance to prove myself, even with a label on my forehead.

My faith is not a bunch of rules; it is a living relationship with God, and it's real. It changes you from the inside out. To me, that's the Christian life; the other is religion, which is going through the motions, not living it for real. The people that just have religion are miserable. For me, this came about while I was imprisoned. When I went in there, like, I realized I had lost everything—at sixty years old. My family was gone; my business was gone; my house was gone—everything was gone. When you get to that place, when you hit absolute bottom and you got nowhere to look but up 'cause there is nothing left, you got two choices—you will turn bitter or you will turn and get better. When I lost everything, that's when I realized that God was still there, waiting for me, to wake up and turn to him. When you turn to Him, you realize He's all you need. And it's true, absolutely true.

As I grew up, I always had a job, my own house, always had a vehicle. Now, I have none of it, and I can't explain how free I feel. The pressure is off! God supplies my needs, and I don't have the pressure that stuff owns you. God is my insurance for it. Look at that store—it was a beautiful business, but it owned us and I would not go back to that if you offered it on a silver platter. So, that is what was so neat. I realized when you have a purpose in life and know what it is, God is meeting your needs. Life is good.

There is a church I go to now, and I am really impressed with them. Even when I explained all my charges, I was so impressed with the pastor there. He said he was humbled and honoured that I would choose to come to that church. He didn't try to belittle me; he said that is what the church is there for. You are broken and hurting; if you can't walk into a church and be welcomed, that church needs to look at what they are there for.

Now that Richard has been released from the halfway house, he is on statutory release and will be until his sentence is completed. This is a form of conditional release, subject to his good behaviour in the community and his following specific conditions:

- Not to own, use, or possess a computer,
- Not to have direct or indirect contact with the victim or their family,
- Avoid contact with children under eighteen years of age, and
- Not to possess weapons.

If he is not of good behaviour or violates any of the conditions, he faces the real possibility of his conditional release being suspended or revoked, and then being returned to the penitentiary to serve the remainder of his sentence in custody. In short, if he screws up anytime in the next three years, back to prison he could go.

RICHARD NOW SPENDS HIS DAYS in the community. He can travel freely around the city, using the transit buses and the light rail system. He was asked to visit a man who tried to commit suicide and who is now in a care facility due to brain damage. Richard visits with the man and they play games. He hopes this will be a regular activity. Richard also has high hopes he will be able to attend a weekly Bible Study class at the church. First, however, he will need the permission of his parole officer to do so. Just as when he lived at the halfway house, he needed permission to attend a Sunday church service from both the manager of the halfway house as well as the parole officer. Now, he has permission to attend that particular church only, no other churches, for the Sunday service only.

Richard explains:

All in all, I am enjoying life. I got no pressures. I can do what I want and go where I want, within certain limits, of course. I've got a yearly bus pass so I can travel anywhere I want in the city. Over all, one of the biggest plus on the whole experience is I learned to enjoy the day, enjoy the trip, rather than I gotta be here and do this, do that. When I go out, I am just enjoying my day, whatever—go have coffee with who-ever, do this, do that. I have some friends who I see from time to time, and now I know this guy who tried to commit suicide and has some brain damage. His sister, who lives a five-hour drive away, is trying to find someone who will just be with him—try and help him. I met with him once, and I go back to see him this evening—just see if I can help out. If I see someone with a need, or whatever, I'm free to help or encourage somebody, and I love it. The fellow I am living with is also a senior, retired. The biggest thing I am shocked at, even though I don't have to go to work; it seems you do two things and the day is done. I got no struggle staying busy.

I have a lot of interests. I think it goes back to when I was growing up with nothing. I've always been grateful to say this—I never get bored and I love it. I read lots—I have a lot of books. I come from the insti-tution with six big boxes—mostly Christian books, a few on photography. There's also two or three stores in the city where you can buy books, just super cheap and you can fill a big shopping bag full for five bucks— that's about thirty cents a book. So, every so often, I go there and get anything of interest. I like to read, I like to write, I like photography. I'm loving it because now I have no trouble living on my income and I've got all day, every day so I am not going to spend my time being bored. For the first time in my life, I can go out and just enjoy every day.

There are no specific conditions on his parole for counselling, therapy, or programs related to his offences. He is on his own to find ways to live a law-abiding life in the community. I asked Richard, "In terms of something therapeutic, you have your faith in God—is that enough?" His reply was:

Yes. If anybody knows how to treat you from the inside out, He does. When He does it, the change is real; and I know that, so I don't worry about it. I have learned, I guess, I see how, as humans, we are all fallen creatures. I'm not saying I'm perfect; I could never do anything again, but I sure know that with my faith in God, He truly has given me a second chance. I firmly believe that day is going to come that when I stand before Him and account for everything I haven't repented for and asked his forgiveness, I'm gonna answer for it. I do not want to stand before Him and explain how I went down the same road again. That's the biggest deterrent. I'm not going to say why I flushed that one down the toilet—the second time, how much worse? So, there's my biggest deterrent, right there. I think I've learned enough going through the time in jail. I can go back on the street. My wife sees it. I might fool the cops, the parole board, you. I might fool everybody but I won't fool Him. And He's the one I'm scared to face.

I had no programs in prison. I am okay with what my faith in God did for me and what I learned in the institution by helping other people with their programs. I see where I went horribly wrong, and I know there is no cure for a pedophile and you're branded for life. I know I can manage my risk, with my faith in God and I see how I hurt my family so there's no way ever—I simply will not go down that road.

I believe society's got me labelled for life but I can live with that, too. In some ways, I almost like it. Okay, wherever needed, I'll disclose my past; and you want to put up a big wall, well okay, you are a waste of my time, too. Obviously that person feels I'm a waste of skin. And my opinion is you are a waste of my time because you will not look at me who I am now. You have this label on me, and that's how you judge me— that's how you treat me. You want nothing to do with me, and I want to have nothing to do with you. Really, to me, now, I'm sorry you feel that way; you are also wasting my time.

I'm going to go slow with things, like the Bible Study group in the church I go to now. I know I can because I don't want to raise any red flags with the parole officer. I need to show people I can be trust-ed—I have to earn their trust.

Richard made some concluding remarks:

At the institution, others had the option of programs but not me. I do not understand why, my caseworker didn't understand why; for some reason, others had to go through all the programs but not me. I believe I got everything I needed by helping two guys with their program and just the faith I have in God. I will never understand why I didn't get the programs, even when I asked. 'You don't qualify,' they said. Like why? I didn't have to go to programs, I didn't have to go to work, I didn't have to go to school, all of it just shocked me. I was just put in a cell and left alone. I got what I think

I needed but I don't think I will ever understand why I was treated so different from everyone else. I was the exception. I'm not complaining. The whole thing turned into a positive thing except for how I hurt my family. I had no experience before with the prison system, criminal justice, I was as green as grass.

I don't understand why I got a ten-year sentence. But I'm not upset by it. I was eligible for parole in 2016 and I got out in 2019. I just didn't feel the time was right for me to apply for parole any earlier—I didn't want it yet. I did not find my years in prison stressful. I can honestly say I felt the Lord was telling me, 'Not yet.' In 2019, I felt it was time, and it went good since then. I made the right decision at the right time.

I'm a long way from being broken and hurt, like I was before.

Richard reflected on what lies ahead:

My wife sees the change in me is real. I realize I need to prove myself to her and to everybody that the change in me is real. Since my release, I've just talked with her on the phone; and talk, I guess, is cheap so I got no struggle with that. I'm just happy to find somebody who is willing to give me a chance to prove to them that the change is real. As you watch me over time and spend time with me, the real person comes out. And I don't struggle with that. I struggle with people who just stick a label on your forehead—they've got you wrote off. All I'm asking is watch my life, and you'll soon know that there's a real change and thank you for giving me the chance to prove that.

I guess I'd have to say that most people would say I need counselling. But my biggest deterrent is I stand before the Lord and explain all I've done. I'm confident I can handle my risk factors, if you want to say that's still there. I'm comfortable that I'll be okay on the street; everybody is safe. There's that and then there's my family. If I go back on the street and get caught doing things again, especially if they are starting to trust me now— *(trailing off)*

I talk with my wife on the phone but my kids, not as of yet. I have no idea if it will ever happen or not. My point is that I hurt all of them; even worse if I'm back again, can I even ask anybody to give me another chance? Yes, I made a tragic error in judgment, I'm paying for it and I'll pay for it the rest of my life. I have found out that once you come clean, you have nothing to hide, and life becomes enjoyable. If I'm hiding things, stress is there. If I am transparent and wide open who I am, I can sleep good at night.

NOW, I WOULD LIKE TO offer some final remarks regarding Richard's journey. Looking at the first question at the start of this chapter, do you see how this happened? For at least fifty years, Richard led a stable, productive and fairly common life in a small community. So far as we know, he had no involvement with the criminal justice system during this part of his life. Then, according to his account, he found himself facing more and more stress that was related to his lifestyle. I think most members of the community can relate to this feeling, to find it understandable.

He also found that viewing readily available adult pornography and masturbation offered temporary relief from the stress. Might some members of the community be able to relate to this, to find it understandable to some extent? Gradually, this extended to child pornography and, ultimately, to his taking inappropriate pictures of a child. I think most members of the community would have real difficulty understanding how this could happen, how it could extend this far.

Let's look at Richard, himself. Is he a monster? A low life? Maybe it would be easy to conclude yes if we look only at his criminal conduct. But what if we look at Richard as a whole person, warts and all? This assumes we all have some warts—is this a realistic assumption? For most of his life, he led a fairly normal, law-biding life, did he not?

What lies ahead for Richard? I have the sense that he is pretty confident about his future. He seems to be concentrating on living a simple life, one day at a time, enjoying whatever comes his way and, most importantly, living according to his faith in God and in Christian teachings.

Can you accept his view of his world? Can Richard live this way successfully in the community? Can the community be reasonably assured that Richard's risk of re-offending is manageable? Check back to the title of this story—is Richard bitter or better?

I now offer a final comment. You will recall that Richard wondered if things might be different if he had been able to get some help before being arrested. I posed the following question to Dr. J.Thomas Dalby, a forensic psychologist: "Is help available (counselling, therapy, treatment, etc.) for those using child pornography prior to coming to the attention of police?" Dr. Dalby's reply was:

> I can't think of a single case where someone using child pornography reached out through the 'normal' system of mental health. There are individuals working in forensic services who do this sort of work but since possession of child pornography is an offence in itself, a person who has not been 'caught' would not be accepted. The short answer is:

No help is available unless through some back channels (some churches?) who do not want to be involved with the law.

As a member of the community, are you satisfied with the reality identified by the forensic psychologist (No help is available...)? Should we, as a community, continue to rely solely on imprisonment, where some help is available in some prisons to some inmates, in dealing with child pornography? What about turning our attention away from punishment to focus more on prevention? Surely the professions of psychology and psychiatry could provide valuable direction on how to deal with users of child pornography, especially before things get to the point where law enforcement agencies become involved. The advances in the fields of mental health, addictions and substance abuse tell us that positive impacts are possible, despite the challenges that are present.

Think back to the previous chapter about Juanito. He was given a choice, basically an ultimatum: Go to drug court or go to prison for a long time. His incentive: Get his life back on track and face one day in jail. Juanito made the choice to get back to being normal, with lots of help from community agencies. It took over a year, but he overcame the barriers that stood in his way. He personally faces a bright future, and the community now does not have to worry about its safety because of the past chaos in his life.

Might this approach be worth considering for those who use child pornography? What if we could use or develop community-based supports for this group of people who commit this crime? Could the faith sector of a community play an important role here? Rather than reacting to only the offence, how can we as a community react to the offender and help in a return to normalcy?

CHAPTER 13

JOSEPH: I KNOW WHO KILLED MY BROTHER

I FIRST MET Joseph when he was referred to me by one of my friends who knew I was writing a book about people who committed crime. He said Joseph currently worked for him on a major construction project in the city. My friend had worked for many years in construction as a labourer and as a general foreman, both in the city and at fly-in sites where he lived in camps. Whenever he and I visited over a beer, my friend talked about, among other things, some of the characters he worked with in his career. He said he had come to know Joseph quite well and was impressed with him as a worker. Joseph eventually told my friend that he was on parole; and, when he learned about the book I was writing, he was interested in talking to me about his life.

I texted Joseph and we made arrangements to meet at a coffee shop near where he lived in the city. I wanted to hear directly from him that he was in fact on parole, that he really did want to have his story told and that he would be comfortable having me doing so. As well, I wanted Joseph to hear from me that his story would be told without disclosing his identity.

We first met in the evening after he returned from work. Joseph struck me as being energetic, intense, somewhat impulsive, and cooperative. He seemed well-spoken, and he spoke quickly, spicing up his sentences with lots of "fucks" and with interjections like, "You know," "Man," and "Bro," (most of which have been edited from his story).

His conversations jumped around a lot, as if he had trouble staying on one topic for very long.

Joseph was of slim build, five feet eight inches tall, had short dark hair and a neck full of tattoos that disappeared into his t-shirt to emerge on his forearms. His jeans were tight fitting and he wore a black ball cap and running shoes.

He wanted to get started on our interview right then and there in the coffee shop. I directed that we would meet later in a quiet place where our conversation would not be overheard. In my view, a coffee shop was no place to talk about one's personal history or crimes. Other patrons do not need to hear bits and pieces of that type of conversation. Joseph agreed and we decided on a day and time to meet in the local library not far from his apartment. Our follow up interviews were held again in the library and at his apartment.

JOSEPH WAS KEEN, even excited, to tell his story. He told me that he'd pleaded guilty to being involved in a home invasion. He and some accomplices, armed with a shotgun and some knives, entered a house in the middle of the night wearing dark clothes and balaclavas in a community near the city. They were looking for money, drugs, and jewelry. A fight broke out when the home owner confronted the intruders and the owner was stabbed and taken to hospital but eventually recovered from his injuries. Joseph fled the scene when the fight first broke out but he was arrested when he turned himself in to police two months after the incident, following an extensive police investigation. After appearing in court, bail was granted and he was released with numerous conditions designed to achieve two objectives—to protect the public and to ensure his appearance in court as required. He did not have a criminal record at the time of the offense.

Home invasion is a serious charge. It involves breaking into a residence while wearing a disguise. Breaking into
a residence and then committing another serious offence
carries a possible sentence of life imprisonment. Wearing
a disguise carries a possible sentence of ten years imprisonment. Such serious charges bring up a host of questions:
Who would do such a thing? Why would someone do this?
In Joseph's case, what actually took place? How bad were
the injuries? Were there more people involved?

We begin to look for answers to these questions by
looking at Joseph's early years. Here is how he described his
early years:

> I was born in a northern city. My dad is from the east
> coast. My mom is from a northern town. She grew
> up on a reserve then moved off the reserve to go to
> the northern city—that's where my mom met my dad
> in the early eighties. They were together for a while
> and then I was born. My mom told my dad that my
> step-brother was his son, but later on it turned out he
> wasn't. They divorced when I was two years old. They
> got a blood test for me and him; my brother wasn't his
> and I was. My dad wasn't letting me go with my mom
> when they separated. I've been with my dad since I
> was two years old. My dad raised me by himself (did
> the best he could) up until I was fourteen.
>
> My dad didn't want my mom to be part of my life
> either because of the way she was like. She would say
> something then never show up. I never got anything
> for my birthday or anything like that. Biggest memory
> I have was being like five years old and I shit on my
> bike, pretty bad, and was crying for my mom. My dad
> looked at me, 'Stop crying,' he said, 'she's not coming
> back,' and told me to quit crying. So I stopped crying;
> I would only cry in the really stressful times in my life,

like a death or something. Even then, I was taught not to cry at an early age. It's hard when you keep all that shit inside you your whole life. You have a meltdown. When I was ten, he met the woman he is with now; and he moved her out west, out here. When I was fourteen, they packed up and moved back east. Dad asked me if I wanted to move with them and I said, 'No.' I told him I wasn't going to move out there—I didn't know anybody back east and I didn't like her at the time.

I was always looking for that approval; and I never had it, you know. I always thought I was useless. But my dad never told me I was useless; my step-mom used to always drive that into my head. I'm never going to be anything; just totally all useless. Just because I was an asshole. A complete liar, you know.

Joseph decided to remain in the northern city as a teenager, rather than go down east with his dad and step-mom. His dad arranged for him to stay with a guardian, and Joseph pretty well had the run of the place. He came and went as he pleased with few rules or expectations from adults. It was during this time that Joseph became involved with buying and selling drugs.

So I stayed in the northern city when they left. My dad would come up here to work and visit me once in awhile. He didn't leave me in a bad place, just left me with a guardian who let me do whatever the hell I wanted to do, as long as she got her six hundred bucks a month for housing me. It was all good. My dad would give me one hundred dollars a week for school. I was a bad kid and would take that hundred dollars, buy dope, and then sell it at school to make more money and then get a part time job. I said I was working, you know, but I wasn't. Oh, I'd work for two weeks then quit. Dad would never see me and he didn't ask questions. He knew what I was up to, but he turned a blind eye. That went on until I graduated. I didn't graduate with the best marks, but I did graduate. I struggled with most classes but that's because I didn't do the work. I didn't want to help myself, I guess.

The guardian became a mother figure for Joseph for the three years he lived with her. He became close to her son, too, who Joseph came to see as a brother over time.

The guardian was a good family friend. She used to be my baby sitter when I was a little kid; she lived two houses down the road from us. She was nice. She passed away when I was twenty-two, she died of cancer. She was pretty much the only mother figure I had in my life. She used to decorate for weddings, taught me a lot of stuff like that. Yeah, I would just come and go on the weekends, no need to call in or anything, show back up on Sunday evening and go to school. She didn't care. She'd cover my ass; lied to my dad. She was pretty solid like that, but I could have taken a few kicks in the ass, I guess.

When Joseph became an adult at age eighteen, it seemed like the patterns in his younger years had become fairly well entrenched and he carried on doing pretty much the same things.

When I turned eighteen, my mom started coming around in my life. It kinda made things worse, I think. At first, I would let her in my life a bit but it would go shitty. She made false promises so I'd close the door on her and let her back in here and there. She was always around, in close vicinity, but she had never made herself a part of my life.

After that, at eighteen when I graduated from high school, my dad gave me a thousand bucks; told me to start my life. So I took that thousand dollars, bought a bunch of dope, started selling dope even more. I was doing alright for a while then the ship went south, went downhill. He got me in the union which was good. I've been in the union ever since, but I'd just use it as a fall back—do a shutdown here and there, make twenty or thirty grand. I wouldn't work the rest of the year—just sell dope. I did that for a lot of years.

Joseph's drug use started when he was fifteen years old in grade nine at school. That quickly turned into drug abuse when he started selling drugs, in addition to using. His abusive use of drugs lasted for eight or nine years until Joseph was in his mid-twenties.

I was handed a dope phone at fifteen years old. They gave me a phone that profited sixteen hundred dollars on a Thursday night—pay day night in the northern city. 'Here's the phone; come on back when you need some more'. I was hooked. I was a fifteen year old kid going to high school in grade nine. I had sixteen hundred dollars in my pocket on Friday morning, going to school. Gold chains, the nicest clothes. I didn't know what to do, you know; I was lost, got sucked in, you know. And later on in life, I'm sitting there, (Some of this shit my dad still doesn't know) but I'm listening to him and there's this program about biker gangs on TV. They grab the kids when they're young and they corrupt them young. It's the guys under them that corrupt the young guys and suck them in. That way, the gang keeps their hands clean.

Then one day my dad said, 'Come on I'm gonna take you pipelining'. I was already too far gone. I was always on the dope, making three grand a week, drinking it, snorting it, and gambling. That's where my paycheck went for a good three years. I could have bought a house, had my truck paid off. I had to learn that stuff. Some people never learn it. I was lucky to wake up when I did.

I was always working and dealing—half and half. I was flying under the radar—working part time as a teenager and being a bad kid at the same time by selling dope. I never had a steady job, right, until I hit the pipeline and then it was always good.

My guardian's son—I've known him since he was in diapers—was struggling. I loved him as a brother—I considered him a brother. He was lost. His mom had passed, right. I was on the dope and I was sending him money so he could just get dope and then sell it. You know, I'd get my cut. I said fuck it—I got tired of it. Then I got sucked into the home invasion.

Up to this point, Joseph had lived a contradictory life. For years, he bought, sold and used drugs extensively but was never caught. He had completed high school and he worked about half the time, thus maintaining a front of respectability, of being ordinary. He saw his mom and his dad from time to time but stayed aloof from them. As he grew older, he was getting tired of the lifestyle. It seems he started to give some consideration to making a lifestyle adjustment, although just what that would look like was still unclear.

It was his relationship with his "brother," to whom he felt a loyalty and a protectiveness that he believes got him directly involved in the home invasion.

One day, my brother picked me up at camp at five in the morning. I'll never forget that because he got the truck stuck in the mud on the camp road. Had to get it towed out. Big ruts, in the spring. I quit that job, hopped in the truck in the middle of the night and said, 'Let's go'. I had a big bag of dope waiting for me. We had rented this house in a town not far from the city for like two months. We upgraded to a bigger house and we had some more guys with us and then everything was going smooth. I went away with my mom to my grandparents' sixtieth anniversary. While I was gone, someone home-invaded (broke into) my house and stole everything—all the clothes, tied my brother up, beat him up bad—didn't kill him, didn't stab him; I'm surprised. So, we were left broke. A couple of days later, my brother come up and said he knew some guys who had some shit (valuables) and I told him, 'No man—we'll get it back. We're not going to go and do that.' A week went by. I was drunk. It was like midnight. Him and another guy came to my room. For two hours straight, they come up and down, up and down, hounding me to go. And then I did. I gave in 'cause he was dead-set determined to go and I couldn't let him go. I loved that kid to death. I wasn't letting him go alone. So I went. Before, I had told his mom I would protect him at all cost—I promised her before she died. So I went.

That night, Joseph and the others left the community they were living in, and drove to a nearby community.

All I did was just walk into that house, that's all. I didn't have a weapon, I didn't take anything. I seen somebody got stabbed, and I just got out right away. There was an altercation. I vaguely remember going in 'cause I was so messed up. I remember seeing that guy get stabbed and then it was like I sobered up real quick and saw what I was doing and then just ran out. What have I got myself into? I couldn't sleep for awhile after, man. I was just fucked right up.

Joseph ran from the scene of the home invasion and several of the others were quickly arrested by police. An extensive investigation by police was launched and police eventually determined that Joseph was involved. The pressure on him was building. He continued using, and he felt like his life was a mess. Then came the overdose.

An overdose occurs when there is so much drug or mixture of drugs in the body that the body is functionally poisoned and, to protect itself, its systems shut down. Basic physiological functions like breathing and pulse are compromised to the point that death is a real possibility. Overdose is a critical physiological condition.

I was getting more and more screwed up. Then I went to a rodeo with a bunch of dope—I did an ounce of cocaine for myself in a day and a half, which was unheard of. I had an eight-ball left so I swallowed it, then it blew up in my stomach and that's how I ended up in hospital. That was the overdose—that's what pushed it over to the edge. That one bag blew up in my stomach. It ruptured my guts—I was puking blood. My nose was a faucet, bleeding like it blew up. I was hallucinating, couldn't stop throwing up blood—it was just like someone cutting a vein, just coming out. I looked at my hand; I was totally covered in blood, right down my arm. Once the ambulance got there, they tried to put an IV in me. They moved the rig for ten minutes, trying to poke and get the IV in me. They got the IV in me. The cops showed up first, and

I told the cop, 'Yo, my phone is not working'. I was like, 'can you call my dad? Call him and tell him I am sorry.' The cop wouldn't call him—wouldn't call my damn house. You know what I'm saying? I still don't get it. You know, what the hell? Call! It was practically my last dying wish for someone to call my house and nobody did. You know what I mean? Only the nurses called when I got to the hospital in the city. They called home when I was in hospital. They put me in that room to die.

For my overdose, when that happened, I had a cocaine problem—big time. It started at the age of fifteen and it didn't end until I was twenty-four years old. At the time, I thought it was a good run.

I woke up when I seen my dad cry after I got out of the hospital from the overdose. He drove across the country in four days to come and see me. He said, 'I don't ever want to see you overdosed again.' He was crying, said he was supposed to die before I die. It's going to be a hard day.

My mom showed up at the hospital the day after I overdosed. My dad got a hold of her somehow, so she left work and drove all the way to the city and got there when I was in the emergency room. They put me in a room to die. They told me I was going to die. They told my mom they don't know why I am still alive and that I'm gonna die. I'm sitting there and I'm all messed up. My eyes are rolling in the back of my head. I just remember they put me in the room to die, man. My system was dying, starting to fail and she come in there with my step brother and one of my uncles. They just rubbed me with holy oil and prayed for a few hours. Then the doctor come running in and said, 'Okay, we're going to take him into surgery'. They took me in and they told me I might not wake up. I said there was a good chance, whatever. I'm already this far gone—you might as well try.

I was told I was a walking miracle. God has big plans for me. That's what I was told. The doctor at my overdose couldn't believe it. Every blood vessel in my face was collapsed, my whole face was purple-veined, everywhere. My eyes were just black. I weighed like about one hundred and twenty pounds. I don't ever want to see anyone's face like that again. I never want to look at myself like that in a mirror. I looked at myself the next day in a mirror and said I should be dead.

At this point, Joseph did not care if he lived or died.

Up to now, Joseph had not been too interested in or involved with his Indigenous heritage. He was aware of his background but it had not been an important part of his life. That now was about to change.

I pulled through. My mom, my step brother and my uncle told me they seen life come back into me. Then, after that, she took me to see a medicine man. A couple of days later, she took me to a ceremony. We offered him tobacco. I got doctored. I asked to be forgiven for everything I'd done in the past. I didn't want those demons with me anymore. I didn't eat anything white or anything. I took some medicine, and it wasn't white; and what I threw up were big chunks of white—I don't know what the hell it was.

The medicine man was quick to scoop it up and go bury it in the woods. It still boggles me to this day. I asked for the demons to come out, and I seen some shit come out—it is pretty crazy. I didn't believe in that stuff up until that day. My dad told me it was sorcery, but, at the end of the day, that is my heritage. That got me a little culturally attached. Later, I would go see that medicine man once in a while when I was on day parole.

When I went to jail, I stayed away from cultural stuff until I got to minimum security, a healing centre in the city, and then I started going to cultural programs, sweats and other ceremonies."

I haven't gone to sweats or ceremonies in a long time—I'm due. I've been working so much. I don't really do much for myself either. Just come home from work after up to twelve hours on the job, spend time with my fiancé and that's it.

When a person is arrested by police, the officers make an immediate decision either to release the person on a summons or appearance notice or to keep the person in custody to ensure his/her appearance in court. Keeping the person in custody until their court appearance is a common police decision when the charge is a serious one, such as a home invasion. After Joseph turned himself in to police and was then immediately arrested, he appeared in court where his case was adjourned a number of times. At one of these appearances, Joseph's lawyer submitted an application to the judge to have him released on bail, also known as judicial interim release, rather than continue to keep him in custody. The judge, after hearing from Joseph's lawyer and the prosecutor, eventually approved the application and released Joseph on bail. A number of conditions were imposed on Joseph such as a curfew (be home by 10 p.m.), abstain completely from the consumption of non-prescription drugs and alcohol, report any changes in address or employment to police, not to be in possession of sharp items with sharp edges, no contact with co-accused, and attend court when required to do so. These conditions are in place to protect the public and to ensure the accused person's appearance in court.

Like I said, I pulled through that and then went back on the pipeline and this time I was with my dad the whole time. I went working for a couple of months then got a phone call from the cops about the home invasion and turned myself in. So I went down there. Everything was on the table. The other guys had talked. The cop left the room. He left his binder on the table on purpose. I reached over, turned his binder over and I opened the pages. There were pictures of me—what I was wearing, everything, a bunch of statements.

Then I made bail. My dad was scrambling to get bail money. He hit every ATM he could find to get the bail money. He bailed me out. I was on bail for two years before I got sentenced.

While on bail, his case slowly wound its way through the courts for a period of two years. Joseph complied with all the bail conditions, and he was steadily employed for most of the time that he was on bail.

Many people experience an event so profound that its memory stays sharply in their mind forever. For Joseph, one such event was the death of his little brother.

In that time on bail, my little step-brother died. He got shot. You know, I'd told him to change his life, 'Change your life man, it's not worth it.' A year or so after I'd been on bail, I got a phone call—he's dead. Someone shot him in the head; someone kicked in his door and shot him."

When I think about it now, this is another stepping stone in my life. If I wouldn't have changed, if no one had been willing to help, and I didn't help myself, I would have been sitting right next to him and who knows what would have happened. I might have been the one who got shot, or I would have seen him get shot. I would have grabbed the gun, and I would have shot back. I probably would have killed them all. It was up north. And to this day, I know who did it. I know where they are right now. I've seen them. But I don't blame them—they have to live with that. You know, I don't have that weight on my shoulders. They do. Every time I see that person, I want to fuck him up, I just hold back because I know it's not worth it. At the end of the day, he made that choice. Him and his partner made that choice. My brother made that choice—he did not want to change. I was told he was trying at the end but he didn't try fast enough, man. He should have listened.

He was one of the guys who badgered me into the home invasion. He was shot a year and a half after I was on bail—because of something else. I don't know the full details, I don't know why, I choose not to know why. It is better that way. A friend called to tell me he was gone and because I had to be home every night and things like that while on bail, I didn't even bother to go. It would have been too hard. Like, I went and visited his grave for the first time about three months ago in the summer. I drove there and couldn't even get out of the car. I broke down. A big factor in my life, after that. It's not worth going back to that lifestyle 'cause you end up like that, or in jail, and the next time, who knows, I might be doing a life sentence.

Some people look at me like I'm weak 'cause I'm not retaliating but this is just what it is. It's not worth it. I've been in jail and I don't want to go again, man. It's not worth it. Just sit in a cell and look at bricks, someone telling you when you can go eat, door opening and closing, you know what I mean?

Joseph was sentenced in 2016 to four years imprisonment for the home invasion charges. He began the sentence in a medium security penitentiary where he spent a year working in the institution's employment program.

In 2017, he was transferred from the penitentiary to a minimum security healing centre in the city. Here, he was classified as an inmate for five months, then was released on day parole for six months. On day parole, Joseph worked in a cafeteria and as a construction labourer during the day, returning to the healing centre in the evening.

> When I got sentenced, I went to a medium security penitentiary for about a year. After that, I transferred to the healing centre in the city. That place was good. They helped big time, you know? Took us out, which was nice. Have a lot of faith in people, which is good. My Elder was good. It was good in there. I went and grabbed a spirit name, an animal; went fasting for three days in the woods. Built a hut, man, out of willows and pine branches. Nice round hut. I made this door that I could prop open with two sticks on the side. I had my one door; you're not supposed to cover it so I left it open. So I could have a fire in my hut which was dangerous but I still had a fire going 'cause it was cold. All I had was sleep—no water, just a sleeping bag, a foamy, and my fire. And I had to stay in the circle—my boundaries that I tied my cloth in that area. Some other people would come and bring me firewood when I needed wood, right. People come and checked on me. Three days. On the third day, I was starting to hallucinate, I can tell you that much. My lips were just pasted. I remember being so dehydrated that I couldn't pee. Just this little bit would come out— yellow and green. Holy shit, my kidneys are going to fail. It was good, a good time, man. After, I drank lots

of water, and we had a sweat. I'd go to sweats every week when I was in there. When I got on day parole, it was once a month for sweats. I did five months there at the healing centre and then six months day parole there, too, and then full parole to the street.

It has now been about four years that Joseph has been clean and sober. Two years of that time were while he was on bail and under the watchful eye of police and court officials. During the past two years, he has been under the watchful eye of prison and parole officials. During the entire time he has been involved with the criminal justice system, he has not been found to have committed other crimes. It seems he has been able to refrain from using drugs and alcohol—a remarkable achievement considering his previous extensive use of substances for eight or nine years.

Also, during this time, he has faced a traumatic family event—the shooting death of his little brother. In my view, he made a wise and thoughtful decision not to 'get back' at his little brother's killer. This, too, can be seen as a remarkable achievement, given his previous criminal involvement.

Since I've been doctored, you know, I've had the urge to do drugs about twice. There is a lot of things that I wouldn't have given a care about and now even a year after I went back to my dad's, some of my old friends there on Christmas Eve, they were all drinking and I wasn't allowed to drink. They were all drinking and then one dude shows up with a big bag of dope, throws it on the table, started chopping out lines for everybody. I got up and left. 'Look boys, I gotta go.' Still my friends, you know, but I know when to distance myself. I know when to leave. That's a tough choice for a lot of people. I was a heavy user. I would use anything—I didn't care. You put a drug in front of me—I didn't care, okay, let's do it.

In the past, I didn't care if I lived or died at one point. I didn't care about anybody around me, I didn't care about my family. I thought they all abandoned me. Well, kinda was abandoned. But, you know, the second option when I was fourteen, that was my option. I let them abandon me. I thought I would be better off. Who knows? Maybe it would be worse. Maybe I wouldn't even be here if I had been over there in the east—a lot worse. I've got to think of this from every perspective I can. That's how I was taught. That's one thing my dad taught me. That is try to think of every worse-case scenario. The one time in my life I didn't listen to him, and that's how I ended up in jail. I always crossed my toes—everything. I made sure I thought of everything—what could happen if I did this or that. I was always good at getting out of anything. That time, I put my life in someone else's hands, and I'll never do that again.

Joseph is living in an apartment with his girlfriend. They met at a church service while both serving time in different prisons. This relationship has lasted for about two years.

I have a girlfriend now—a fiancé. She's good. She has been on parole. She went to jail. I met her at church on a pass. The healing centre really didn't like that, though. However, it is what it is. I'm one of the only few that went to visit another inmate. I was on day parole and I was allowed to go and visit her. But only 'cause I was doing so good. I'm happy I met her. Sometimes, she struggles. She's been done parole for a while now. She has her moments. That's fine. She doesn't use. Like, the one thing I told her—if you use, you gotta go. I do love you, I will try and help you but I gotta keep my distance. She understands that. She doesn't want to use again. She's been to hell and back, too. She lost her father while she was in jail. This still affects her big time. She's finally reconnecting with her mom, again, you know, and her sisters. We're not perfect but we're making the best of it. They say two wrongs don't make a right, but two wrongs are making it right now. For once in my life, we both did wrongs and look at us now—on top. Not a lot of people can do that shit.

I prayed for a long time to meet somebody who knew the same stuff as me and has the same outlook on life. Someone I can relate to. She is finished parole. She's not working now and that's alright. She's come from selling drugs, living that lifestyle. It's hard for a person to re-adjust. I make enough money so I told her to stay at home—it's cool, I'll take care of you.

Joseph has lived an interesting life, full of turmoil, trauma, and substance abuse, along with some ordinary achievements like regular work and finishing high school. In the past three to four years, he seems to have regained control over his life and a pro-social focus. He now can be somewhat analytical as he reflects on his life journey.

I met some pretty interesting characters on my travels, man. I was a pipeliner for three years straight, every little small town, partied it up with all sorts of people, some people you wouldn't even think of, can't even imagine. But that's the kind of shit you bring towards yourself when you are in that lifestyle.

I was no saint, man, I needed to go—I'm not going to lie—I needed to go to jail. And I accepted that. I made a mistake and I owned it. I was told always to own everything, you know what I mean?

My dad wanted me to be tough, grow up tough, be able to do shit on my own, not have to ask anybody, so I, like, never asked him for anything. That's why I went and sold drugs 'cause I'm not just going to ask him for money. I'm just going to have to pay it back anyways. He doesn't have to do that. Like I said, that's what makes me who I am. I admire him for it now, but I went through some hard times not wanting to call home just to get lectured. The help was there, but I had to go through shit to get the help, you know what I mean? I had to get yelled at, or something, and then I'd get help; but to me it wasn't worth it. Fuck it; that's what I would say!

Joseph has developed a certain philosophical view about his life. He is not angry at anyone. He does have some frustrations with the justice system, based on how some officials dealt with him, but Joseph has come up with a way to put his life into perspective.

To do it all again, honestly I would not change a thing. I wouldn't be here today, the strong person that I am. Maybe I should have taken some alternative routes, made better choices but I'm not the only contributing factor. I'm not playing the blame game either. It is what it is. I can only do so much. I tend to laugh and joke about this, but you know, my brain—I'm twenty-eight years old but my brain is older.

For that period of time that I used drugs and stayed up all those times, all the stuff that I have seen and learned. Mentality wise, it is older but it might be a little underdeveloped because I used drugs since an early age but once you stop, it comes back. That's pretty much a proven fact, actually. You just have to focus. I know a lot more now, too. I'm still naive, I know that and I can admit that.

As for my time in the northern city, it was just

partying. I was living the high life but not really, you know, it was just a mirage.

After I almost died from the overdose, I tell my dad I love him almost whenever I talk to him. He's the same thing. It takes a real wake-up for everybody.

I'm just a labourer out here now, struggling, but I'm doing okay. I was struggling, but that's only because of my poor choices. I'm a foreman now, but that's only 'cause I'm sober. The trust—it took me a long time to rebuild my name. I'm happy now, you know, better job all the time, no worries. I'm not scared about not showing up for work. I'm not going to be all screwed up— can't pass a drug test.

Now I work, I crash. I watch TV. Hang out with her on weekends. Try to enjoy some weekends when I can. I just bought a motorbike, actually a 1974 Suzuki. It wasn't road legal, and I made it road legal. It cost me eight hundred dollars, just for the bike. I already put in like six hundred dollars to make it road legal, and I got to put another five hundred dollars in for finishing touches so I can actually go on the road with it. At the end of the day, I'm nineteen hundred dollars into it. It's a collector's item, road legal, and I can get three grand for it any day. It's a vintage bike. But I'm going to keep it. That's one thing my dad always taught me—take care of my stuff. Always take pride in your stuff. Be proud. My grandpa was a proud man. I'm happy I got to see him when I was on bail, and that was my biggest fear, like, he made it to ninety-seven years old. My biggest fear was that I would be in jail and couldn't be there for my dad at his funeral. I wasn't there for my grandma's funeral 'cause I was too messed up. My dad offered to take me but I said no. I kick myself in the ass still today. But I was there for the old man. That one, that was a hard day, too. I seen a lot of stuff, man. I've had a lot of friends die over stupid stuff, like overdoses, drowning, drinking and driving on quads, stuff like that.

In the future, I'd like to get a house—that's the next big-ticket item. I don't care where—I'm gonna get a house. Just a bit out of the city, so I am away from everything. Hop on my dirt bike and go for a ride with no one bothering me. Maybe I could go snowboarding again. I loved that.

My life has been a roller coaster. Now, I think about things, second guess, and anticipate what is going to happen. I try to think things through, trying to look at the down-side of things. Some guys do the first thing that comes to their mind; they don't give it a second thought. That's how you fail. It is hard to do. I don't risk it, man. I know better. It's not worth it. I've come this far and I'm not going back.

In 2018, Joseph was released from the healing centre on full parole to serve the balance of his sentence in the community under the supervision of a parole officer. There are a number of conditions relating to his release on parole: Report to the parole officer, a lifetime ban on possession of weapons, and no contact with known drug users. The four-year sentence will be completed when Joseph completes parole in 2020. If he "screws up" and does not successfully serve his sentence in the community, he will be returned to a prison, likely the medium custody penitentiary where he started his sentence, to finish the remaining portion of the four year sentence in custody.

Joseph's parole officer shared his thoughts with me:

Joseph is doing well on parole. My job is to make sure he is following the conditions of his release from prison and that he is behaving himself. I also try to help him with situations that come up that might steer him off track. He has some trouble with blurring boundaries on some issues like who is a good friend versus who might be manipulating him, so I work with him on things like that. When he was first released on parole, he was required to report to me at least once a week; now his reporting requirements have been reduced down to once a month. That is a remarkable change, that doesn't happen very often.

Now, he has a prescription for medical cannabis from his doctor—he has trouble sleeping at night, worrying about his work now as a foreman. I'll have to work with him on that so he doesn't blur those lines.

I think the parole officer has assessed Joseph very accurately. Joseph is doing all the right things: He is working steadily and has the support of his employer, he seems to have a stable and positive relationship with his girlfriend and they have lived in the same apartment for over a year, he doesn't use street drugs or alcohol, and he is developing some constructive activities in his spare time.

Something the parole officer is concerned about is what he calls Joseph's tendency to blur boundaries. This concern is well-founded, in my view. If Joseph is not careful, he could inadvertently drift across the boundaries that are in place to help him lead a law-abiding life. Joseph talks about how he has learned to think things through in his mind so this attitude will be helpful in keeping him from drifting too far off course. This will help him successfully finish his sentence in the community. Hopefully, this will help him in the future to lead a law-abiding life style where the community is no longer at risk from his behaviour.

So far, so good.

CHAPTER 14

RYAN: THE WORLD BY THE BALLS

*"If I was doing back then what I was supposed to be doing,
I'd now have the world by the balls."*

I MET RYAN through a referral from his father, a friend of mine who works in corrections. His dad and I have known each other for many years and, at a social event, I told him about the book I was writing and that I could use another story. My friend commented enthusiastically, "Oh, you should interview my son! He has quite the story—three times in the pen but he has settled down now, doing pretty well. Just about has his ticket."

It took three months to connect with Ryan but we finally agreed to meet via FaceTime. He is thirty-five years old, a big man at 230 pounds, with a husky muscular build, bald, and tattoos on his neck and upper body. He says that when he was younger and using crystal meth, he was skinny, about half the weight he is now. At our first interview, his year-old son crawled all over Ryan as he sat in front of his cell phone, joyfully making typical one-year-old noises and squeals, pulling and poking, rarely sitting still for more than a few seconds. Ryan took it all in stride, very patiently.

He spoke about his motivation to share his story:

Whatever I can do to help people figure out their way, a better way, I'm gung-ho for that. Before, when I was into the street drug scene, I always thought that was the lifestyle I would die in, what was I supposed to do?

193

His acceptance of a criminal lifestyle is not uncommon. Sadly, a surprising number of people like Ryan who commit crime see themselves in a situation that they came to accept, despite all the pain and negativity. They reach a point where they don't see a realistic alternative or achievable option. They don't have much hope of anything different.

When I reviewed the requirement of confidentiality for the people in the book, he responded:

> I'm pretty open with my story. You don't really have to go in leaps and bounds with the confidentiality. I own what I did. My story will help explain why I'm a 35-year-old apprentice when most people my age are foremen. The other thing is, like, it will help people understand my tattoos and stuff. I own everything, so you don't have to worry about confidentiality—for me, it is not that big of a deal.

Ryan and the others in this part of the book represent, in my view, a substantial proportion of offenders who become locked into a criminal frame of mind and associated behaviours and then, after a while, they decide to get away from that and go on to be crime free. In Ryan's story, I have evoked confidentiality, despite his view that it is not that big of a deal.

As our initial interview progressed, he seemed to have difficulty from time to time answering some of my questions. He took long pauses; and it looked like he was thinking, recollecting, even struggling, trying to come up with answers. It was like he experienced scrambled speech and thought patterns. Then Ryan explained:

> For a lot of the time, it's kinda all a blur. There were times when I remember being up for fifteen days without sleep. I can tell you little bits and pieces of

what has happened—little snippets. I had done so much damage to my brain to that point.

As in the other stories, questions emerge right away. In Ryan's case: How did he go from a pretty-good childhood to a teen with a serious drug problem and living on the streets? He admits to being a monster; how did he get this way? What factors contributed to him settling down and moving away from a criminal lifestyle?

Let's start exploring some of these questions by examining his early years, starting with his account of these times:

> I was born in the city and before I was a year old, my parents moved down east. My dad was from the city and my mom grew up out east. We moved near a small city there and I spent the first ten years of my life there. We had a good time there—lots of close family and friends. My parents owned a couple of gas stations and convenience stores. My mom did all the discipline. My dad would agree with the discipline but then when she wasn't around, he would kinda spoil us. Her parents were immigrants, working in agriculture and they had a very harsh upbringing. So mom would spank us a lot, probably most of it deserved but a lot was over the top, too much. Me and my sister got it pretty good, not so much my brother. Altogether, though, I thought it was a pretty good upbringing. I have a younger sister and younger brother. We weren't neglected or anything. I was getting good marks in school until we moved back to the city.

Nothing in Ryan's early life hinted at the dysfunction that would soon dominate. His schooling would fall apart. He started using drugs at age fifteen and within a year he would be homeless, living on the streets in the city.

When I was about ten years old, we moved back here and we lived in a small community near the city. I went to school out there. I was really excited to move back but before long I just didn't really fit in with most of the kids. I started to get into fights. I don't know if I was expecting something different or what. But everything changed then. I went to a couple of schools near where we lived and then started high school in the city. I went to a couple of high schools actually, then eventually dropped out. That's when I kinda gave up on school, at seventeen. I found a crowd, started to smoke lots of pot and stuff, then progressed to finding the rave scene in the city and meeting kids there and started doing acid and ecstasy and eventually I started doing meth, all the time. That was pretty much where it started—I tried meth when I was fifteen years old and then within a year I was out of the house and living on the streets in the city. I didn't get kicked out of the house, I just left on my own. I would sometimes stay at a youth shelter and places like that. Occasionally, I would come back home just to sleep for a week at my parent's house. In the city, I was pretty much doing meth all the time. To get money when I first started, me and my friends used to rob people. We did this for about a year.

At seventeen, I just started selling meth—that's how it kinda started. After selling meth for a year or two, I had a buddy I worked for and he wanted to get into the business of selling crack. Within a couple of months, I realized there was way more money to be earned in selling crack than meth. It was a little bit easier, too. I didn't do crack, so I didn't have to worry about using my own stuff—I didn't smoke crack. With crack, people were only high for about ten minutes and then they needed more so it was kind of a perfect money-maker. The other thing I noticed with crack that I found; there was way less chance to get caught with it because you can hold bags of crack in your mouth. That's what I did in the bad neighborhoods. You held the crack in your mouth and if the cops come, you just swallow it. After they let you go, you drank a bunch of water, put your finger down your throat and puke it all back up. You couldn't do that with meth because you would probably die."

Ryan continued reflecting about his life on the streets. Notice how his perception of things led him to distort the reality of his circumstances.

On the streets, I went with a friend to the city and he had some PCP to sell; and I offered to go sell it. One time before, my dad had told me a bit about a place, how rough it was, so that's the place I decided to go, with all the drug addicts and guys selling drugs. I walked into that place, a restaurant and bar, at age sixteen, and tried to sell the stuff; but I ended up getting robbed in the bathroom by these guys. I told my friend I lost all his stuff—they robbed me at knife point. He wouldn't go in there. He said, 'No problem, don't worry about that—it was all crushed-up Tylenol.' Our idea was if we let the guys try it, and if they bought it, then they were just idiots that should have their money taken away anyway. So, we crushed up a bunch of Tylenol and went to a rave club that night. There were guys buying it off us, smoking it in pipes. We used the money we got to go buy some ecstasy. The next day we went to a big shopping mall to see if we could make any money there. The kid I went with disappeared on me and I haven't seen or heard of him to this day—no idea where the hell he went or what happened to him. That still kinda sticks out in my mind. I met the worst people then.

I got in with the wrong kind of people and started selling. Me and another guy would beat people up and rob them all the time for fucking nothing. I'm surprised we didn't kill anybody, all for twenty bucks. Basically, we would find just about anybody our age, not regular adults, say, waiting for the bus, who had something that we wanted and sometimes other drug dealers that we knew. We would just lure them somewhere, tell them we wanted to smoke pot with them or something, get them into an isolated area and then we would beat them with a wrench or pool ball in a sock. We would just wail on them with whatever we had until they were down on the ground. Then, we would go through their pockets and take what we wanted. If they had shoes that we wanted, we would take the shoes. Lots of times, we took their drugs or if they had a Discman or something, just anything we wanted. We were just thorough little bastards, real monsters. We were doing crystal meth back then, and it was better quality than today. We would be up for seven to fourteen days, high, without going to sleep. That's the best way to describe it—we were just f'n monsters.

After that, my buddy eventually got out of the scene, and I got into selling drugs. Once in awhile, if things were going really bad, I might get up early in the morning and go to one of those temp agencies, just trying to get a short-term job and some money. That didn't happen very much—maybe once or twice. I'd have a good customer who was working and would only party on the weekends and who had a job and his own place so I would ask to rent a room. I'd give him money and then on the weekends, whatever—I'd give him dope so he could go on working. I remember being like a vampire then. There would be people just getting high on the weekends, and I'd rent a room off them. Within a couple of weeks, they'd lose their job and I would have to move on.

Ryan led this lifestyle for about three years, from the time he was sixteen years old until he was nineteen. It was then that he encountered his first drug charge.

The first charge was trafficking. I didn't know about the charge at first. I was sleeping in a parkade, and I got woken up by the police. There used to be a spot where I'd go and crash at the top of the stairwell. A janitor must have found me or something and called police, who came and told me that I was wanted for trafficking. I said, 'What do you mean?' The cop told me but I was high, and so I said 'Yeah, it might have happened.'

I had heard all these stories about prison—you get all you can eat, you get paid for work, you eat in your cell. So I said fuck it, that sounds good so I should cop out to two years and just do that. On my third court appearance, I talked to duty counsel, I didn't even get a lawyer, I said, 'Yeah, I'm guilty, I want two years.' They said okay. So the judge gave me two years. All the local jails were full so they sent me to a penitentiary in another jurisdiction. I was there for a month and a parole officer came and talked with me. She asked if they ever caught my co-accused, and I said, "What are you talking about?" She read the disclosure, and it turned out that it wasn't even me who sold the drugs. But I was with my buddy who sold the drugs. They said we were partners and I copped to that without even thinking. I felt really stupid about that. After two months, I was transferred to a penitentiary closer to the city. So I got fast-tracked for parole and was out in six months. I went to a halfway house in the city. I went back to prison sixty days later—I got arrested for being super high. I had been awake for four days. Later, they let me back out and but I took off from the halfway house in the city. I didn't last long in the community until I went back to the pen.

Notice that Ryan made the decision not to fight the trafficking charge, not even to hire a lawyer on such a serious charge. To his credit, he did speak to the duty counsel in court that day. It seems that by then, he had enough of living on the streets. I suspect that, in his mind, being in prison was going to be better than the streets. Interestingly, he made that decision on the basis of rather sketchy and simplistic perceptions of what being in prison was actually like. Still, he wanted to get away from the streets, even if that meant going to jail. However, this thinking did not last too long. His buddy on this offence had also been in the same penitentiary and had been released a week before he was.

When I got out of the pen to go to the city, my buddy was working in a town nearby. He met me at a bus stop with some crystal meth so I was high before I even got out of town. It was super bad. I made a lot of crappy decisions.

Ryan completed that first sentence in January, 2006. He explained what happened next:

As soon as I got out, I went right back to selling crack and doing meth. I then met my daughter's mom. In an attempt to clean up, I went to her dad's reserve. That's when she got pregnant with my daughter. I then moved back to the city and started working and stayed working until my daughter was two years old and then went back to selling drugs again. I worked as a baker, then had a job doing concrete, then building log homes. My daughter's mom moved back to the city to be with me—no work on the reserve, but rent was low. Her family all were drunks. The plan was that she would stay there and I would go earn some money. I moved to the city to work and she later came with me. I made enough money to get our own place in the city.

Then my daughter was born. Her mom was using crack and stuff, lots of drinking, and we started fighting all the time. She started using again—way before I did. Then I got started selling and using—they go hand-in-hand for me. I can't do one without doing the other. I moved out 'cause of all the bullshit and got a different job. I took my daughter to my dad's place, got her out of that mess, and I lived there for a while, too. I just started getting high and eventually quit even coming home to my dad's place. Then I was living here, living there. But at this point I was selling more drugs so I had more money so I could stay in better people's places. At one point, I had three different places to stay and a vehicle, too.

The three-year period, 2006 to 2009, saw some big events for Ryan. He lived with the lady who bore their daughter but who was very unsettled herself. He worked steadily at a variety of jobs, something he hadn't done before. However, the structure and beginning stability in his life were fragile and he eventually slipped back into living on his own from place to place and selling drugs. Describing this he said:

In 2009, that second charge—this is another smart move for me. I just came back from my stash house in the inner city, my safe house and I had a fair bit of crack on me, hid in my underwear, so if I got patted down, they'd think it was my testicles or whatever. So, I met somebody who had fifty bucks and he wanted to buy. Usually, I would give three pieces of crack for fifty bucks but I was feeling cheap, so I gave him two pieces. I had this one piece of crack in my pocket. I was near a liquor store, waiting for a friend who had gone inside to buy booze. A cop drove up, and he knew all about me. He searched me, but I tossed the piece of crack on the ground behind me. But he found the crack, so I knew I was gonna get a charge and go to jail. He arrested me, then took my phone which was ringing. He started talking to people and making deals with these people on the phone. The people didn't put two and two together—they were actually doing deals with the cop on my phone. The cop took me to the police station, and that's where they found the rest of my drugs in my underwear. I was charged with possession for the purposes of trafficking.

His sentence this time was two and a half years, thirty months, for another serious offence. Now his criminal record showed two drug convictions and two penitentiary terms. Does the account of his lifestyle to this point support a conclusion that he is, or is becoming, a proficient drug dealer? Or does it support the notion that Ryan is inept as a drug dealer? From his earlier comment ("another smart move for me"), I think he is getting the idea that maybe he is somewhat on the side of ineptness. Looking back over the past ten years that he has been dealing, what does he have to show for it? Virtually nothing!

At this point in our discussion, Ryan became reflective:

My thing is the remembering, like, towards the end of it I was using so much meth, I am surprised I can

still recall so much. I'm surprised I can be a tradesper-
son. There is no way I should be getting through the
schooling, getting to be a journeyman. I am truly lucky
but remembering some of the stuff that happened back
there is difficult. I remember bits and pieces.

He served his sentence at another penitentiary:

At this pen, I decided to get lots of tattoos done—that
was kind of the main focus for me while I was there.
I met an old friend from the street who was in the
tattoo business. There's the thing about tattoos—you
get one, and then another, then another. You start
with one then it goes on from there. I like the way
they look on me. I did get some to make a statement,
and I regret a few of them. I planned to get clean, too.
I found that take the drugs away and I did pretty good.
I did a substance abuse program and passed that, and
I worked in the kitchen. For my last two or three
months, I was moved to the minimum security annex
before my statutory release.

It was not long before Ryan was back to his old ways,
even though there were some fleeting signs of stability:

After I left that pen on statutory release, I wasn't supposed to see my daughter's mother but I did. My dad
found out and made me tell my parole officer. I was
staying in a halfway house but got kicked out for lying
where I was so I got into trouble for that. Then I went
to move in with a friend of mine, the same friend I
used to rob people with, but he had straightened
his life out way before this so I stayed with him and
started working, doing concrete for a guy. I was doing
well, got a bunch of raises and stuff and then winter

happened. I went from working five ten-hour days a week to working short shifts during the night. I started running out of money, and I decided I was going to sell drugs again.

While I was both working and selling drugs, I got arrested for breaking my conditions of my statutory release—not hanging around with certain people like other offenders, drug addicts or gang members. They didn't catch me with drugs 'cause I swallowed it all. The parole officer sent me back to the pen. As soon as I got out again, I started selling drugs. I only sold to people I knew, and some customers even hid me in the back of where they worked when the cops were around. A bunch of middlemen around me got arrested but I didn't because I didn't do any hand-to-hand with these guys. Lots of times, I was stopped by beat cops who wanted to know who I was. I had other problems arise later down the road. I knew a lot of the native gang guys from the institution and from the area I sold in too.

There was one guy who really didn't like me. He called me one time and picked me up as well as the guy I got my drugs off of. I met up with this guy, not realizing how shady he was. He drove me to a house and said a friend of mine was in there, so I went in to see him. When I went inside, I got beat up and stabbed. I was made to take a shower because I was so beat up and bloody, then they beat me up some more. This went on for about three or four hours.

The guy who masterminded this whole thing left. I don't know to this day whether that guy meant to kill me or not. I almost had PTSD because of that. It seemed to me that everybody who used to work for me now worked for that gang. All these close friends and acquaintances, people that I had trusted,

started working for them so I couldn't trust anybody. So then I moved my base to another area of
the city—there weren't so many of the gang down
there. It wasn't as good as my old area but it was
okay.

I knew a bunch of people there, so I had a place
to stay at. I knew meth dealers in that area, so I
could go get my fix of meth. Then one of my good
friends got out of jail, and he started to hook me up
with really good prices. The gang guys didn't mess
with him—he was willing to shoot them all.

Things were going pretty good for a bit, and I
was high all the time. My friend couldn't get any
coke so he started to give me meth to sell. I could
take an 8 ball of meth, about 3 ½ grams, in the
palm of my hand, and I could crush that all up and
snort all that in one line. I did it as a parlour trick,
just to freak people out, a couple of times a day.

Some days I would go out and make a bunch of
money and that would be awesome. Other times, I
would get paranoid and go to try and find a place
to hide the rest of my dope. I would find an open
apartment building and find a place to hide my
stuff. Then at night, I'd go move my stuff—gotta
leave. This would happen on a regular basis when I
was doing these big honking lines of stuff. It would
turn me into a paranoid retard, basically. So my
buddy couldn't get coke; I wanted to make money
so he would give me meth and lots of it. I was doing
so much of that. Sometimes I would be doing okay;
other times I wouldn't be good at all. One time, I
had this old man that was a customer of mine. He
would sleep on the couch; I would get his bedroom.
I would pay him in drugs every day and he was fine
with that.

By this time, Ryan was very entrenched in the drug scene. He had fleeting contact with his family:

My dad was an excellent source of money every couple of weeks. I would go to where he worked, just wait for him and ask him for money, and ten times out of ten he gave me what I wanted. My mom would tell me later on that she would get mad at my dad—like why is he giving me money? He knew where that money was going to. About every three months, I would ask to go home and I would like sleep for a week, usually after something really crappy had happened or if I needed to lay low after something happened. There was a time that I was just dead to the world and I needed sleep. Every time I really needed to go home, they were there to let me go home. But it never lasted. Once I was all slept up and ate up, I would be gone again.

Back to the streets he went. To this point, he had been in the drug scene for about ten years:

One time I was at a guy's place—me and about five friends sitting around in the living room, including a guy who was working for me, my girlfriend and a couple of other girls—and there was a knock at the door. I'm not the kind of guy who sells drugs where I was sleeping. Whoever knocked on the door stepped out of the way and my friend opened the door. It's policemen. They came in, no warrant. One was a beat cop who always bugged me. They were searching everywhere, and they found all my drugs. They were talking on my phone. I thought I was done. Then, all of a sudden, the one cop says, 'You are a fucking idiot, there is a warrant for you, failing to show up for finger prints. What kind of stupid shit is that? You go deal with that right now.' He let me pack a bag and leave but they kept all my drugs and I hadn't paid for them. My buddy was pretty good about it. Me and him went back a long time. He says he understands. Down the road, I'm selling meth again but not doing too well. He says I am the best crack dealer but the shittiest meth dealer he ever met. I says, 'Yeah, because I do too much of the meth.'

I remember the day I went to the parole office for the last time, the last day I got pinched. I had this one big bag of meth, instead of a bunch of smaller bags of meth. I don't usually bag up the stuff ahead of time so I don't get charged with possession for the purposes. But for some reason, this time I did. I go ride my bike to meet this buddy. I sold him what I was giving him. Then I got a text from that other buddy who said he was getting some coke tonight, so he could get me some crack. I'm extremely broke now because I had only been selling meth. I owed this guy money because how shitty I was at selling meth. He's gonna have crack for me—that's awesome news! Then I see a cop car so I disappear into a little shopping centre—I'm gonna get rid of the dope I have in my sock. The cop car goes straight past me, then stops right in front; and he jumps out. He says he has a warrant and then he arrests me. He asks, 'Where is your dope?' I say, 'What warrant?' knowing full well there was one for that shit. He pats my socks, finds everything, looks on my cell phone and sees a text I forgot to erase ordering an 8 ball. 'Here you go—you are pinched.' From there, I went to the remand centre in the city.

I signed up for a boot camp type program— maybe I can get some time knocked off this bit. I had kind of a shitty lawyer. He said maybe he could get me off, maybe I could go to drug court. I called my dad and said, 'Dad, I'm fucking done, I'm not doing this anymore. I'm done! There is nothing I miss about this anymore. No matter what happens, I'm done'. He said if I needed help, just let him know.

I put off my case for about three months. My lawyer didn't really know what he could do so I said, 'Well, can you get me two years today?' I didn't want to sit there for months wondering what the hell is going on when I could just go to the pen, get programming to finish my high school and get out. He got me thirty months. The judge mentioned I was a seasoned veteran. By this point, I was worried about the beef I had with the street gang, with some of the members. When the parole officer came and saw me, I told her that I don't want to go to the pen I was last in. 'Okay,' she said, 'I'll put you in another institution where you haven't been'.

By now, Ryan had seen the worst of the drug scene in the city. He was well-known to police, had the reputation in the courts of being a seasoned, veteran offender, had been severely beaten up and wondered if he would be killed, and just kept fumbling his way from one crisis to another. All his former clients were now buying from rival dealers in a street gang. He felt that all his former close friends would now turn on him, just to be on the good side of the gang. But, now he had declared to his dad that he was done with the scene. This time, when he went to the pen, he had a different attitude:

I went to that pen and met some of the most influential people in my life. For the first week I was locked in my cell. When I could get out of my cell, a guard asked me if I wanted to go to safety training, a safety school. 'You'll get paid,' he said. I said, 'okay'. I went to the computer room and staff there talked with me. I said, 'This is my third pen bit, and it is going to be my fucking last. I don't have my high school diploma, and I really want to get that while I'm in here. If there is anything you can do to help me along, I'll work hard, whatever I can—I just want this time not to be a waste of time.' The teacher had me in school within a month. He started me off with math, adding and subtracting, like in middle school, and I did that. He and a lady teacher there both helped me so much and let me take some coursework home just so I could get my diploma. I have to thank the teachers. Other inmates said she was stupid, a bitch. But they sure set me up to get through high school and into a trade. I did the work and they did everything they possibly could to make sure I passed and that I was finished in time for my release. I didn't get any more tattoos, and I worked in the kitchen, too.

While I was in there, I had to take an advanced substance abuse program which taught me something very important. Before, everything was the 12 Step meetings, all AA, CA, and NA that made you believe you had to go to these meetings all the time to stay clean, that you were powerless to your addiction, that addiction was stronger than you—without them and the meetings, you could not be sober. In this advanced program, they teach that you learn to be a drug addict, that you didn't learn to be an addict overnight. You couldn't sit there and do a line the first time you did it—you had to learn all that shit. So, I liked that, if you could learn to be an addict, you could unlearn to be an addict. I liked that better than going to a lot of meetings for the rest of my life. I also did a lot of body building. School and body building—that's what kept me going in this bit.

During this prison sentence, Ryan did the work he needed to do to benefit from the program opportunities. Staff went to bat for him, something that never happened before because he had no interest in this in the two previous penitentiary sentences. He earned his high school diploma, developed some helpful insights into his addiction and took steps to build up his health. A new Ryan seemed to be emerging as he was released once again.

I was released and my plan was that I was going to be a welder. Then I heard about a trades recruitment program that aimed to get guys into the trades with unions. I was in classes with welders, boiler makers, electricians, and a millwright. I went to write an entrance exam for one of the unions but all I had was my parole identification. Later they said I failed that test. I do not believe I failed that test because there was something funny about all this, something else was going on. My trades program went to bat for me and said I was a smart guy, a good guy, so let him do a re-write next Tuesday. This was on a Friday.

On the weekend, I was on a date and the cops stopped me. I showed them my parole ID. They checked the girl and found there was a warrant for her. So I was arrested for failing to avoid certain persons, ones with criminal records, and I was thrown back in jail. They let her go.

My parole officer was really good. I called her on Wednesday, the day after I was to re-write. She was upset because had she known sooner, she could have got me out. When I did get out, I went to the trades recruitment program. They pointed out that I missed the exam—too bad. I asked, 'What are my options?' They said either quit the program or write an exam for another trade. They said I was smart enough to be in another trade. So I did. I now tell people I originally wanted to be in one trade but another trade chose me to be in theirs. My new trade gave me a reference and some tools so I could work non-union to start me off. They helped me find my career so I was very happy with that trades recruitment program, even if they didn't find me a job.

I did some dating, then I dated another lady, now my fiancée and we plan to get married in a few months time. I first met her when we were fifteen—we were both in the scene. Both of us have been to the pen, except she went for a really long time whereas I went for three small bits. I knew her from before but we never dated but I kinda wanted to so when I saw the opportunity, I got in there and now we have a new son. I also have a step-son and she has a step-daughter.

Ryan now has his own family, a blended one, and he is enjoying this experience:

Now, I get up every day and see my kids; this is won-derful. I know we as parents are not supposed to have favourites; but the baby, my youngest, just watching the world pass by his eyes is amazing. My step-son is just so inquisitive and nothing gets past him. My daughter lives with my dad. She's a teenager and I see her on the weekends but I don't get the same experi-ence with her as with the two boys. Watching both of them, they watch everything, see everything. I'm so proud of everything they do. I missed that with my daughter because I was still being an idiot when she was young. I really take everything in with the boys, especially the baby. He's walking around and he's climbing things. He does his baby sign language, speaks a few words. It amazes me every day. I came into my step-son's life when he was three. I was there to see him toilet trained and watching him as he goes through school. He is just so inquisitive, so smart. He's the kind of kid you can't get one over on. One time, I told him we don't have any more popsicles, and he says, 'Well, I want to see in the box.'

They are the ones getting me through this. My wonderful fiancé, I love her so much. We never fight. I've been with her almost two years and it has been absolutely wonderful. She works in harm reduction, in a house that has hard-to-house drug addicts, people with mental problems. She loves the job. She's the bread-winner now, and I'm the house husband for now. She never complains; she just stepped right in and took the reins. There are no complaints.

We do lots of stuff as a family. We do a lot of video games, TV, stuff like that. When it is nice out, we go for walks. My fiancée always has things planned for the weekends. She takes them to play places. My fiancée does lots of crafts with them, too. They did an Easter mural on the front glass door.

We have a close group of friends who actually all know each other from the meth scene. We've all gotten straightened out. We go out with them and have kids the similar age to ours. We get together on the weekends—have some drinks. They are all pretty close by. It's nice.

Earlier, Ryan spoke about the importance of body building as a very helpful activity while he was imprisoned for the third time. He still talks about the importance of body building in his quest to stay clean, albeit his circumstances have changed.

I used to do a lot of bodybuilding. Now, with the younger kids, I haven't been able to do that as much but I actually plan to get a set of dumbbells and bench and stuff so I can do workouts at home. My fiancée works from 4:30 in the afternoon until midnight on weekdays. I usually got home from work at supper time so I'd put the kids to bed. I used to go to the gym all the time, often at 3:30 a.m. before going to work. And I loved doing that, especially when I first got out of prison. Then, bodybuilding kept me clean. With the baby, now, I've had to put that stuff on hold. I'll get back into it when all is said and done. Now, getting high is not an option. That would be like jumping off a building right now.

Ryan is drawing employment insurance at the present time as he has been laid off. He is not negative or pessimistic, but realistic about his employment prospects.

I'm now on EI with a good sized outfit, but there is no work now. I have a feeling that with the economy down, I may have to go look for work in the commercial side of the business—there is nothing industrial right now. I worked there for about a year and a half—the longest I ever worked steadily in one place. I certainly do really like the company. They are paying me a hell of a lot more money than that last company I worked for, and I got to do a lot more interesting stuff. I like the nature of the work and the safety standards. I would really like to continue working with them, but I don't really know what is going to happen over the next couple of months. Some supervisors have told me to keep my skill set up so I can get a job anywhere, especially when there aren't a lot of jobs coming up. Work is harder to find now.

As he looked back on his journey, he shared some insights he had gained in the process:

My mom still asks if there is anything else that she could have done. The answer is, 'No.' Nothing more she could have done would have moved me away from the scene. I say to parents and others, 'Be prepared to watch the train derail and hope for the best'.

For a drug addict/robber/dealer, the worst thing you can do is enable them. If they are hurting, you take them in. If you let them live in your home, giving them money, whatever you are doing, you are saying that they are kinda okay with this because they are still helping out. There is no problem helping them out, but it has to be for their betterment. Help them out by driving them to treatment. Helping them out by saying, 'As soon as you get clean, I can help you. You can stay at our place until you get on your feet; but if you are still using and out there, then no you can't'.

Because drug addicts, crooks, they are vultures taking advantage of anything that you let them do. They will walk all over you. If you have them stay in your house, if they can deal from their mom's house, they are never going to f'n change. They need to hit rock bottom. My rock bottom was three pen bits on top of almost getting killed. Plus watching everybody I know turning into absolute snakes that would help these gang guys f'n find me. If I was doing back then, in my twenties, what I was supposed to be doing, I'd now have the world by the balls. I'd be getting a couple of tickets for different trades so that I would always have a job. You know, I lost so much time.

You can't help someone to smarten up because they are doing what they want to do. As long as they want that, as long as that is in their head, they're going to f'n do it. Nothing you can do is going to change that. You just gotta pray for them. Let them know that you are there for them but until they are clean or sober, you can't really do anything. That's not your son anymore, it's not your brother, it's an addict. They would burn so many bridges with their parents, you know, steal off them, sell drugs out of their house.

For me, if you were to talk to me when I was in that lifestyle, I would have told you that first of all, in my mind, I wasn't a drug addict, I was a dealer, that God made me a drug dealer. That's all I was good for and that's all I was ever going to be. I believed that in my head for years, even when I was in jail until I had my breaking point, until I said there has got to be a different way—I can't do this anymore. But if you had asked me that then, I would have told you that is what I wanted to be. It was like I was lying to myself to say that I was going to be sober or go to work. Now, I honestly believe I just sold myself short. That's even the same place I was in with my ex—I had to accept the way things were, what I deserved. Now, I want people to think—don't sell yourself short.

As on the first page of this story, Ryan had some expectations that telling his story would have on others.

Even if my story puts the bug in somebody's mind, I will be happy. If someone says they have a brother in the scene, all you can do is hope for the best, don't enable them. Wanting to change has to come from within. If you can put the idea into one person's head when they hit the bottom, such as knowing this guy who changed his life and is doing good, maybe they can do that, too. If that happens, then it will all be worth it for me. I never thought it could be done, that I could change. What were my options? I feel I'm too old to go to university so the trades are the only option I know how to do. I just sold myself short all these times. That's what people do—sell themselves short.

There is something you can do that will make you just as happy as you were with drugs, even more. Don't get me wrong—I liked being a drug dealer, I did! Otherwise, I wouldn't have done it for so long, wouldn't have thrown my life away doing that, doing that shit, going to jail. But it's all fake. You only see all the good things. You don't see all the bad things that everybody else sees—like, you don't see your kids, or your girl is f'n the next guy. In reality I was selling myself short.

Ryan raises a powerful question: Do we as parents, family members, community members and corrections workers set our expectations too low for our young people or for anyone for that matter in the community? Could we realistically set the bar higher? Could we expect more and then see people rise to the occasion? Are we enabling drug users?

CHAPTER 15

BRANDON: PARDON ME

IT WAS MID-JULY on the prairies, in a village located in farm and ranch country. The population of the village was listed in a government publication as "32 inhabitants, with 12 residences." There was exactly one store selling gas, and groceries; a run-down church; five abandoned buildings, and a bar. The land surrounding the village was flat— so flat, in fact, you could see for a long way in all directions. Jokes about this type of landscape were ever-present, "You can see a dozen coyotes lined up to take a pee at the only tree around here for miles." It was late in the evening, getting quite dark, and the sounds from birds, vehicles, and humans were subsiding.

"Oh, shit!" slurred 24-year-old Brandon as he glanced in the rear view mirror of his old, beat up, rusty pickup truck that was parked outside the bar. He saw a blinking light, rolling out red and blue flashes that bounced from the other buildings in the village, coming from the roof of a car that pulled up behind his vehicle. He was in the driver's seat, digging the keys out of his pants pocket.

"Cops!" he mumbled. He had a sinking feeling that this was not going to be a pleasant ending to an enjoyable night at the bar as he had expected.

He tried to focus on the flashing lights in the mirror as he pawed the seat beside him, searching for the twelve-pack of beer he had purchased just a short time ago just as the bar was closing for the night at eleven o'clock. He and his friend, who was far too drunk to drive, still shared the idea to have just a few more beers at home before they called it a night. They had reassured themselves that, yes, they did have to be at work in the morning; but they figured there was time for one or two more beers before crashing.

Two young officers from the detachment in a town about an hour away sat in the car parked behind Brandon's truck. One officer stayed in the car while the other, from the driver's side, got out of the car and approached the driver's door of the pickup, where Brandon was behind the wheel. He had cranked down the window.

"Good evening, sir," announced the officer, "how many drinks have you had tonight?"

"Lots," replied Brandon, who was both flippant and honest in his comment.

Sitting with me and telling the story, Brandon recalls that, "Right then, the waitress came out from the bar, saying she would make sure we got home safe—she called us "the boys." But the officer just said, "Thank you, ma'am. We'll take care of them from here." Brandon continues:

> I knew there was no getting out of it. The officers were quite nice actually. They didn't have a breathalyzer with them so they had to drive me all the way to the detachment in their town. They put my friend in with me in the back seat of the police car and we talked with them all the way to the police station. The two cops talked like normal people. When we got there, they sat me down and I blew .18. I figured they were stalling 'cause I think they wanted me to come down from that. We must have waited an hour. Maybe they were thinking that this guy, me, is a nice character and this is a one-off so maybe they could straighten me out about this. I blew again and it was .14.

Based on the breathalyzer readings, Brandon was legally impaired and was charged with impaired driving, contrary to the Criminal Code. In Brandon's words:

> The officers told me, 'You've got two options now. We can call your parents, and they can come and get you or you can sleep in the drunk tank tonight.' So I said to them, 'Ah, geez. Not the parents thing! Any chance you're heading back out that way to our village?' Then one of the officers said, 'Alright, you guys seem like decent guys.' It hadn't really hit me yet as to what had just happened.

So, in the middle of the night, the officers actually drove Brandon and his buddy all the way back to the village and to Brandon's residence where the boys crashed out for what little remained of the night.

The period between his arrest and the subsequent court appearance was a time of intense reflection for Brandon.

> I was thinking about how I'd be able to cross the border. I had committed to going to a music festival across the line. I was scared the border officers could send me back. We were going to the west coast to cross over. I'd paid good money for those tickets so what was going to happen when I got to the border? Would they tell me to get out of there?

He also thought about his past, looking for some perspective or maybe an explanation, for his drunken behaviour.

> I was born in a rural northern community into a family full of fishermen, farmers, and labourers. My dad owned an apiary—a bee farm. His pride and joy was an old Ford truck. We lived in a small trailer. Later, we

moved to a very small town, and dad worked away on the oil rigs and then in construction, which is where I ended up in the long run. I have an older sister and an adopted younger sister too. She was a foster kid to start with and came into our family when I was thirteen. My folks fostered two other kids for a few weeks. It was so devastating for my parents to have these two around and start to love them and then, all of a sudden, they were swept away in the foster care system. That hurt us kids too, right, 'cause you started to care for them as well.

We moved to a bigger town so my mom could get work. Both my parents worked a lot away from home so my sister and I got used to that, raised ourselves a little bit by cooking, cleaning, plus going to school. We learned how to fend for ourselves. It was a large shock learning to fit into a larger community with the existing people and a new school. I remember doing some things to fit in and be cool, not real bad things, like starting to smoke at fourteen, just following in my sister's footsteps. This was cool—an identity thing.

Another thing I did was skip school on track day which was a shame. I was really good at track. There was a time when everyone was gonna go fishing. The boys who were going fishing were a little older than me. So, I skipped out of grade seven and eight track because the boys who were in my sister's class and were three years older than me were going fishing and drinking beer. So I'm gonna do track if there's fishing and beer? Nope that's where I'm headed! I ran a race in the morning 'cause I didn't know they were going yet, and I got first. So I was supposed to be in the next heat. But, by then, there was heat #8— and there was no Brandon. I'd already gone fishing by then. I got into trouble over that.

There were other goofy things like in the back of the bus on band camp or field trips we were on, laughing and giving the finger to the driver behind us. A guy was actually following us and picked us out when we finally arrived. I did not want to get off that bus. You know; silly things like that. And fighting all the time, continually in fights until they realized nobody could beat me.

I always looked up to my dad because I thought he was tough, working so hard all the time, and we could see the change in our situation—moving up in the world to live in bigger homes in bigger communities. He would do all his own handiwork and he would do a very good job. So, he was a jack-of-all-trades. I wanted to be like that. He would always say, though, 'Oh, you don't want to be like me. This is no way to live your life. You don't want to end up shoveling ditches, you need a good education.'

I did fairly good in school, especially gym and physical sorts of stuff. I graduated from high school and decided to take a resource management program at college. After the program, I ended up taking a job in fisheries which I did for four years. It was a hard job, not for the weak-at-heart or weak mentally.

He turned his thoughts to the culture in the region of young men and alcohol.

At that time, guys from the region with a bit of money and a cool job could get into trouble. Not so much me, but lots of other guys. I stayed out of it pretty much. You get drinking and far away from home. Every small town has a bar and everyone you know has an impaired charge so that's the standard. It was not even a big deal mentally if you get one, until you get one.

Then, that's a different story. Everyone talks tough about it or talks big about it, but that's not necessarily the case.

That summer, we had a lot of parties and a lot of get-togethers, almost to the point of out-of-control drinking. It was an absolutely quiet community and not much going on. Then all of a sudden, all these young, strapping, well-paid boys show up and move in—we just took over the village. Everyone around knew who we were. Instead of driving our vehicles down to the store, which had everything—videos, mail, snacks, gas—we would just ride the lawnmowers down to there, fill up, get some snacks and then head out. We made race tracks in the field next to the village; we'd do time trials with the lawn mowers and things like that. We weren't quiet by any means. The young ladies sure appreciated us being around. Everybody knew when we were off work. We would flood the place, go in and hoot and holler, but we never got complaints, really, so that was good.

We would drink all the time just because this one person wanted to drink and he was feeling okay that day, then that kind dragged everyone else in there. They'd harass you, 'Don't be such a wimp,' or they would literally come and haul you out of your room. There would be girls outside and they'd be hooting and hollering. What do you do if you can't beat 'em? Join 'em, right? That was the whole basis of what we were up to—work and drink. We'd even set a TV up outside and watch hockey games when it was near freezing. We'd be sitting drinking beer out there, out in the yard; we were outside guys. I guess almost all of our money went into drinking. Even if you didn't have money or whatever, they'd sucker you, 'Oh, no, we're buying or this person is buying; that person owes a case of beer because he was late for work and they covered for him or something', so stuff like that. It was almost like a spiral sometimes where there were times when guys, like, would vandalize stuff or get caught driving drunk out of that group. It was just a matter of time before this person or that person would get caught. It would spiral down quickly.

Before long, Brandon had his day in court.

When I went to court for impaired driving, I took my friend, made him take the day off work, 'cause he was part of the whole gig, too. Now, I can't drive. I pleaded guilty. In my mind, I didn't care if I could get away with it or not, I was going to face the consequences 'cause I needed that lesson—that was the lesson to myself. I had to pay a fine at the courthouse, then I had to attend a two-day seminar on the effects of drinking and driving, what it can do to you and your family and the consequences. I lost my licence for a year. The worst thing about it was that I had let my mom down because her father died in a drinking and driving accident (he wasn't the driver). I did the worst thing I could possibly do to my mother.

Now, some of the realities of a conviction for impaired driving caught up to Brandon.

So then, everything was affected. At my job, they wanted me to run to the city lots of times to pick up stuff or drop stuff off. I couldn't do that, so I'm not as valuable as the next guy who has a licence, so there's those implications. Then how do I get to work? I live out in the middle of nowhere. So, what do I do? I had to depend on everyone. My parents and a lot of my friends lived about an hour away and my work was about ten minutes away. How would I go anywhere? I'm stuck in a village of thirty-two people so I need to depend on people to get to work. I can't work over-time. If whoever I am riding with is on a bit of a different shift, that causes problems. I'm asking for rides everywhere. It was just very, very difficult. I couldn't afford a 'blow box' 'cause I was paying off a student loan so how could I afford all this stuff? If I had to go to the city, I had to get a ride with someone. There was a courier service that would go around to all these small towns so I'd jump a ride with them. The driver knew my parents so he did me a favour by picking me up. I'd buy him a couple of beers or something. It was just really, really hard. When you don't have a licence in the middle of nowhere, what do you do? Where do you go? People get annoyed. You don't want to bug people but how are you gonna get from point A to point B? I limped through that year—it seemed it take forever. Then I got my licence back.

I heard you are not eligible for seven years to get a pardon, so I just put that idea on the back burner, anyway. At that time, I'm not thinking down the line about the consequences for having a criminal record.

Changes were about to unfold in Brandon's life.

Around that time, I had a job offer to work on the railway so that is how I ended up out here in the city. They promised me a lot of money, and I would be doing maintenance on the track. So, I decided to jump at that and I worked at the railway for a few months. Then a superintendent with a construction company saw my work ethic and wanted me to work with them.

I worked for that construction company as a

labourer, then a foreman, and then a general foreman at massive industrial sites, both near the city and up north, making really good money and starting to realize that I have potential here. I've got the responsibility of leadership and managing groups of people.

Things were going pretty well for Brandon at this point, and he gave only fleeting thought to his criminal record. His employment, travel, associations and daily routines were unaffected by his record.

I got married in 2008. We were told we couldn't have kids—it just wasn't going to happen. The chances of that happening, in my mind, was you might just as well plan on winning the lottery. Then one day I got a phone call from my wife when I was working up north. She was pregnant! This was after eight years of being together. We would be having a girl! I was sort of blown away and very happy. But somewhere in there, my world just changed—everything changed. I didn't have to live for just me anymore, I had to live for someone else, my daughter. There are a few things that go through your mind, like what schools are we gonna have her in, what activities or whatever?

Additional realities began to sink home:

In planning this stuff, I thought, I have a criminal record. What if I want to be a chaperone at something? I can't be. A field trip? Girl Guides? What if I have to change jobs? She'll have dual citizenship, she's going to travel; what if I can't? I could miss out on stuff like that. Do I get turned away at the border when she's with me? Or, dad's gotta go home and you get to go here? What kinds of questions will I have to answer then? And how many people do I have to tell now? Do I tell everyone? How will they look at me? Whether it's an impaired or a drug charge, some people just get it in their mind that you are a criminal.

Brandon began to think more seriously about his criminal record. He paid close attention to what those around him said about criminal records in their everyday conversation.

I heard it was seven years before you could get a pardon—not an easy process. It was going to cost a ton of money, and applying was just not worth doing. The attitude out there was just don't do it. There is a stack of papers on somebody's desk that is a mile high and you're going to be the last one on the list. It's going to be another ten years before you get your pardon. I started hearing things like it's not called a pardon any more. It's called a record suspension so people can still see that you have a criminal record. Because you have a record suspension, it's gonna come up that you have a criminal record.

One day, I was looking in the classified section of a newspaper and saw an ad or an article that it was $3,000 or some number like that for assistance with a pardon/record suspension application. A lot of people can't come up with that amount of money.

I started digging around a bit to see how much it would cost. It just seemed so much because someone else was doing the work. It's like when you take your vehicle to the garage—it costs $300 for a part and $1,000 for the mechanic to do the work. I decided to be the mechanic. I talked to a friend who said, 'Why don't you go to the office of a non-profit society that specializes in criminal justice services—they can help'. I didn't know anything about the place. I walked in and went to the front desk and asked if they had any paperwork on pardons or record suspensions. The lady just went, 'Sure, no problem' and she printed me out a lot of paper. I wondered how much this was going to cost, and I got scared again. It turned out that the copies were free.

That night, I sat down and read it over. Sure, I needed help with a couple of things but it wasn't crazy. I lumbered along with it and within four or five months, I had the thing filled out. Waiting for things like the official conviction from the courthouse was the longest part. I heard stuff like they are going to send it back to you three or four times because you used the wrong coloured pen, or you used white out.

The questions were actually quite basic, and I sent it away. The whole process took about a year and about $600 for the government's fee, from the time I got the paperwork until I got a letter saying my record suspension was approved. I was shocked it only took that long.

It was nice to close that chapter, just to be done with that. That stuff can weigh in the back of your mind for a really long time. I work with lots of people who have criminal records who will never do anything about it. When I tell my story, they go 'Really? Oh, that doesn't seem too bad'. I've had people ask me for help with it. I'm amazed there are so many misconceptions.

Now I can take my daughter to Girl Guides or anywhere without worrying about the ever-increasing requirement of criminal record checks.

Brandon is like most citizens who do not realize the bigger-picture ramifications of a criminal conviction. Once caught up in the justice system, they focus on immediate issues like arrest, court appearances, plea, sentence, and the immediate consequences of that sentence. Only later do they come to realize that they may also have to deal with other possible consequences of a criminal conviction:

- Deportation and denial of re-entry to the country,
- Denial of citizenship and immigration, including sponsoring someone,
- Difficulty gaining employment since some employers screen out those with criminal records,
- May not be eligible to serve on a jury,
- Restricted travel—may not be granted permission to enter some countries,
- Denied access to jobs dealing with vulnerable people or children,
- Prevented from entering certain occupations or professions or from entering certain training programs,
- Accommodation—landlords can refuse to rent to people with criminal convictions,
- Insurance and bonding—insurers can refuse to insure people with criminal records,
- Adoption—it may be difficult to do this, and
- Refusal to grant a permit or license to purchase or use a firearm.

Brandon has provided a commendable service to members of the public, especially those with criminal records, by allowing his story to be told. By being open about his criminal behaviour and the resulting criminal record, he has shed important light on some of the myths and misconceptions that are so rampant in criminal justice.

CHAPTER 16

PAULA: FREEDOM FROM A FPS#

"We all have life stories, right? How we got to where we are, both personally and professionally. We have to wade through all that stuff to get to a certain point in life. A reflection for me is I want to be mindful of what is shared, what is talked about, the scope of the sharing; to be comfortable with it. I didn't get to where I am gently, so I don't just give it away."

WITH THESE COMMENTS, Paula opened her FaceTime interview with me. She is a Métis woman, fifty years of age and, as we shall learn, spent twenty-two years in and out of the criminal justice system, both as a youth and as an adult. She expressed the hope of getting one's FPS# (Finger Print Section number) off people's back. This is a number assigned by the national police service to people charged with and/or convicted of criminal and quasi-criminal offences. Paula was known by her FPS# for many years and her last FPS entry expired twelve years ago.

She began "wading through stuff" by outlining some of her childhood experiences:

> Some of my earliest memories were the smell of alcohol, arguing, violence, fighting, all around me. I don't have a lot of memories from age ten and under. I remember feeling displaced all the time, on-the-run. My folks were into their addictions. Although I self-identify as Métis, it was never spoken about in my upbringing as dad did not live his life as a Métis man. Part of our family

heritage is we are Ojibway but that caused discord in our family as dad did not acknowledge his background. After age ten, I remember building relationships with other kids that were having problems at home as well. I was out of the house as much as possible because there was no guidance there, no nurturing. It was confusing for me to be at home. We grew up in small towns and I never felt then that I was from anywhere. My older brother once said that we moved twenty-one times in one year. At age twelve, we were in a town for a while— that's where I had a sense of community. I felt semi-rooted. But by now, my parents had separated and that changed the course of my life. Now, I really needed attention. I was a little kid, I needed love, somebody just to listen to me. The only thing I knew how to do was to reach out in a negative way.

Paula explained some of the negative measures that she used to get attention:

I started doing crime and hooking up with kids who were doing break and enters, stealing liquor, whatever. The kids I hung out with smoked weed or drank. I did not know how to manage my feelings. By age twelve, I started skipping school. My life was a free-for-all. I was doing my own thing. I learned to react with violence. I remember being in a rage and beating up one of my friends. I had rages like that for half of my teen years. I picked up traits of insecurity, victim mentality, violence, no communication skills at all. All I knew what to do was yell and scream. I spent my childhood inside my own head until I was about twenty. I never talked about anything I felt. I kept it all inside and it came out as violence. It came out in me stealing cars. And I learned how to charm, to be a hustler, like my dad. That's how he survived in his life. That's what we kids learned. That created all the insanity in my brain the whole time in my teens. I was very violent, despite not being very big. I was so full of rage. I was a force of energy that was insane.

As she reached age thirteen (she was now old enough to be considered a young offender), her behaviour became increasingly problematic. By sixteen, she was in youth court:

I had years of seeking attention. I was just priming myself to enter the young offender system. It progressed from breaking into garages to stealing cars. By age fifteen, I could roll into a car dealership with a hustle, like, 'I'm graduating this year and my folks are buying me a brand new ride and they told me to come down here to check it out'. I was very good at what I did! That's how I got about half of the vehicles I ever stole. The dealer would put a dealer's plate on a vehicle, hand me the keys and I'd go for a ride.

Later, I would get the keys, steal a vehicle and then get involved in a high speed chase. The cops knew me because it was a small town. They caught me, gave me shit, but never charged me.

At age sixteen, I worked in a restaurant. The owner treated us like we were garbage so I finally quit, then broke into her café. I had two side-kicks and we stole all the cigarettes. The keys to her car were on the wall, so I grabbed them and away we went to a nearby city to a car dealership. They saw the nice car I had and I said I wanted to trade it in. I was awful to think like this, but I was good at it—a charmer. I put a plate on a new vehicle and took it for a test drive. We went back to our home town and went joy-riding for two days. Then, the cops saw the vehicle and the chase was on. The police caught up and surrounded the vehicle with guns drawn. When they opened the door and recognized me, one officer ripped a strip off me; he was so mad. 'You f'n little brat!' he screamed. Needless to say, I was charged as a youth with theft of auto, break and enter, and endangering the public. That's where my criminal justice life began.

Now, Paula had earned her FPS#, one that would follow her for the next twenty years:

I entered the youth system. I figured I was old enough to defend myself, that I was a big girl now, and nobody's going to fuck with me. I never wanted to break into that lady's restaurant. I never wanted to do anything to harm her—she gave me a job; she fed me, she gave me money, even if she was an old crank. I never had money before in my life. This was my first job. I did the B & E because my whole life was in turmoil.

I stepped up my level of criminal activity. It got me away from my mother. I remember still today, thirty some years later, standing in the courtroom and my mother was there, disgusted with me—how could I be so bad and embarrass her. The judge asked my mother if she wanted to take me home, and she stood up and said, 'No—you guys take her. I don't want her anymore'. My mom didn't know how that would affect me. She couldn't handle me, at all.

Paula had entered the youth justice system at age sixteen and she spent the next two years in custody, beginning in a group home and ending two years later in secure custody.

On this first bit, I got four months open custody in a group home; but I took off. For this, I got six months closed custody in a youth centre. They caged us in the basement of an old building. By the time I became an adult at age eighteen, I had several escape charges. I was then transferred to a more secure youth centre for a year. I was always looking for a way to escape. By age seventeen, I was big and bad.

Just before I turned eighteen, I escaped again. A few months later, I was arrested and charged with escaping lawful custody. In court, the judge asked me what I wanted to do. Since I was big and bad and tough, plus having some youth time left, I chose to do adult time. I was sentenced to eight months in an adult prison.

Paula's FPS# followed her into the adult justice system. Her first adult sentence of eight months turned into imprisonment for two years:

Now it was a whole other ball game, being in adult prison—more manipulation, more trauma, more deviancy. I released my rage and violence against staff and inmates. I was rank, and I created quite the reputation. I was segregated many times. This started paving the way for another twenty years in the system. My first adult sentence lasted almost two years, 'til I was twenty.

I experienced crazy people, trauma, riots, fights, staff being injured, inmates injured, being caged because of my behaviour. That part of my life was really impactful and really messed with a lot of things for me. I raged—I never talked. I would freak out when they locked me up, do anything to pound out the door or scratch the window, anything to get out. I felt like a mouse in a cage, trying to eat its arm off. This was a whole new level of trauma. I know my behaviours got me there but I never knew things like this before, so it created a whole new level of shit.

One staff member, a woman, would talk to me. She would come to the cell door and talk and talk. I would never talk. She wanted to get to know me. She obviously had something on for me but I didn't understand it at that time. Now that I reflect on it, I was fresh meat then. It took me years to see this. I was getting institutional charges for not obeying orders, for disrespecting officers. I was a jerk—all I knew how to do was to yell and scream. I was creating the reputation in the institution as violent, and she was creeping on me the whole time I was in lock up.

At this point in our interview, Paula became somewhat subdued and quiet, more thoughtful, and less expressive. She reflected:

My childhood was a prison, my fears were a prison and now I was in a prison within a prison. I got used to this, I felt safe and comfortable because I was locked away from everyone else.

Staff working in correctional centres have really tough jobs. They have to control inmates in order to protect the public, the staff and other inmates, as well as help inmates prepare for release, better equipped to live a law-biding lifestyle. Thus far, staff had decided the best way to deal with Paula was to keep her locked up. This met the criteria of control and protection but did not meet the criteria of helping people adjust in a positive way, especially in the face of her fast-approaching release date.

Paula explained that staff then developed a new correctional plan for her that focused on getting her re-integrated into the general inmate population and into the community:

Lo and behold, I worked on my reintegration. Nine months go by and I'm back in population. I still get locked up once in a while; but people would come and talk to me, and I was grateful for that.

I'm nearing the end of my sentence. I guess my rage and violence was harnessed, put it in a cage. People were still scared shitless of me. I created a reputation of 'Don't fuck with me.' It kept everything away—friends, family, education, staff, even my self-worth. I was screwed up mentally, physically, socially and spiritually.

Even though I was full of rage, there was still some space for a few staff to connect with me, to see my spirit and my heart. They took the time not to take advantage of me, to guide and nurture me. I will never forget them.

Upon her release, Paula stepped tentatively into the community. She hadn't spent much time in the community in the last four years. A lot would have changed. How would she adapt? She explained:

Now I'm twenty. I've been in jail since I was sixteen. I've got nothing other than a few friends. When I was released, I went to the life I knew—the partying, drinking at the bar, watching people inject drugs.

I was living a double life—crime, drugs and violence was more normal to me than going to school and getting a regular job and training. I was back in jail seven months after release—for assault. I didn't drink before, but now I drank for three people for a good ten years.

The double life thing—that goes back to the guard who had been grooming me for the last couple of years. I was residing at her place, living in her basement. She showered me with jewelry, dressed me up like her little puppet. At that time, I didn't know it then, she was just another person who wants to use me and that is what I am used to. I sold the jewelry because I had no attachment to it. I was at her place for a couple of months. I was too into the street life. A lot of the people that I hung with were older. I sat back and watched and learned. I was violent and people would call on me to do certain things and I would be mean to people, beat them up. It felt good because of where I was in my life and what had happened to me. That was my way to take it out on people, to release it.

Paula somehow stayed out of trouble with the law for the next four years, bouncing around from town to town and then settling with a friend:

I started taking pills with the alcohol. You don't feel anything. It was Ts and Rs (Talwin and Ritalin) back in those days. It was a way for me to express all of that pent-up rage, the abandonment, everything I had experienced. Alcohol gave me that excuse to pound the shit out of people. That's how I operated for quite a while up to 1994, after I had been out close to four years, no more charges. One time I was drinking and got into a fight, beat somebody up real good and ended up getting charged with assault. So, I hit the justice system again.

This time, the court was lenient with Paula and took her youth record into account; she received a suspended sentence and probation. As she said, "They were still giving me chances."

She spent the next couple of years going from town to town and into another city, partying with the same friends. In 1996, Paula got a charge of failing to comply with the conditions of her probation order and then picked up an armed robbery charge:

At that time, we were partying and everyone was running out of money. I was a rager and didn't care, and I knew what to do. I went in and robbed a convenience store. I was half in the bag, walked in there and robbed them. I was sentenced to 18 months and sent to the same jail where that female guard worked. This was traumatizing. The people who were supposed to be reforming me were actually re-victimizing me—locking me up in a cage, talking my ear off about love, how beautiful I am— all this weird stuff. It confused me and creeped me out.

Paula began journaling, putting her thoughts and feelings down on paper. She felt good about finally being able to "get things out", something she had not been able to do before. One theme she journaled about was the female staff member, now a senior official at the institution, who continued to creep Paula, and now, another female inmate as well. Someone found her journal, read it, then wrote a letter of complaint to the warden. The warden attacked her credibility and announced she was being transferred out. Just hours before the transfer, two guards who Paula liked and trusted suddenly took her to a room in the institution and locked her inside, instructing her to pick up the phone and call the number written on a piece of paper. Paula briefly wondered what was going on, but she trusted these two staff so she called the number. In Paula's words:

I called the number and it was the frick'n Ombudsman. They wanted to know what was going on so I told them—I opened up a real can of worms. It felt so good to finally tell my story. Finally, somebody believed me and was listening. I reflected on whether I really wanted to go ahead with this. I said to myself, "F'n right, let's open it up." I took responsibly for it. I was using her back—tit-for-tat. I was surviving.

Paula was transferred to another adult correctional facility in another jurisdiction. She had no connections in that city. At that centre, she took a few programs like anger management, addictions, and a thirty-day treatment program. Paula worked closely with the Ombudsman—it took nine months to complete that investigation. She was alone, with just the Ombudsman to talk to. She tried to slash up a few times. Paula was released right after the Ombudsman's investigation was concluded. They called her just before her release and said it is maybe not what she wanted but they have now implemented a policy about segregated inmates and about proper relationships. Paula commented, "This is the way it rolled out, and it will help people in the future. I was happy with it."

Upon release, Paula moved to another city to live with a friend. She noticed a pattern emerging with this relationship. The woman showered her with gifts and encouraged her drug abuse. She decided to end the relationship the only way she knew how—fighting back. So, she took the friend's credit cards and removed several thousand dollars via ATMs. Police were called, and Paula was charged with theft of the credit cards. In court, she received a suspended sentence and probation. After court, her friend, the victim of the credit card theft, took Paula shopping and gave her $5,000 cash.

Paula partied with the money. She was injecting drugs like cocaine. Paula still raged but now tempered that with cocaine—she felt she could float away for days on end. She got very deeply involved in the drug scene and experienced psychosis from doing so much cocaine, including blacking out and even going blind for a while. Her lifestyle continued as it had been for many years, even as she returned to her hometown, tired, hungry, and malnourished after several years of steady drug use. In 2001, Paula's drug use opened up a whole new level of addiction, trauma and survivor skills:

I started getting into poor man's heroin. I got introduced to downers, to morphine. It numbed me; I couldn't feel a thing. I was in a relationship with a drug user as well, just motoring along in my addiction; and it progressed from cocaine to opiates.

That kept me right into the life of crime—I was addicted, had to have it. I never got busted with anything—I just didn't get caught. I was going into stores to steal shit, steal someone's wallet. I didn't have the guts to go do a robbery, so I stayed with petty thefts—ten bucks here, twenty bucks there—anything to keep me rolling.

I really liked that it suppressed all the layers of stuff that I was dealing with—way better than alcohol or weed. Now I needed to make sure I had opiates on hand, especially early in the morning. All the people around me were just getting right into it so now I had a new circle of friends that were into that addiction and lifestyle. The second year there, I was well into my addiction and started to do more crime.

In that year, Paula witnessed a lot of stuff going on like robberies, people getting hurt, beat up or stabbed. She usually drove and assisted in some way. She hid her addiction well until she didn't have an income to support her habit.

Then, she started getting back into crime, petty thefts like stealing work boots—walk in and get a pair of high-end work boots, walk out and sell them for half price; that would do her for a day. A couple of pairs of boots—that would be good for three days—hooray! *(Here, Paula laughs)*.

Paula's addiction to opiates continued and, not surprisingly, her criminal activity increased in severity. No doubt the police were running out of patience as they saw the public increasingly at risk from Paula's destructive behaviour:

I'd been at this for a couple of years, deep into the addiction, got into robbing. Now it's 2002. I've got more skills and criminal talents under my belt, so now I start selling cocaine. I was withdrawing pretty bad, I had no friends, I was so sick. I walked into a convenience store and robbed the clerk of money at knife-point. I literally walked out of there; then ran to the railroad tracks. I needed to feel better—I didn't care what I would do. No one was hurt. I was more of a threatening big mouth, scare tactics and rage to get what I wanted. The police station was a block away. It was a matter of one minute before the alarms went off and the cops are coming. I'm running down the tracks like a bat out of hell—they could easily see me. The police knew me. I started my criminal record here in 1986. The two cops didn't like me—I was an arsehole and pretty violent. They are standing there, guns drawn, telling me I am under arrest for armed robbery.

Paula was remanded in custody as her case worked its way through the court. She was in the correctional centre where she had served previous sentences. Here, according to Paula, she and some of her colleagues had two correctional officers who brought in drugs and were very well paid to do so. Here, as well, she was able to withdraw from the drugs she used on the street. She was sentenced on the armed robbery charge to thirty months imprisonment in December 2002, with her sentence to be served in a women's penitentiary in the city. Her first reaction to being sentenced to the pen was:

Wow! Yahoooo! I was in my glory. I was in my man-hater mode *(Paula laughs)*. Now in my thirties and sentenced to a women's pen—sweet! I didn't engage in the programs that were offered—I wasn't ready for that yet. I was still living a criminal lifestyle even though I was doing time. Being a first-time penitentiary offender, I qualified for parole within eight to ten months. In the pre-parole time, I faked it. I would not admit I was an addict—I was not going to share that weakness with anybody. I wouldn't do programs; and I told them what they wanted to hear. I wasn't in the mindset to be released to heal. I was still operating with a criminal mindset that was still addicted to opiates, even though I hadn't done them in a while. Now I'm in full rein where drugs are coming in.

By the time Paula hit the pen, she stopped trying to escape, and she stopped beating people up. She was coming up for consideration for parole and was encouraged to apply for day parole. What happened next was one of those things that planted a seed in Paula and got her thinking about new influences, new directions for her life. She explains:

I started working with an Elder. She talked about culture and ceremony. I was mad at God for quite a few things and I was confused about spirituality and culture and ceremony. I connected with the Elder and we created an awesome relationship. She was a beautiful mentor. She helped me understand so many things about myself and where my life was headed. She helped me see that the shenanigans I was doing, both on the street and inside prison, being with multiple women, were a huge distraction that prevented me from looking into the mirror and seeing who I really was.

She was amazing. She changed my life—she planted a seed. I started going to ceremony and I started doing sweats. I was the fire keeper. I did one round of a sweat and then got out—I was freaked out. In that first round, I heard a baby crying—this child-like crying for help—and it freaked the hell out of me. Today, I know what it is but back then I didn't understand. The Elder really assisted me. There was a pull there, it was real, something exciting I felt. I started thinking about spirituality and looking at Creator, at medicine, prayer and ceremony—all this stuff really works.

Paula was granted day parole and was transferred to a halfway house in the city. Within two months, her day parole was revoked because she violated one of the conditions requiring her not to use non-prescription drugs—she was caught using weed. Paula reflected on this:

> Looking back on my record, remembering into childhood, how could I follow structure and stuff like that? I was never taught it. By the time anyone attempted to teach me structure, I was in corrections and I was pissed off. I was revoked and sent back to the prison, right back to where I was comfortable. I didn't know what to do on the street. I was told and directed to do all these things but I had never done them before. In my view, the arseholes sent me back. It was everybody else's fault.

Paula did not get full parole due to her conduct on day parole, her institutional record over the years, her drug use and her defiant attitude. She was released in 2004 on statutory release with a bus ticket to her home town. Back in her home town, Paula not surprisingly returned to her lifestyle of drugs and crime. She explains:

> One of my best friends overdosed and passed away. I attempted to commit suicide by overdosing in a basement. I remember running to another city and into crack addiction. I spent four months there, working in crack shacks, witnessing major violence, trauma, people getting broken arms, the crack shacks surrounded

by people with guns who wanted to rob us. I was very violent. We were raided by police. One time, a cop had me sitting up in handcuffs. He asked me why I am here, why am I doing this to myself. He was an awesome cop, he spent time with me when all around us was crazy— addicts, police dogs, guns, people bleeding—all this chaos going on—and that cop sat with me, wondering what I was doing. He said, 'You are in the crack capital of the country. You seem very smart, you are communicative, remorseful, you're telling me you're an addict and this is where you feel you belong?' He made me open my eyes—another seed was planted. Because this cop is taking ten minutes to bring me back to another reality, I felt really good. What he did for me spiritually was beautiful. He never arrested me. But I went back home, the only place I knew, even though I got right back into selling cocaine again.

One day, Paula and a friend went looking for their dealer at a hotel to stock up. The dealer did not show as planned and they were vomiting and withdrawing. Paula continues:

We took off from the hotel and I went on a rampage. In a four block radius, I was kicked out of another hotel, stole some gift cards from a gas station convenience store and stormed into a coffee shop. I was mad, raging and thirsty. I was trying to sell the gift cards in the coffee shop, and one guy was laughing at me—the cards had not been activated. I walked into a mini mall, one with small stores and the first thing I seen was a lady walking with a cash register, getting ready to start her shift. I walked up to her and just nailed her, both hands together as hard as I could on her shoulders. I hit her so hard that her feet went right out from under her— her whole body was airborne and she hit the cement floor. The till landed on the floor and everything went flying. I bent over and swiped some of the bills—and I said, 'Sorry',—so polite and charming, eh? *(Here, Paula chuckled.)*

Paula jumped into a nearby cab and headed toward her dealer's house. She got out of the cab in the alley, then fell to her knees in the gravel and put her head in her hands:

I was laughing my ass off. Then I saw the police cars coming. Here I am, a violent offender, just committed a robbery and the cops are taking precautionary measures, like guns drawn and pointed at my head. All I could think of is to scream 'Fuck!'

This was in 2006, two years after being released from the pen. Here I am in my home town, where it all started. I was coming to the end of the trail. I had a vision—a girl in it was in shoes that were tattered and torn, she was dusty and tattered, just about done. That's how I felt. I was getting to the point where I was done with this shit. I just picked up another robbery—this is three times now. I'm thinking I'm in real trouble here.

Six weeks later, Paula case is set for sentencing. She is delighted to learn that the judge who will sentence her was, many years ago, her lawyer when she was in youth court. Paula describes how the sentencing hearing played out:

The prosecutor painted a nasty picture of me, went back to 1987, especially the violence and the assaults, the robberies and the fail to comply. I have twelve entries on my FPS. Now, I was scared shitless—I thought I would get ten years—I'm too old for this shit. My lawyer spoke, then I got the floor. It was the judge and me. The judge seen me and he heard me. He said 'I know your life, what you endured, and what you put people through as well. I want you to take this sentence and change your life—I'm giving you an opportunity right now. I'm giving you thirty months because I believe you can change. Now I see a different woman. Take care'. You could have heard a pin drop in that courtroom, and I thanked him.

I got a big break. The honourable judge was in my life again. As a youth, that man is one of the people that planted a seed—he told me I was worth something. I took what he said then, and I will never forget him. I actually wrote him a letter a few months ago to let him know where I am today. I wanted to give him thanks because he played a part in getting my shit together.

I was ready to change. I was tired of that dusty trail. But if I'd have gotten ten years that day, my brain would have switched to resentment and anger and fuck you attitude. I would have shut down completely and that's the gift he gave me.

Paula went to the women's penitentiary, again; and, once again, she felt right at home. But this time, she felt that something was different. She did some shenanigans in the first six months of that sentence. Then, according to Paula, something remarkable happened:

One day, something came over me. I was walking in a hallway in the prison. I stopped dead in my tracks. There was nobody around me, no noise—and I was done. I wasn't comfortable any more. This wasn't my home anymore. I didn't belong here anymore. So now, 'What the fuck are you gonna do? Dummy up—now it's time to go to work.'

This was a turning point in her life. She got to work by taking programs whole-heartedly and finally admitting her addiction. Paula took some core programs, worked with a women's organization's worker, and a trauma therapist. She started working though her resentments, hurts, abandonment, anger, and rejection. Paula was ready to trust some people. There would be people now, not to judge her, but to help her work on things, show her and teach her ways to deal with them.

> I quit all drug activity, well, for the most part *(a giggle here)*. I stopped engaging in shenanigans; I stopped beating people up. I stopped female relationships—I needed to look at that part of my life. I threw myself fully into programs and talking and shedding layers, sharing. I used that time to do good things for myself and for switching my whole vocabulary, my thinking processes. I engaged with the new Elder that was there, doing culture and ceremonies that worked.

Paula walked out of the penitentiary better equipped than on any of her previous imprisonments. Unfortunately, she says, she went back home again. Paula got into opiates again but she quickly realized what was going on. Paula completed her statutory remission in December 2008. This was her last FPS entry.

Despite having developed remarkable insight into her past and having a clearer picture of what might lay ahead, Paula continued to struggle with drugs over a period of several years. She enrolled in a methadone program, however she found that methadone blocked all her emotions—physical, emotional, and spiritual. She was ready to take her own life, so she decided to use that to motivate herself and weaned herself off the methadone.

Paula went looking for work, something she had not done for many years. She found employment—milking cows. She explains what a great job this was for her:

I got connected with this farmer. He took time to see me and planted some seeds in my life. I worked for him for just ten days; however, we had conversations, shared a bit of our lives and the family loved me. They knew I was rebuilding my life and they gave me a hand up. They didn't care what colour I was or how many tattoos I had. They didn't see that. They seen me and they seen my spirit. This was part of my launching pad; they helped me a lot.

She found work in other areas—heavy equipment operator and server at a coffee shop. Paula did a lot of thinking, a lot of reflecting. This was new to her, a long way from the anger, drug abuse, violence and chaos that filled so many years. She came to a conclusion: She wanted to give back to the people who helped her. In looking for work possibilities, she spotted the web page of a human service agency that was looking for staff at the courthouse in a small city. Paula continues:

They wouldn't hire me because of my criminal record but they said I could volunteer with youth at the courthouse to build up my skills. I continued to work at the coffee shop. I was mentored by an agency staff member. One thing she did was to take me to Value Village and taught me how to dress. I was used to snazzing up in rock and roll, leather, chaps, a Harley jacket, whatever. She took me under her wing and got me dressed-for-the-work. The next day, I walked into work and saw the lady. She just stood there; she was in complete shock. 'Wow,' she exclaimed, 'you are meant to walk in here, with that confidence. I look at you, thinking that you fit in here except for your criminal record.' I would bring my co-workers coffee and donuts, started meeting lawyers, having conversations with judges. I love talking with my clients, guiding them, and learning about the

justice system on a whole new level. I get to form relationships with people, and I have my own caseload. I
get to help them, love them where they are at today.
Now I can give to people that need it—I can see what
they need. I needed that too, damn it, so here! I'm
going to cry in joy and give you what I got.

Word spread among the community agencies about
"the new girl" at the courthouse. A manager from another
human service agency asked her for a resume. Paula reflects:

All I had on my resume for work was equipment
operator and coffee shop server. To be honest, I felt
ashamed of my resume. But he saw past that, and he
saw me. Then I got a job interview and they wanted
to know my criminal history, my life experiences, my
trials, tribulations, and triumphs. We talked about real
life, about conquering addiction, about coming to culture and ceremony, the beginning part of my healing
journey—and I got the job, working with Indigenous
youth in March 2014.

I did that for two and a half years. When I worked
with youth, I walked with them. It taught me a lot.
This healed the youth in me that I needed when I was
a youth in jail, youth in trouble, youth abandoned, all
that trauma. I needed that, and I was put in that very
position to give that. So, not only did I get the bless-
ing of working with the kids, it was reciprocal—I got
healing there. I was a part of their lives and tried to
steer them away from that, or to plant a seed. I knew
some of them had mental health issues so they needed
connections. In working with youth, I gave them
everything I had. I'd answer my phone at three in the
morning. I was in my car at four in the morning. I had
guns pointed at me by adult gang members because I

was working with their youth members. I was there to steer them out. I said look at what's happening—is that what you want?

Paula continues, outlining some of the things she did in her job and the attitudes she brought to the workplace:

I was trained to the max. I went back into sweats with my co-workers and with the kids. I walked with the kids on that land and I prayed with them, cried with them. I saw changes through the sweats and the real growth happening in the ceremonies. My employer provided so much for me, and the Creator was leading my life. They believed in me. My skills were noticed; they saw my gifts to come out strong, communicative, a go-getter. All the skills I had developed in a negative way, I began to refine in a positive way. I was an advocate for these kids, protecting them from predators in the system, in their families, and among their friends, giving them voice so they could heal parts of themselves. They had their mouths shut all their lives; me, having a big mouth for them, gave them action. I was blessed to have so many Elders to work beside. God bless the agency for bringing me in, training me, believing in me. I was creating connections with lawyers, cops, teachers, judges, social workers, youth workers, housing—all in the same city where I had been homeless. It all came back full circle, guiding the youth and families, giving them a piece of me so they could walk down those streets in a different direction. I was blessed to do that and it empowered me.

And there is my dad, cheering for me, so proud of me. I had moved in with my dad and his wife. He was now my biggest fan and told everybody about my work. I proved to him that my will to help people was stronger than any addiction. I did it because there was something bigger than the journey I was leading; it was meant for good. I believed all that trauma and shit was for something.

In 2016, Paula received an unexpected phone call. Her dad had just dropped dead. *(Paula goes quiet in the interview. I can hear quick breaths, like quiet sobs).* He recently had a clean bill of health. Paula fell into trauma as the course of her life changed, again. She decided to quit her job. Her reality is that she lost her dad for a while as a little girl when he left and now it had happened again. In her grief, she started drinking. She explained, "I was in such a dark place and fighting those demons that if I didn't deal with things, I would probably be dead or in jail for the rest of my life.

Her previous employer kept in touch with Paula over that year, checking how she was doing, encouraging her. In 2017, she was offered a new position in housing, working with the most vulnerable people in the city. She received healing, more training, sweats and ceremony and culture. It was through the sweats and ceremony that she gave up drinking. Paula was facing cancer. They did a prayer ceremony at the sweat lodge, a blanket ceremony. She had the full hysterectomy and everything was clear. When Paula was working with the homeless, she noticed a change in how she saw things:

> I knew I could reach people on a different level. I had the energy, the ideas and the passion to do more. I thought I could write programs based on my own experience, like self-worth because my self-worth was blown for forty years. It took me time to build it up again and to understand my energy. My employer totally backed me. I figured I was going to get my own

business licence because I knew in my heart to aim at the communities that don't get what we have in the city, to rural people, youth, whoever needs them. I had this stuff all wrapped up inside me, I wanted to give it away. I knew as a human service provider that you don't get rich but you are enriched in working with people with love, in spirituality.

In 2018, I bought a business licence. I had done a lot of healing after losing my dad. All of my past comes flooding in for me and that brought me to now when I was back in the human service field. I'm sober, I am cancer-free, and making all these connections. I registered my company, getting the name from what dad used to call me, my nickname.

Now, Paula has started on another path. She transitioned her skills and go-getter attitude from a court worker, housing worker, and a trauma worker to that of a business woman. She does things now like a professional, not a seventeen-year-old girl like before. Paula can now have conversations as equals and she feels confident to say what needs to be said in a kind and gentle, yet firm, way.

I always will remember my FPS#. It is entrenched in my mind, but my vision is clear. I'm free of resentment and being pissed off. I use that number to teach and to guide, to use pieces of me, to bring people to reality. I use my passion to take my story to people. I want others to feel it. But you know that it's real, there was a price paid to live that story.

This is Paula's story. As she spoke, there were laughs as she reflected on some of the things that happened to her and the goofy things that she did. There were some tears, when the memories washed over her. In one sense, her story in remarkable—several times she said she does not know why she didn't die. I find her story remarkable for the challenges and barriers she overcame to be at a point now in her life where she is poised to take on the challenge of being in business.

On the other hand, I find her story rather ordinary. Her reflections jolted my memories of other young women I met in my career who behaved in ways I just could not understand. Why did they take off? Why didn't they trust me? Why did they keep on doing stupid stuff? Paula's story starts to steer me to some answers. Her accounts of the transformations she achieved are wonderfully typical—many people who were offenders do turn their lives around over time to become valuable members of the community. The public rarely hears about these success stories, despite the fact there are lots of them.

Over the years, I met quite a few former offenders who said they just were not ready to share their stories, even though there were happy endings. Thanks, Paula, for not being reluctant to tell your story, both the good and the not-so-good parts.

AS I REFLECT ON PAULA'S STORY, and indeed on a number of the others in this book, I wonder why we as a community find it so difficult to pay attention to how we might respond in a preventative way. Why are we so reluctant to consider extensive interventions to strengthen individuals, families and communities? We seem to be content to "call the cops" and "throw away the keys." To me, we pay a hefty price for this attitude. Surely there are better ways that would yield better results.

I am impressed by Paula's resilience. She overcame circumstances that would destroy others. In her case, I think there was a little girl, bursting with enthusiasm but had no one around to steer her, guide her, to mentor her in a positive way. She turned inward on herself and had over twenty years of turmoil, chaos and anger. But, Paula overcame these forces and learned how to manage herself to become a contributing member of the community.

I think Paula is very clear in her message to those of us working in criminal justice. We don't have magic wands that turn these people who we call "tough cases" into success stories. What we can do, to use her words, is "plant a seed" in their minds. All of us in criminal justice—police, judges, and corrections—can take the time to listen, empathize, and treat them with compassion and respect. The tough cases will remember this when they are finished, as Paula says, with the shenanigans that have ruled their lives. When the tough cases like Ryan and Paula "are done," they are ready to change. It is then that we have a terrific opportunity to teach them new knowledge, attitudes, and skills.

We have to be patient, sometimes for a long time and be ready to pounce when the tough cases are ready. Members of the community, be they coffee shop servers or farmers, can support and encourage all offenders, no matter what their FPS# shows. Paula worked for an agency that really cared about their employees and it would be to everyone's benefit if there were more employers like that.

Maybe we need to pay careful attention to the observations of former Judge John Reilly. In his book *Bad Law: Rethinking Justice for a Postcolonial Canada*, he urges us to focus on repairing the harm caused to the victim and to the community by crime rather than concentrating on punishing the offender. Paula seemed repeatedly hell-bent for jail until she had the help of others to learn to see things differently and to learn how to behave in a socially acceptable manner. Notice the key word here—learning.

Judge Reilly, along with many others, including myself, are horrified by the over-representation of Indigenous people in the justice system. With rates of male and female Indigenous offenders in custody increasing noticeably over many years, questions emerge, like, "What the hell is going on here? How can this be? What needs to change? How can we do better? No doubt you, the reader, can come up with a few more questions. Hopefully, readers can also come up with reactions and suggestions that will contribute positively to this discussion and will lead to initiatives and practices that will make a difference.

Might this be a good time to review the Calls to Action of the Truth and Reconciliation Commission? Might this be a good time to reflect on the findings and recommendations of "Reclaiming Power and Place," National Inquiry into Missing and Murdered Indigenous Women and Girls?

I draw the readers' attention to an observation by Det. Debbie Doyle in her afterword:

> Ordinary people commit crimes due to their circumstances. We aren't born criminals but learn by watching others' behaviour or realizing that without criminal activity, we are unable to survive in these increasingly difficult times.

As my friend and colleague Howard Sapers advised in his foreword, we journeyed beyond Paula's crimes to take a look at her life and her ambitions.

Thank you, readers, for being along for the ride.

AFTERWORD

DETECTIVE DEBBIE J. DOYLE (RETIRED)

WHEN ONE READS a story about the triumph or failure of the judicial system, judgments are made. If an individual who was charged with a heinous offence is convicted and sent to jail, part of society will be happy but another part will not. Sentence lengths, victim impact statements, and lasting or life-long physical and mental injuries inflicted on the victim are difficult to deal with. How can any sentence ever provide justice for decade-long sexual assault perpetrated by an adult on their four-year-old child, now a young adult? Is a three-year sentence substantial time for a sexual assault against a woman or a man? And what should be the punishment for the perpetrators of a home-invasion? Would it matter if the victims were criminals or law-abiding citizens; should the sentencing reflect this?

There are no simple answers to these questions, but endless hours of debating could occur with each sentencing. Should a full-scale investigation be conducted on each convicted criminal to determine how they were raised, whether they have any learning disabilities, whether they were physically or sexually abused, or whether they exhibit psychopathic behaviours?

When criminals are convicted, serve their sentence, are released back into the community and then commit more crime, society becomes enraged and may blame an organization or an individual other than the one who committed the crime. Blaming the victim for dressing provocatively, or a witness for testifying poorly, or the police for not solving the case sooner or a lawyer for defending the criminal are commonplace. This is an easy way for members of our society to judge without comprehensive factual information. When has society accepted the blame for an individual's actions? Does society confess to not providing the necessities of life to everyone so that people have adequate food, shelter, and access to medical services? Will society accept the blame when children commit suicide?

Rarely do individuals want to accept blame for their behaviour, especially when it is criminal. On many occasions, people will downplay their negative behaviour in order to justify their actions. Whether an individual is an ordinary citizen who was caught for speeding or a criminal who has committed a dozen break and enters, excuses and minimization are provided to the police. "I was late to pick my daughter up from daycare." "I was abused as a child, now have a drug problem and need to commit crime to feed my habit." When individuals are caught, they minimize their involvement or downplay the severity of the crime. Sex and child offenders may blame the victims or their spouses for not tending to their basic sexual needs. Property offenders may blame employers or society for their lack of employment or unwanted drug addiction. Bank robbers may claim that the money is being taken from an institution that exploits their customers. Everyone has a story and every story contains factual and fictional information.

While reading the collection of stories, many of our own beliefs, experiences and prejudices are applied to judge the story, the criminal, the victim and the judicial system. "Why did he act that way?" "Why didn't she change her situation?" "How could he have been so foolish?" Unfortunately, everyone doesn't grow up in a perfect home or environment, nor with the same mental capacity or ability to learn. Being genetically or nurtured to be predisposed to certain behaviours impacts our actions in adulthood. It is difficult to comprehend the actions of others when we have not been subjected to their upbringing.

How many people have been charged with a criminal offence and have pleaded guilty because they don't understand or are afraid of the legal system? How many individuals are embarrassed by their actions and don't want others to know they have committed a crime? Although in saying this, the "shame factor" in our society has diminished over time. Even though the accused may be guilty, there may be mitigating circumstances whereby the individual did something wrong to do something right. This information may never be presented or disclosed in a courtroom upon sentencing.

I will refer to the story of Mary in chapter six. There are a host of questions that each of us may formulate in our minds regarding her intellect, child-rearing ability, cleanliness, and ability to engage in an equitable relationship. Does Mary suffer from any psychological issues or mental disorders, and if so, do they manifest themselves in her decision-making process? People may express their disapproval of Mary's housekeeping abilities or lack thereof, however, what if she was raised in a similar environment? Would there be any reason for her to change or to even know any difference? Other readers may be concerned that she is being exploited and controlled by her husband who has an advantage due to his age and life skill over this period of time. Is Paul interested about parenting or does he expect that Mary should already know this?

This story was told by author Doug Heckbert, who, at the time, was a probation officer, not a marriage counsellor, nor an expert in child-rearing or sanitizing houses. He had a case load that was extensive and time-consuming. He didn't have the time to delve into all of the issues surrounding Mary's behaviour, nor the crimes she committed. After reading this story, we have to ask ourselves, "Is Mary a criminal? Will she ever commit another criminal offence? Should the legal system be involved in dealing with this crime or is it a waste of taxpayers' money?"

Many may argue that Mary is a criminal because she was charged and convicted of a criminal offence. Others may declare that she is an unfortunate victim of the many circumstances that surround her life. Both views may be correct but did they matter when she was sentenced? If Mary had a little more money, would she have committed the crime?

If we want to ensure that this type of situation doesn't occur with other women, what are we, as a society and as individuals willing to do? Will we agree to have our tax rate increased to hire more Children's Services employees to conduct home visits on all parents and ensure that the environment is a clean, safe and healthy one? And at what point would this interfere with the Canadian Charter of Rights and Freedoms?

I continue with the story about Ron, in chapter two, who was an emerging adult with two younger siblings and parents. While one parent worked, the other remained home to raise her children and ensure stability within the family. What incident or series of incidents made Ron want to engage in criminal behaviour? Is a life full of financial stability and nurturing parents a recipe for acting out and seeking adventurous criminal activity? Was Ron bored or was he trying to fit in with a specific group of people? It is an easier task with this story to lay the blame solely on Ron? In saying this, however, individuals might criticize Doug for not reporting Ron to the police after being shown all of the stolen property. After all, possession of stolen property in this amount would warrant substantial jail time. How many crimes had Ron committed? Should this activity be ignored because of his family's standing within the community and his polite behaviour? In this particular case, Doug saw the positive result of his decision to take no action against Ron and it was a story about the positive results when the law wasn't entirely followed. This is what occurred when Doug, who was still a young man at the time, was working for the government and made a decision that he believed was right. Further to making the decision, Doug sought advice from a senior employee who agreed with his actions.

A comparison of criminal activity was made with Fred, also in chapter two. Is there any difference between Fred and Ron's criminal behaviour? Were Fred and Ron being transparent with Doug? Why did it take Ron so long to confide in Doug? Unfortunately, as individuals reading these stories, we are unable to delve into the minds of Ron and Fred and determine why they committed the crimes. This would make it easier for us to judge each individual and then judge Doug's actions.

If we continually engage in corporal punishment with our children when they make mistakes, how are they supposed to learn? Instead, if we turned the discipline into behaviour modification through constructive learning, would they refrain from negative behaviour in the future? Children revert to behaviours and acts that they see or have experienced; this has been proven in a variety of studies. If Ron was punished for being honest, would he continue to be honest or would he contemplate the outcome of his honesty prior to acting on it?

What would have happened if Doug had seen Ron's name in the newspaper years or decades later, being convicted of a host of crimes? Doug would have originally thought he made the correct decision but then realized that he failed to ensure the safety of the community. A judgment call was made; an olive branch was presented, accepted and retained. This won't always happen but we need to understand that there may be options other than jail.

The Juvenile Delinquents Act was replaced by the Young Offenders Act and then replaced by the Youth Criminal Justice Act. Even the name changes over the years have softened, ensuring that the spirit of justice should prevail, although in reality, this isn't always the case. Wouldn't it be nice to have a second chance at an action we have committed as adults – that momentary lapse in judgment that may brand us for the rest of our lives?

AS IN MOST CREATURES on this planet, we learn how to survive by watching and being taught by our parents. In the animal kingdom when parents are unable to properly raise their young, in many instances, their young perish. Humans have come a long way and ensured that even though children may not be raised properly, we need to ensure that they benefit from other members of society raising them or being given a chance to learn in their teenage years.

Adults make mistakes on a regular basis but expect that children should be perfect. Children's brains are still developing in their twenties which means that until they are legally adults, they should be treated differently than adults. Even though the law may not have condoned this behaviour when Doug enacted it, the result was positive. Was Ron a criminal; is he now?

How different are Ron and Mary from Barry; or are there similarities? In reading the story about Barry, my first thoughts revolved around Barry's mental development. Does he have any learning disabilities or does he suffer from Fetal Alcohol Spectrum Disorder? My thoughts then turned to his childhood and I cannot help but wonder why he was originally placed in foster care. There is always a concern when a child is placed in numerous foster and group homes, has poor hygiene, and engages in minor impulse crimes, specifically thefts.

Should we consider Barry a criminal, a victim or both? Would his life be different had he been fostered and raised in Ron's household or would it have mattered? An unstable childhood, lack of education, and potential mental and psychological disabilities are a perfect combination for an individual to be exploited and then subsequently engage in criminal activity. During Barry's youth, he may or may not have been exploited but his history of crime reveals poor reasoning and judgment. Unfortunately, when children such as Barry age, they may become targets for career criminals—our jails are full of individuals who suffer from FASD and have been exploited by other criminals. Will Barry continue to commit crimes? Will they become more severe or will they only be limited to minor property crimes. In his early twenties, Barry has a long life ahead of him but what does his future hold?

The story about Peter is a sad one because we know the outcome. Was Peter a criminal? Was he defending himself against unwanted sexual advances or a potential sexual assault? Would it have been different if he hadn't been drinking? This is a real-life story about unfortunate circumstances that befell on a man; those circumstances eventually led to his ultimately death. When reading about Peter, I didn't' perceive him as a bad man, merely a loner due to his lifestyle. Many people thrive by being on their own or having limited contact with others. It may not be what the majority of society yearns for but a small sliver of society thrives in that environment.

Peter had to journey to the city to meet with a specialist regarding a medical issue. Due to insufficient funds, he was unable to afford a more reputable hotel, which may have prevented the fight from occurring. Even though he wasn't sentenced to serve time in jail, Peter's incarceration in a facility close to the city was detrimental to his psychological well-being. Critics of this story might indicate that assaulting a male by kicking him while he was down and then assaulting a police officer should warrant jail time. This is true and once again, we see a criminal, who before his journey, wasn't. We observe a man who had lived in isolation his entire life, deteriorate and die after living in a situation that was completely foreign to him. Did the punishment fit the crime?

Now it is time for us to reflect on each of these stories. Should we feel sorry for any of the individuals involved in criminal activity? Should we trust their confessions and turn a blind eye to their circumstances or punish them to the full extent of the law? And why should we even care?

We live in a democratic society where social values are important. Canadians are renowned for their community spirit, helping others, and volunteering. We are twice as likely to volunteer as our neighbours to the south. Almost half of all Canadians are or have been involved with volunteering. What does this have to do with crime? It is in our nature to ensure that others are provided for. As a society, we have eliminated corporal punishment against prisoners and abolished the death penalty. This is not to say that criminals shouldn't be punished but the way that the judicial system is operating at present time is not working as well as it should. It is not only the judicial system that needs attention, but our society.

If an individual steals to feed his or her family, it is a crime they commit against society. But does society commit a crime by not providing enough resources to ensure that people have food, shelter, and medical care? If everyone was provided the basic needs, would people steal food to eat or money to pay the rent or buy work clothes? How much should our society provide to individuals who are involved in the criminal element?

The medical profession speaks on a continual basis about prevention; if we exercised several days a week, didn't smoke, ate more vegetables, and lost weight, we would be healthier. Even though our society speaks about pro-active policing, they rarely speak about pro-active positive behavioural reinforcement. Eliminating fundamental issues in its infancy will ensure that problems don't occur in the future. If all children were raised in homes without alcohol, drug abuse or violence and had parents who wanted and loved them and wanted to ensure their well-being, how many of them would become criminals? But what would that cost society and how much are we willing to allow the government to take as taxes to make dramatic judicial and social reforms?

In today's difficult economic state, the majority of Canadians are trying to ensure that their families are provided for, even when job losses are high. They aren't willing to give more of their diminishing incomes to the government to help criminals. I understand this completely and don't blame anyone for thinking this way, but if we allow society to continue in this fashion, more ordinary people will become criminals and their arrests and incarcerations will use more taxpayers' dollars when prevention is readily available.

I do want to reiterate, like Doug has, that not all criminals are nice. There are individuals living among us who are robbers, rapists, murderers, and child sex offenders. Even with early intervention, not all of these individuals could be prevented from committing crime. There are people in our society who are bad, mean and evil. These individuals should be incarcerated to protect our society.

Probation officers, police officers, judges, and lawyers, to name a few, look back and wonder if they made a difference. Rarely do they see the final outcome of the individual they found out, like Doug did, that an individual is doing well in society. All of us wonder, "Did we make the correct decision?" "Should I have sentenced him to a longer jail term?" "Should I have defended him when I knew he sexually assaulted all of those children?" "Should I have arrested him for stealing apples from an apple tree because he was hungry?" And in most instances, we will never know the answer.

One person can't change a nation but with the help of others, small changes can slowly be implemented. We are all members of society and can make changes by becoming enlightened, sharing knowledge with others and contacting politicians to recommend and even force change when circumstances are biased against groups of individuals. Unlike in television and movies, all people who commit crimes are not bad and not all crimes are heinous. Ordinary people commit crimes due to their circumstances. We aren't born criminals but learn by watching others' behaviour or realizing that without criminal activity, we are unable to survive in these increasingly difficult times.

The next time you see an individual in handcuffs, don't immediately judge them. Reflect on the stories of the people in this book and their circumstances. Know that they and we can learn from our biases and prejudices and through education, we can make society a better place to live and raise the next generation.

— *Detective Debbie J. Doyle (retired)*
Edmonton Police Service

REFERENCES

Chapter 10. "Paul: A Ten Year Journey to Normalcy"

Thistle, Jesse, *From The Ashes: My Story of Being Métis, Homeless, and Finding My Way.* Toronto: Simon & Schuster Canada, 2019.

Thanh, Yasuko, *Mistakes To Run.* Toronto: Penguin Random House Canada, 2019.

Chapter 17. "Paula: Freedom from a FPS#"

Reilly, John. *Bad Law: Rethinking Justice for a Postcolonial Canada.* Victoria: Rocky Mountain Books, 2019.

Truth and Reconciliation Commission of Canada. *Final Report of the Truth and Reconciliation Commission of Canada:* Summary: Honouring the Truth, Reconciling for the Future. Winnipeg: Truth and Reconciliation Commission of Canada, 2015.

National Inquiry into Missing and Murdered Indigenous Women and Girls. *Reclaiming Power and Place: The Final Report of the National Inquiry into Missing and Murdered Indigenous Women and Girls.* 2019

Referenced in Acknowledgments

"Turning Points: A study of the factors related to the successful reintegration of Aboriginal offenders." R-112 Research Branch, Correctional Services of Canada. 2001.

"Healing, Spirit and Recovery: An exploratory study examining the lifestyles of aboriginal offenders who have become law-biding citizens." The Nechi Institute and the Aboriginal Corrections Unit, Ministry Secretariat, Solicitor General Canada. 1995.

Healing The Spirit. (Wil Campbell, 1996) Nechi Institute. Videorecording.

ACKNOWLEDGMENTS

MANY PEOPLE helped me think about and write this book. In my career, I had a never-ending stream of clients and, most often, I was too busy dealing with them on a day-to-day basis to check whether they were successful in making longer-term changes in their lives. I had some inkling that I did indeed have a positive impact on some clients. However, it was not until I worked at Native Counselling Services of Alberta that it really dawned on me just how often people do go from being troublemakers to role models in the community.

This realization became firmly cemented in my mind when I was asked by Dr. Maggie Hodgson OC, with the Nechi Training, Research, and Health Promotions Institute to lead research studies and create a documentary video about Indigenous offenders who turned their lives around. I am indebted to Maggie for her leadership, to Anne, Rod, Bill and Darlene for interviewing dozens of offenders, and to Wil Campbell, producer of the video.

My wife, Joanne Heckbert, has been very supportive. She listened attentively as I bounced ideas around and she offered her thoughts and insights. She encouraged my emergence as a writer, sharing the high times ("Hooray, I have a publisher!") and the low times ("Damn, the words just won't come!"). My sons, Scott and Mark, were very interested in my decision to write a book. Mark had questions and always offered support and encouragement. At a time when I questioned whether I should continue writing, Scott gave me a 15cm ancient Egyptian scribe that he produced with his 3D printer. It soon earned a place overlooking my writing desk—and it worked like a charm!

Some parole officers and agency managers referred cases to me. They saw the merit of the book and agreed that the public most certainly needs to hear these stories. They are not named so as to contribute to the confidentiality of the cases in the book.

Jean Jackson and Shauna Young offered editorial services with an insightful eye coupled with a respect for the people they read about. Howard Sapers and Debbie J. Doyle wrote the foreword and afterword to the book, bringing great insight from their professions in corrections and law enforcement. Dr. J. Thomas Dalby, with an exceptional career in psychology and the law, offered his professional opinion on the help available to sexual offenders. Dr. Annette Begalke offered a quick lesson in physiology when she explained how a bullet from a rifle could enter and exit the human shoulder without causing a great deal of damage, which is what happened in the title story.

I pay tribute to Lorene Shyba for accepting my pitch that *Go Ahead And Shoot Me!* would be a nice fit in the Durvile True Cases series. Lorene listened, prodded, advised and inspired me throughout the writing and editing process. Lorene brought others to this process, including cover illustrator Rich Théroux and proofreader Cole Girodat.

Thanks goes to Dr. George Kupfer, formerly with the University of Alberta. I spent a term working with George as his Teaching Assistant where I experienced the joy and power (and the hard work) of writing.

The biggest appreciation goes to the folks who agreed to tell their story in Part II. They accepted my claim that confidentiality would be paramount. They set the bar high for me, and I hope I rose to the occasion. They echoed my concern that the public needs to have more information about people who commit crime and the officials who work with them. These are real people; only their names and other identifying information have been changed for confidentiality reasons.

Other books in the
THE DURVILE TRUE CASES SERIES

**Tough Crimes: True Cases by
Top Canadian Criminal Lawyers**
By Edward L. Greenspan *et al*
Book 1 in the True Cases Series

*"Tough Crimes demonstrates that Crown
prosecutors and criminal defence lawyers
do not escape unscathed from serious
trials. The disturbing memories remain."*
— Hon. John C. Major, CC QC,
Justice of the Supreme Court of Canada.

Tough Crimes is a collection of
thoughtful and insightful essays
from some of Canada's most prom-
inent criminal lawyers. Stories
include wrongful convictions,
reasonable doubt, homicides, and
community spirit.

Edited by C.D. Evans and Lorene Shyba

Price: $29.95, 24.95 US *Paperback*
288 pages

ISBN: 978-0-9689754-6-6 (2014)
E-book: 978-0-9689754-7-3 (2015)
Audio: 978-0-9689754-7-3 (2017)

**SHRUNK: Crime and
Disorders of the Mind
True Cases by Forensic Experts**
By J. Thomas Dalby *et al*
Book 2 in the True Cases Series

*"The workings of the criminally disordered
minds has always been a fascinating
subject. Does our prison system throw
away the key after incarceration, or is it
worthwhile to rehabilitate?"*
— Earl Levy, QC

SHRUNK is a collection of true
cases by eminent Canadian and
international forensic psychologists
and psychiatrists facing the tough
topic of mental illness in the
criminal justice system.

Edited by Lorene Shyba and J. Thomas Dalby
Foreword by Dr. Lisa Ramshaw

Price: $29.95, 24.95 US *Paperback*
272 pages

ISBN: 978-0-9947352-0-1 (2016)
E-book: 978-0-9947352-3-2 (2016)
Audio: 978-0-9952322-7-3 (2017)

**More Tough Crimes:
True Cases by Canadian Judges
and Criminal Lawyers**
By Donald Bayne *et al*
Book 3 in the True Cases Series

*"A revealing, at times searing and
always very human look inside our
criminal courtrooms and the people
who populate them."*
— Sean Fine, Globe and Mail

The third book in the "True
Cases" series, *More Tough Crimes*
provides readers with a window
into the insightful thinking
of some of Canada's best legal
minds from coast to coast.

Edited by William Trudell & Lorene Shyba
Foreword by Hon. Patrick LeSage

Price: $29.95, 24.95 US *Paperback*
272 pages

ISBN: 978-0-9947352-5-6 (2017)
E-book: 978-0-9952322-2-8 (2017)
Audio: 978-0-9952322-9-7 (2018)

Canada   Alberta
Government

Durvile Publications would like to acknowledge the financial support of the Government of Canada through Canadian
Heritage Canada Book Fund and the Government of Alberta, Alberta Media Fund.

DURVILE &
UpRoute Books

Other books in the
THE DURVILE TRUE CASES SERIES

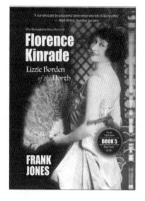

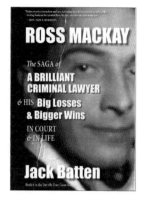

Women in Criminal Justice:
True Cases By and About
Canadian Women and the Law
By Hon. Susan Lang *et al*
Book 4 in the True Cases Series

"The reader emerges with pictures in mind ... women working without respite to achieve just outcomes for the people they deal with often in the face of difficulty."
— Rt. Hon. Beverley McLachlin

Stories in *Women in Criminal Justice* deal with terrorism, drugs, sexual assault, mental disorders, motherhood, child protection, LGBTQ+, Indigenous, and other urgent issues of our time.

Edited by William Trudell & Lorene Shyba
Foreword by Rt. Hon. Beverley McLachlin

Price: $29.95, 24.95 US *Paperback*
272 pages

ISBN: 978-0-9947352-4-9 (2018)
E-book: 978-1-9888241-4-7 (2018)
Audio: 978-1-9888241-4-7 (2018)

Florence Kinrade:
Lizzie Borden of the North
By Frank Jones
Book 5 in the True Cases Series

"Frank Jones has always had a knack for finding the quirkiest and most interesting true crime tales, and relating them with the skill you'd expect from a lifelong, first rate journalist, and this latest is no exception." — Linwood Barclay, Author

In this 1909 historical true crime, Florence Kinrade was a dutiful daughter, engaged to the parson's son. She also led a double life as a vaudeville showgirl in Richmond, Virginia. Florence becomes the central figure in a gruesome crime; the murder of her sister, Ethel.

Price: $29.95, 24.95 US *Paperback*
272 pages

ISBN: 978-1-9888243-5-2 (2019)
E-book: 978-0-9952322-8-0 (2019)
Audio: 978-1-988824-31-4 (2019)

Ross Mackay, The Saga of a
Brilliant Criminal Lawyer
By Jack Batten
Book 6 in the True Cases Series

"Jack Batten marries journalism and law, meticulous fact-driven research, to give us this riveting book on the talented Ross Mackay, who flew too close to the sun."
— Hon. Nancy Morrison, Former Judge of The Supreme Court of B.C

This is the story of his courage and the harsh penalties Ross Mackay paid for the often daring and controversial choices he made in life and in the courtroom. It is also the story of Ross Mackay's dedication to the maxim that everyone is entitled to a defence.

Price: $35.00, 29.95 US *Paperback*
288 pages

ISBN: 978-1-9888243-9-0 (2020)
E-book: 978-1-988824-60-4 (2020)
Audio: 978-1-988824-51-2 (2020)

Book 8 in the True Cases Series for 2021
After the Force: True Cases by Law Enforcement Officers.
Edited by Det. Debbie J. Doyle (ret) and Lorene Shyba PhD

DURVILE &
UpRoute Books

CONTRIBUTORS

Doug Heckbert. Doug's work experience includes probation officer and prison case-worker with Alberta Correctional Services, parole officer with the National Parole Service, staff trainer and program director with Native Counselling Services of Alberta, and instructor with MacEwan University. Doug obtained Bachelor and Masters degrees from the University of Alberta and has taught courses to community groups and conducted research projects concerning offenders.

Debbie J. Doyle. Deb is a retired veteran of the Edmonton Police Service. During her career, she was seconded to the United Nations Peacekeeping force in Timor Leste and worked in the Vulnerable Person's Unit. After serving two tours of duty, she returned to Edmonton, was promoted, and worked in the Child Protection Section and the Internet Child Pornography section. She is currently writing novels and is presently compiling and editing, *After the Force*, Book 8 in the Durvile True Cases series.

Howard Sapers. From 2004 to 2016 Howard was the Correctional Investigator of Canada. He has also served as Executive Director of the John Howard Society of Alberta, was an elected member of the Legislative Assembly of Alberta, Director of Canada's National Crime Prevention Centre Investment Fund, and a Vice Chairperson of the Parole Board Canada. Recently he completed two years as the Independent Advisor on Corrections Reform for the province of Ontario.